Mudville MADNESS

Mudville MADNESS

FABULOUS FEATS, BELLIGERENT BEHAVIOR, AND ERRATIC EPISODES ON THE DIAMOND

JONATHAN WEEKS

TAYLOR TRADE PUBLISHING
Lanham • Boulder • New York • Toronto • Plymouth, UK

Published by Taylor Trade Publishing
An imprint of Rowman & Littlefield
4501 Forbes Boulevard, Suite 200, Lanham, Maryland 20706
www.rowman.com

10 Thornbury Road, Plymouth PL6 7PP, United Kingdom

Distributed by NATIONAL BOOK NETWORK

British Library Cataloguing in Publication Information Available

Library of Congress Cataloging-in-Publication Data Available

ISBN 978-1-58979-956-1 (pbk. : alk. paper)
ISBN 978-1-58979-957-8 (electronic)

♾™ The paper used in this publication meets the minimum requirements
of American National Standard for Information Sciences—Permanence of
Paper for Printed Library Materials, ANSI/NISO Z39.48-1992.

Printed in the United States of America

Again, this book is dedicated to Samantha and Elizabeth,
My primary sources of hope and joy.

Baseball games are like snowflakes and fingerprints. No two are ever alike.

—W. P. Kinsella

Contents

Acknowledgments

I would like to extend a word of thanks to Dan Glickman for fact-checking my work on an extremely short deadline.

I also want to thank Karie Simpson at Taylor Trade Publishing for her tireless efforts in obtaining photos and making this book better than it was before she got involved.

Introduction

The extent to which remarkable things can happen on a baseball diamond is virtually limitless. Records get broken, tempers flare, balls carom wildly, playing surfaces are invaded by uninvited guests; in extreme cases, players meet their demise.

While perusing an old issue of *Sporting Life* magazine a few years ago, I happened upon the following anecdote, which is a testament to just how far things can stray from the ordinary.

> In a nineteenth century game that pitted the University of St. Joseph against the Chatham Stars at New Brunswick, the Stars were leading 2–0 in the bottom of the ninth when a St. Joseph's player named O'Hara (reputedly the team's weakest hitter) doubled to left. The next batter, a man named Robidoux, slammed a ball over the center fielder's head. While rounding the bases, O'Hara suddenly collapsed and died. Robidoux, upon encountering the obstruction in his path, hoisted the corpse of his teammate aloft and carried it with him to home. With the championship at stake, members of the Chatham squad strenuously protested as a village doctor worked on the fallen player. Ignoring their petitions, the umpire counted both runs and ordered the game to continue. An eyewitness concluded that, in scoring posthumously, O'Hara had made "the most solemn, most dramatic and greatest play that baseball has ever seen."

While we are not likely to encounter such a play in modern times, notable events still occur with regularity. If you're anything like me, you find yourself scouring box scores and game accounts to uncover something new or rarely encountered. This book represents the fruits of my labors. If I've done my job well, many of the snippets within will leave you shaking your head in disbelief. Hall of Famer Bob Lemon once remarked: "I don't care how long you've been around, you'll never see it all." I concur. And as an avid proponent of the sport for more than forty years, I've discovered that, when it comes to baseball, the truth often requires minimal embellishment.

Part 1
THE EARLY DAYS,
1846-1899

Timeline of Significant Events

1846   The first "official" baseball game takes place in Hoboken, New Jersey, using rules established by Alexander Cartwright.

1858   A new set of rules is established by the Massachusetts Association of Baseball Players. The "new" game is often referred to as "Town Ball."

1871   The first professional league is formed, known as the National Association of Professional Baseball Players. Batting averages are recorded for the first time.

1875   First confirmed use of a baseball glove by Charlie Waitt, a St. Louis outfielder/first baseman.

1876   The National League is founded.

1882   The American Association is established as a second major league.

1890   Unhappy with baseball's reserve clause, players establish their own league. Most of the game's brightest stars sign up, but by 1891, the only circuit still standing will be the National League.

1893   The pitcher's mound is moved from a fifty-foot distance to sixty feet, six inches.

1895   Foul tips are counted as strikes if caught. The modern infield fly rule is adopted.

In the Beginning . . .

The first officially recorded baseball game took place in 1846 at Elysian Fields in Hoboken, New Jersey. The rules had been established by a New York bookseller and volunteer firefighter named Alexander Cartwright the year before. Any modern fan in attendance would have found the early conventions quite odd.

Batters were referred to as "strikers." Runs were called "aces" or "counts," and outs were commonly known as "hands." There was no defined batter's box, and the striker could move forward or backward from the ball. Pitchers stood just forty-five feet from home plate. They were allowed a running start but were required to deliver the ball underhand so that strikers could hit it. There were no called balls or strikes, and the first team to score twenty-one times was declared the winner. Nine-inning games were still a few years off.

Players were clad in flannel shirts with wool pantaloons and straw hats. Fielders wore no gloves, and catchers stood ten to twelve feet behind home plate without the benefit of protective equipment. A striker could be put out in several ways: (1) a standard ground out, (2) having a ball caught in the air or on one bounce, or (3) being thrown out by the catcher after missing a third swing.

Umpires sat at a table on the third baseline. Their job was to keep a scorebook, make fair or foul calls, and settle any disputes between teams. There were long spells during which they had very little to do.

September 14, 1872

By 1872 the original rules had been drastically altered, so that game play more closely resembled that of today. But situations still arose in which umpires were left scratching their heads. Such was the case on the date in question, when the Philadelphia Athletics squared off against the Boston Red Stockings at Philadelphia. With the A's leading 4–1 in the seventh inning and runners on first and second bases, Philly first baseman Fergy Malone popped up to shortstop George Wright. Wright, an eventual Hall of Famer who resembled the comic-book character Wolverine with his bushy sideburns and unruly hair, decided for some inexplicable reason (perhaps he was showing off) to catch the ball in his hat.

Wright threw to Harry Schafer at third for the apparent force. Schafer then relayed to Andy Leonard at second in plenty of time, but there was no immediate ruling from umpire William Ellis. Arguing his case, Wright contended that a double play should be awarded since the "hat catch" was not a legal out. Completely flustered by the turn of events, Ellis opted for a "do over," sending the runners back to their original stations and allowing Malone to hit again.

The original play proved to be inconsequential as the A's failed to push any runs across in that frame. Boston knotted the score in the eighth, but the A's bounced back for a pair to win the game, 6–4. It was one of only eight losses for the Red Stockings that year as they captured the National Association pennant with a 39–8 record. Fergy Malone must have learned something from the experience as he went on to umpire in the National League briefly during the 1884 slate.

July 24, 1873

The New York Mutuals played host to the Baltimore Canaries in a National Association game at Brooklyn's Union Grounds. The *New York Sun* reported that the Canaries were early favorites, though the Mutuals pulled ahead by the time betting was closed. Two thousand people turned out to see a nail-biter between the two first-division squads.

Baltimore knotted the score at 5 in the eighth, but the Mutuals answered with three in their half of the frame. The ninth inning would prove to be quite memorable as the Canaries exploded for five runs. Play was interrupted by an ugly argument between umpire Bob Ferguson and New York catcher Nat Hicks. During the dispute, Hicks reportedly called Ferguson a "damn liar." Ferguson, who also served as league president, took exception to the barb and hit Hicks in the left arm with a bat, breaking Hicks's arm in two places and keeping him out of action for the next two months. Since Ferguson was a high-ranking league official, no disciplinary action was ever pursued (though he apologized afterward and quit umpiring for good).

Trailing 10–8, the Mutuals tied the score on a series of clutch hits by Bobby Mathews, Count Gedney, and Dave Eggler. With Eggler on second, third sacker John Hatfield hit a liner to short left field that bounced off of Davy Force's hands. According to one newspaper report, Eggler was "running like a deer" and scored the deciding run "under deafening applause and round after round of cheers." Baltimore finished in third place that year with a 34–22 record. The Mutuals were right behind them at 29–24. Ferguson would be best remembered for his colorful nickname, "Death to Flying Things," which was allegedly bestowed on him by teammates, who said that nothing could get past him when he was stationed at second base.

June 18, 1874

In a sloppy contest at the Union Grounds, the New York Mutuals slaughtered the Chicago White Stockings, 38–1. The *New York Sun* made a colossal understatement when it reported that "the Chicagos played poorly throughout the game." Eight Mutuals players had at least three hits apiece off of Dan Collins and Davy Force, who were subbing for Chicago's regular pitcher, George Zettlein. Zettlein had been barred from participating in this game along with left fielder Ned Cuthbert due to suspicious conduct in a game against Philadelphia the previous day.

The Mutuals scored in every inning, plating eight runs in the first and sixth. They pushed five runs across in three other frames. Jim Devlin and Dan Collins were the only members of the White Stockings to finish the game without an error. According to a Retrosheet box score, there were twenty-one Chicago miscues, including five by center fielder/shortstop Paul Hines. This differs significantly from an account provided by Charlton's *Baseball Chronology*, in which thirty-six errors were reported. Either figure would have been somewhat unusual for a single game, though high error totals were not uncommon in the nineteenth century.

Fielders began wearing gloves in the 1870s—thin, fingerless ones made of heavy fabric. Due to the poor design, catching fly balls, line drives, and hard throws could be both painful and challenging. In 1874, the Philadelphia Athletics recorded the fewest errors among National Association clubs—396. That's an average of seven muffs per game. By way of comparison, the most error-prone major league teams in 2012—the San Diego Padres and Colorado Rockies—both averaged less than an error per game.

In addition to the twenty-one (or possibly thirty-six) Chicago errors on that fateful June afternoon in 1874, catcher Fergy Malone added five passed balls. He would finish the season with twenty-nine in forty-seven games, a statistic that would almost certainly have put him out of a job in the latter half of the following century.

August 9, 1882

A battle of the NL's top teams took place at the Messer Street Grounds in Providence, Rhode Island. The *New York Tribune* reported that a "large crowd" was on hand to see a "well-contested" match between the hometown Grays and the Chicago White Stockings. The Grays were ahead of their opponents by one game in the standings and had been idle for three days.

Providence scored in the second frame and held the lead until the fifth, when Chicago tied things up. The White Stockings would tack on runs in the seventh and eighth for a 3–1 win, moving them into a tie for first place. Aside from its impact on the pennant race, the game held another point of interest as one of the Chicago runs was scored in highly unusual fashion.

According to Charlton's *Baseball Chronology*, a man named Donald Patterson was watching the game from the grandstand, having left his carriage in deep center field under a tree that overhung the fence. Chicago's catcher, Silver Flint, launched a deep drive to center that rolled under the hooves of Patterson's horses. Providence outfielder Paul Hines had trouble accessing the ball as Patterson's coachman tried to keep the skittish horses under control. By the time Hines was able to retrieve the ball, Flint had reportedly rounded the bases. Ground rules allowed the play to stand.

Providence managed just four hits that day to Chicago's six. Each team committed three errors during the contest. The White Stockings would go on to capture their third consecutive NL championship that year, moving into first place for good in mid-September. Providence would come within one-half game of the NL lead on September 23 before ultimately finishing second.

Bizarre ground rules would result in more than one unusual play during the nineteenth century. In an 1884 Union Association game, Tom O'Brien of the Boston Reds was allowed to circle the bases when a ball he hit burrowed deep into a mound of dirt near the outfield perimeter and could not be extricated in time.

July 22, 1884

At Providence, manager Frank Bancroft had difficulty controlling his starting pitcher as the Grays bowed to the Philadelphia Quakers, 10–6. Providence led by a score of 6–2 until the end of the seventh, when right-hander Charlie Sweeney staged an open revolt against Bancroft's authority.

The Grays had played an exhibition game in Woonsocket, Rhode Island, the day before. Sweeney, who had reportedly been drinking heavily throughout the game, refused to return to Providence with the team, choosing instead to spend the night with a woman he had escorted to the ballpark. He missed practice the following morning but showed up at the Messer Street Grounds in time for his scheduled start. Possibly still intoxicated, he managed to hold the Quakers to two runs over seven frames.

Bancroft had seen enough at that point and asked Sweeney to move to right field, calling on Joseph "Cyclone" Miller to finish up. Sweeney outright refused, forcing Bancroft to remove him from the game. Rules at the time prohibited substitutions in the absence of an injury, so Providence was forced to finish the match with just eight men on the field. In the only relief appearance of his brief career, Miller coughed up eight runs and absorbed the loss. According to one report, Sweeney watched the game's conclusion in street clothes and then left with two women, who were believed to be prostitutes. The *New York Tribune* referred to it as "a queer game."

Faced with the prospect of a fine and suspension, Sweeney quit the Grays and defected to the St. Louis Maroons of the Union Association. In his absence, the Grays' only other reliable hurler, veteran Charles "Old Hoss" Radbourne (an eventual Hall of Famer), was forced to pitch nearly every game for the rest of the year. This enabled him to set the all-time mark for wins in a season with fifty-nine.

Meanwhile, Sweeney enjoyed his most successful campaign, collecting a total of forty-one wins and fashioning an impressive 1.70 ERA. Before jumping to St. Louis, Sweeney's record had stood at 17–8. On June 7, he had struck out nineteen Boston hitters—a record that stood until Roger Clemens punched out twenty batters in a game during the 1986 slate. Sweeney's accomplishment was less impressive considering that the mound was located a mere fifty feet from home plate in his day. After 1884, he never posted a winning record.

July 30, 1886

An interesting match was played between the Detroit Wolverines and the Washington Nationals at Swampoodle Grounds in Washington, D.C. The park's funny name was derived from the neighborhood in which it stood, located just a few blocks from the US Capitol. The game ended prematurely when the Nationals provoked the ire of umpire Joe Ellick, who put an end to the proceedings by declaring a forfeit.

Detroit jumped all over rookie hurler George Keefe in the first, plating five runs. They led 6–0 before Washington came storming back with nine scores of their own. Dusk began to descend on the nation's capital as the Wolverines staged a remarkable rally, tagging Keefe for seven more runs in the seventh. Anxious to speed things up before the game was called on account of darkness, Detroit's shortstop Jack Rowe walked off of second base, rounded third, and began strolling casually toward home. Washington players made no effort to tag him, so he stopped in front of the plate and stood there idly until Ellick called him out. Center fielder Ned Hanlon followed with a deliberate strikeout to end the visitors' half of the frame.

Irritated with this turn of events, the Nationals refused to take their turn at bat, griping that Rowe had not been tagged. Ellick grew tired of bickering and ended the match in favor of Detroit. A mob of angry fans rushed the field and tried to attack the arbiter, but they were repelled by police. Four men were arrested. Ellick required a police escort out of the ballpark that day. His gift to Detroit placed them three and a half games ahead of the second-place Chicago White Stockings. Chicago ended up winning the pennant anyway.

August 22, 1886

Describing the American Association match between the Louisville Colonels and Cincinnati Red Stockings that took place on the date in question, a *Sporting Life* correspondent reported: "Eleven stubbornly-contested innings replete with brilliant plays were necessary to decide the contest."

Louisville scratched out a run in the second and Cincinnati answered with one in the third. The score remained deadlocked until the tenth, when both clubs put up a pair of tallies. Colonels right-hander Guy Hecker was dominant that afternoon, yielding just three runs on seven hits in his eleven innings of work. In the eighth, he nearly exited the contest when he was tagged roughly by Red Stockings second baseman Bid McPhee. McPhee applied the tag behind Hecker's ear, reportedly knocking the latter "senseless." Hecker recovered sufficiently to collect the victory.

The game ended on a strange note for Louisville when outfielder Chicken Wolf (whose birth name of William Van Winkle Wolf was equally colorful) launched a deep drive to center field. As Abner Powell was chasing after it, he was attacked by a dog sleeping near the outfield fence. The hostile canine grabbed him by the pants, detaining him long enough to prevent a timely relay to the plate. Wolf scored on the play, helping the Colonels to a 5–3 win.

Cheap home runs would prevail well into the next century. During a 1905 contest between the Athletics and White Sox at South Side Park in Chicago, a member of the Philly squad hammered a towering shot that got stuck on a platform used by the scoreboard operator. Since there were no ground rules to account for this occurrence, outfielder Danny Green was forced to climb a steep wooden ladder in pursuit of the blast. Just as he reached the top, the ball rolled back onto the field. By the time it was recovered, the Philly batter had circled the bases.

August 26, 1889

According to the *Random House Dictionary of Popular Proverbs and Sayings*, the old adage "History repeats itself" can be traced to the mid-fifteenth century. Those words are poignantly accurate when applied to baseball. On August 26, 1889, a game between the Boston Beaneaters and Philadelphia Quakers set the tone for one of the most infamous matches of the twentieth century.

The Quakers had rallied for two runs in the ninth, sending the contest into extra innings. In the twelfth frame, King Kelly was on second and Dan Brouthers was on first for Boston when outfielder Dick Johnston delivered a clutch single to center field. Kelly scored easily on the play, and, believing the game to be over, Johnston stopped short of first and headed for the dressing room. Realizing that his teammate had committed a potentially costly blunder, Kelly grabbed the ball from Philly first baseman Sid Farrar, who clearly intended to tag first and appeal the play.

The two wrestled for possession of the sphere as angry Philadelphia fans spilled onto the field. Realizing the danger he was in, Kelly reportedly hid beneath the grandstand under the protection of players from both sides while additional police were dispatched. Order was restored, and the run was allowed since neither umpire saw Johnston miss first. The 5–4 win would prove to be virtually meaningless as the Beaneaters finished one game behind the Giants anyway. An eerily similar scenario would have a major impact on the National League pennant nearly twenty years later.

This time, Giants first baseman Fred Merkle (just nineteen years old at the time) was the blundering base runner. Tied for first in the National League on September 23, 1908, the Giants and Cubs engaged in an epic battle. With the game knotted at 1 in the bottom of the ninth, Merkle sent teammate Moose McCormick to third with a single. Al Bridwell followed with another hit up the middle that chased McCormick across the plate. Ecstatic hometown fans rushed onto the field, and in the resulting confusion, Merkle stopped short of second base and headed toward the clubhouse.

Outfielder Artie Hofman relayed to Cubs second baseman Johnny Evers, but the throw never arrived as Giants hurler Joe McGinnity intercepted the ball and tossed it into the stands. Evers, who loved to argue, was not so easily deterred, securing a different ball and appealing to home-plate umpire Hank O'Day that Merkle had not touched the bag. O'Day ruled Merkle out on a force and declared the game a tie since clearing the field at that point would be a tremendous undertaking. The call was upheld despite a later appeal, and the contest would directly affect the outcome of the pennant race as the Giants and Cubs remained tied for first at the close of play on October 7. A one-game playoff resulted in a 4–2 Chicago victory. Merkle would forever be branded with the dubious nickname "Bonehead."

August 13, 1891

Right-hander Bob Barr made his pitching debut with the Giants at the Polo Grounds after being acquired from Buffalo's team in the Eastern Association (a minor league). He lasted through two and a third innings before sustaining one of the most bizarre injuries of all time. In the top of the third, he yielded a lead-off homer to Cincinnati's Arlie Latham. He had just retired Jocko Halligan on a circus catch by second baseman Danny Richardson when the unlikely injury occurred.

As Barr was waiting for a return throw from catcher Dick Buckley, a fan in the left-field bleachers decided to return a foul ball back onto the field. There were fewer balls to go around in the nineteenth century, and fans were obligated to toss them back, sometimes under threat of arrest. According to a game account in the *New York Sun*, "The person who threw the ball desired to show what a strong thrower he was so he lined the ball against Barr's right temple." The big hurler collapsed in a heap and remained on the ground while Giants personnel soaked his head with water. Unable to continue, he spent the rest of the afternoon on the bench.

Right-hander Mickey Welch assumed pitching responsibilities and gave up five runs in a 7–4 New York loss. Barr would make just four more appearances that season and then finish his career in the minors. He was not the only major league player to be injured in this fashion. On August 18, 1911, White Sox catcher Fred Payne had several teeth knocked out when he was struck in the face by a foul ball thrown back onto the field from the grandstand at Comiskey Park.

September 4, 1891

Cap Anson, the second manager (after Harry Wright) to win one thousand games and the first to reach three thousand hits, was among the game's earliest superstars. Retiring from active play in 1897, he remains the all-time Cubs leader in hits (3,435), doubles (582), and RBIs (2,075). In Anson's day, the Cubs played as the White Stockings and later as the Colts.

By 1891, Anson was thirty-nine years old and his numbers were beginning to taper off. Though he led the NL in ribbies that year with 120, he would never again pace the circuit in any offensive category during his remaining six seasons. There were whispers that he was too old to play the game, and newspapers often referred to him as "the old man." On the date in question, Anson decided to poke fun at his detractors by appearing on the field in a wig and long white beard. The *Pittsburgh Press* reported that his "clown act was loudly applauded" while the *New York Tribune* remarked that he "created a great deal of merriment." A large crowd was on hand to witness the unusual gag.

Wearing the "grandpa" costume throughout, Anson made eleven putouts at first base but failed to contribute offensively in Chicago's 5–3 win. Concerns about about his age would resurface three days later, when he napped through the first game of a Labor Day doubleheader at Eastern Park in Brooklyn. The Colts lost 21–3 without him. Anson showed up at the ballpark in time for the second match and, sufficiently rested, hit a three-run homer in the top of the first off of Tom Lovett to help Chicago bounce back with a 9–8 victory.

May 15, 1894

Tempers were wearing thin at Boston's South End Grounds as the fifth-place Beaneaters faced the second-place Baltimore Orioles, who had administered a 16–5 thrashing the previous day. In the bottom of the third inning with Boston leading 5–3, a hellacious fight broke out between Orioles third sacker John McGraw and Beaneaters first baseman Tommy Tucker. After the scrum had been cleared, a fire started by a cigarette or match ignited a pile of trash beneath the right-field stands. Nobody took this seriously at first, and many of the 3,500 spectators began chanting, "Play ball!"

As the fire began to grow, Boston's right fielder Jimmy Bannon rushed under the seats and tried to stamp it out with his feet. A gust of wind fanned the flames, and Bannon was eventually forced to retreat. Many spectators were driven into the left-field corner due to the intense heat and began exiting through a hole in the center-field fence. People in the grandstand loitered until police and officials ordered them to get out.

The following account appeared in the *New York Sun*: "With the pavilion and grandstand in flames, the fire took a strange course. After the burning of the right field bleachers, the flames ran along the fence at the lower end of the field and from the outside reached the left-field bleachers. Thus, at one time, the fire almost completely encircled the baseball grounds." The *Sun* reported that the double-decked grandstand was "the handsomest in the country" and had been built in 1888 at a cost of $68,000—a considerable sum in those days.

Sparks from the blaze ignited adjacent buildings, resulting in one of the worst fires the city of Boston had ever faced. According to newspaper reports, the flames swept over twelve acres, consuming 175 buildings and leaving more than a thousand people homeless. Games were moved to the Congress Street Grounds until the original park could be rebuilt. Construction took about two and a half months to complete.

Boston was not the only setting for a ballpark fire during the 1894 slate. On August 5, Cap Anson was batting in the seventh inning of a game at Chicago's West Side Grounds when a fire caused by a discarded cigar broke out in the grandstand. The crowd of six thousand began to stampede, injuring many. In an attempt to escape the blaze, fans ripped down a barbed-wire fence that had been installed to prevent spectators from assaulting the umpire. Chicago Colts outfielders Jimmy Ryan and Walt Wilmot assisted in tearing down another barrier to allow fans onto the field. The game was declared official, and Chicago came away with an 8–1 win over the Reds.

June 18, 1894

In the nineteenth century, there was no such thing as a "relief pitcher." Hurlers were expected to pitch until their arms fell off in good times and bad. This unspoken code produced some interesting results over the years.

On the above-mentioned date, the Boston Beaneaters celebrated Bunker Hill Day in Boston by sending twenty-two men to the plate against Tony Mullane in the first inning. By the time Mullane had recorded the third out, Boston had scored sixteen runs on eleven safeties, seven walks, and a hit batsman. The sixteen tallies were a record for the first inning of a major league game. Hugh Duffy, Bobby Lowe, and Herman Long all reached base three times in the frame.

Though it was clear Mullane was tossing lollipops to the plate, Orioles manager Ned Hanlon stuck with him anyway, finally lifting him in the seventh after he had staked Boston to an insurmountable 24–4 lead. Bert Inks mopped up in the 24–7 loss. In the second game of this doubleheader, Baltimore exacted revenge with a 9–7 victory.

Playing in his last season, Mullane compiled a 6–9 record with a 6.31 ERA during the 1894 slate. He had definitely seen better days. In his prime, he had earned the nickname "the Apollo of the Box" by winning thirty or more games in five consecutive seasons. An interesting claim to fame: Mullane was one of few ambidextrous players and used both hands to throw during a game more than once.

July 20, 1894

A hotly contested match between the Pirates and Reds took place at Cincinnati's League Park. One reporter declared that "errors at critical times nearly defeated the Reds today." There were four Cincinnati errors in all as the hometown crew barely escaped with a dramatic 7–6 win.

Pittsburgh led 5–3 before the Reds answered with two runs in the seventh. The score remained that way at the end of regulation. The Pirates plated a run in the tenth, but a Farmer Vaughn homer knotted the score again in the bottom of the frame. With two outs, shortstop Germany Smith hammered a long shot into the left-field bleachers. According to Charlton's *Baseball Chronology*, peculiar ground rules allowed outfielders to retrieve balls from that area, and Pittsburgh's Elmer Smith tried valiantly to do so. He wrestled with spectators and fended off several with his fists before one overzealous (and possibly insane) Reds fan threatened him with a gun. Realizing the gravity of the situation, he beat a hasty retreat.

According to the original box score, it was a shaky outing for Pittsburgh's Red Ehret as he walked eight, hit a batter, and uncorked a wild pitch. Ice Box Chamberlain was only slightly better for Cincinnati, yielding six runs on seven hits and four walks. Cincinnati stranded seven runners to Pittsburgh's eight. Many of the 1,200 spectators stuck around to witness the game's bizarre conclusion.

June 23, 1895

In colonial times, strict religious laws formed the framework for how Americans (specifically Christians) were expected to conduct themselves. Referred to as "blue laws" by those who found them oppressive, codes against sports games on Sunday persisted into the nineteenth century and were adopted by the National League when it was founded in 1876. Even after NL officials lifted the ban on Sunday baseball, local religious chapters found ways to meddle in the affairs of various teams.

On June 23, 1895, a game between the Chicago Colts and Cleveland Spiders was halted after the third inning when the "Sunday Observance League" successfully lobbied Chicago police to arrest the entire hometown squad for "aiding and abetting a noisy crowd on Sunday." Colts president John Hart agreed to submit quietly to arrest if bonds would be issued on the spot. Those conditions were accepted with warrants being sworn out by local justice Frank A. Cleveland.

To the delight of 13,800 noisy fans, the game resumed, and the Colts handed out a 13–4 pasting to the Spiders. Eight of nine Chicago starters had at least two hits off of left-hander Phil Knell that afternoon. Meanwhile in St. Louis, another NL match went off without a hitch as the Browns defeated the Reds, 9–3.

A similar scene unfolded in Cleveland on May 16, 1897, when a scoreless game between the Spiders and Senators was stopped after the first inning by law enforcement officials. Nine thousand fans were already seated when police closed the gates of League Park, leaving thousands more clamoring for admission. More than a dozen players from both teams were arrested along with umpire Tim Hurst. Bail was set at one hundred dollars per player, and it cost Spiders owner Frank Robison a pretty penny to secure their release. No attempt was made to play the game afterward. An example was made of Cleveland's rookie hurler Jack Powell, who was found guilty of playing ball on Sunday and fined five dollars.

On June 19 of the following year, players in Cleveland would again be arrested for violating Sunday blue laws. The game was preempted in the eighth inning with the Spiders leading, 4–3. According to Charlton's *Baseball Chronology*, the stoppage was a ruse concocted by Cleveland owners to assure victory for their club.

June 19, 1896

Dissension broke out in Cleveland during the seventh inning of a game between the Spiders and Colts. With two men out, Cleveland catcher Jack O'Connor caught Fred Pfeffer leading too far off of first. His snap throw to Patsy Tebeau was in plenty of time, and umpire Thomas J. Lynch promptly called Pfeffer out. As the Spiders were exiting the field, Lynch reversed his call, deciding that Tebeau had violated the rules by completely blocking Pfeffer's return route to the bag. Tebeau, who also served as Cleveland's manager, pleaded his case but was ordered back to his defensive post. In the meantime, Colts outfielder George Decker (who was stationed at third) scampered home with a run.

The dispute between Tebeau and Lynch turned ugly when Tebeau commented that he would "like to wipe the earth" with Lynch. Lynch challenged him to do just that, removing his chest pad and mask. According to newspaper accounts, a fight was narrowly avoided when police and players from both teams intervened. Lynch refused to finish the game, however, prompting the Spiders to lodge an official protest and request a new arbiter for the next day's match. Cy Young of Cleveland and Con Dailey of Chicago were recruited as umpires to complete the game at hand, which ended in a convincing 8–3 Colts win.

A hard-nosed player with a penchant for causing trouble, Tebeau would appear before a Louisville judge to answer charges of disturbing the peace in the wake of a brawl that took place during a game against the Colonels on June 26. He was fined one hundred dollars. Three days later, the NL board of directors imposed another fine on Tebeau for rowdyism. He refused to pay it and announced his intentions to seek legal counsel. When league president Nick Young suspended Tebeau for various indiscretions on July 13, the incorrigible player/manager ignored the penalty and suited up anyway after securing a court injunction.

July 17, 1896

The ninth inning proved to be quite eventful in a game between the Phillies and Pirates at Exposition Park in Pittsburgh. The Bucs led by a run entering the final frame, but Philly batters rallied for three runs off of a tiring Charlie Hastings. In the bottom of the inning, Pittsburgh loaded the bases on a disputed call. Philadelphia players argued strenuously with umpire William Betts but neglected to call for time. Pirates shortstop Bones Ely snuck home while the dispute was in progress.

Infuriated by this development, Philly hurler Jack Taylor punched Betts. His battery mate, Jack Clements, would have done the same had player/manager Billy Nash not rushed onto the field and grabbed him. Both Taylor and Clements were ejected. Kid Carsey took the mound as Mike Grady assumed catching responsibilities. Things fell apart in a hurry as Carsey was called for a balk, allowing the tying run to score. Again, Betts found himself surrounded by angry Philly players, and police were summoned to calm things down. When order was restored, Pittsburgh's Jake Beckley delivered a game-winning single. The *New York Sun* reported that "the game ended in a most disgraceful snarl."

Carsey was not an ideal choice as a closer. He was a highly erratic right-hander who averaged fourteen wild pitches per year between 1891 and 1896.

Using a sidearm cross-fire delivery, he consistently walked more batters than he struck out. "Sometimes I'd get 'em out and sometimes I wouldn't," he told *Baseball Digest* in 1951.

June 1, 1897

The Pirates squandered a game to the Giants at the Polo Grounds when several players became incensed by the officiating of umpire Michael McDermott. Staked to a 7–0 lead in the sixth, Bucs southpaw Frank Killen lost his effectiveness, giving up four runs before recording an out. With New York's Ducky Holmes on first, catcher Parke Wilson hit a grounder to second baseman Dick Padden. Padden raced in and appeared to tag Holmes before relaying to first. McDermott called Holmes out initially but changed his ruling a couple of seconds later, contending that Padden had missed the tag. Pittsburgh players felt that Holmes had run out of the baseline, and this touched off a major dispute.

McDermott was mobbed by angry Pirates, who jostled him roughly. Though Padden, Killen, and manager Patsy Donovan were fined twenty-five dollars on the spot for the use of profanity, their vulgar tirade continued unabated. Ejected from the proceedings, all three refused to leave. McDermott warned Donovan that the game would be forfeited to the Giants if play did not resume promptly. Ignoring the threat, center fielder Steve Brodie joined the dissenters, shouting to his teammates, "Don't play!" McDermott then handed the contest to the New Yorkers by a score of 9–0. The *Sun* reported that "the Pittsburgs came to their senses, but it was too late. They had thrown away a chance to win by sheer block-headedness."

McDermott was involved in another ugly dispute in New York three days later, when Louisville's player/manager Jim Rogers became furious with a questionable call and had to be physically restrained by teammates. A beat writer commented: "There was another disgraceful scene at the Polo Grounds yesterday caused by the apparent incompetency of umpire McDermott. The fair-minded ones in the crowd of 1,500 who saw the game will back up the statement that McDermott's work all through the game was what has been often termed poor umpiring." McDermott would not be rehired by the National League in 1898.

June 29, 1897

The Colts demoralized the Louisville Colonels at Chicago, setting a National League record for runs scored in a 36–7 romp. The *New York Tribune* referred to the game as "the greatest picnic of the season" while the *Sun* called it "the sorriest kind of farce." Fortunately for Louisville, only two hundred fans were on hand to witness it.

Seven Chicago players scored four or more runs, tying the all-time mark set by an earlier Windy City squad. According to the original box score, shortstop BarryMcCormick enjoyed his most productive day of the season, scoring five runs on six hits, which included a homer and a triple. Charlton's *Baseball Chronology* reported that the winning pitcher, Nixey Callahan, went five for seven and would go on to amass five hits in a game twice more in his career—a record for hurlers.

On the losing side, Louisville staff ace Chick Fraser didn't last through the third inning and had staked Chicago to an 8–0 lead by the end of the second. Jim Jones came on in relief and was forced to endure 6.2 brutal innings, facing forty-five batters while yielding twenty-two runs. It was his only pitching appearance of the year. Nine Louisville errors led to a total of twenty-one unearned runs that day.

August 4, 1897

One of the most irritable umpires ever to don a mask, Tim Hurst caused a serious disturbance in a game between the Reds and Pirates at Cincinnati. The Reds had breezed to a 14–3 win in the opener of this doubleheader and were leading 4–1 in the second contest when Hurst called Cincy's left fielder Bug Holliday out at second. Holliday protested, insisting that he had been tripped by second baseman Dick Padden, but Hurst stood firm on his ruling. The crowd roared its disapproval, and an unruly fan tossed a beer glass onto the field. According to one newspaper account, "The glass rolled near [Hurst] and did not seem to be swiftly thrown." Hurst lost his cool anyway, whipping the glass back into the stands.

The projectile struck a local fireman named James Cartuyvelles over the right eye, opening a deep gash that bled freely. Believing the fan to be seriously hurt, police took Hurst into custody, carting him to the Oliver Street station house in a paddy wagon. He would be charged with assault and battery and fired from his job. In his absence, Red Bittman took over. The game was called in the sixth inning with the score tied at 4–4.

Hurst would manage the Browns to a pitiful 39–111 record in 1898 and then serve as a boxing promoter/referee before reappearing as an umpire in the American League. He would end up being fired again for an unpleasant incident that took place in a game between the White Sox and A's in 1909. (Details of that game appear later in this book.)

April 16, 1898

A looming hazard of the wooden ballpark era, fire destroyed the grandstand, pavilion, and bleachers at Sportsman's Park in St. Louis. The Browns were batting in the second inning and had shortstop Russ Hall on first base when the blaze was first spotted by someone in the bleachers. Spectators remained relatively calm until a wall of flame shot up through the floor of the grandstand to the roof. Mass panic ensued.

The stairways quickly became clogged with bodies as the crowd began to stampede. Men were seen taking women in their arms and tossing them over the railing onto the field—a drop of twelve feet. Several panicked patrons jumped from the rear of the grandstand to the ground some forty feet below. Reporters in the press box, which was located on top of the grandstand, escaped injury by jumping onto the roof of a maintenance shed. As a stiff breeze whipped the fire into a fury, players worked together to pile their benches against the railing of the grandstand. Numerous women and children used them to slide to safety.

No deaths were reported, but there were many injuries, mainly broken bones sustained by jumpers and cracked ribs suffered by those crammed into the stairways. Browns owner Chris von der Ahe, who lived in an apartment suite above the clubhouse, lost most of his possessions. "I haven't a shirt to my back," he told a *Sporting Life* correspondent. "All my papers, everything is gone."

A rebuilding project began immediately. By midnight, an army of carpenters had reconstructed the fence and erected temporary box offices. By the following morning, several thousand circus seats had been assembled. The unfinished game was replayed at 3:30 that afternoon. The Browns would have done well to postpone it as the Chicago Orphans (formerly known as the Colts) handed them a humiliating 14–1 loss.

May 3, 1899

An anonymous Pirates employee helped secure a win for the Bucs in a dramatic finish at Exposition Park in Pittsburgh. The Pirates had managed just one run on four hits against Colonels southpaw Pete Dowling through eight innings. With a 6–1 cushion, Dowling became rattled by a pair of Louisville errors as the Pirates suddenly lit up the scoreboard. Following singles by Bones Ely and Frank Bowerman, outfielder Tom McCreery smashed a homer to tie the score. With two outs, Jack McCarthy hit a deep shot to right field, receiving a little help from the stadium crew.

McCarthy's drive rolled to the right-field gate, where (according to members of the Colonels) an unnamed employee opened the doorway to assure the ball's entry and then closed it immediately afterward, barring access to Charlie Dexter, who was in hot pursuit. McCarthy circled the bases with the winning run. Feeling cheated, Louisville lodged a formal protest that was upheld a month later. League officials ordered the game replayed.

In the final analysis, the contest was meaningless to both clubs. Pittsburgh finished in seventh place with a 76–73 record. Louisville ended up three games behind them at 75–77. The two clubs would face each other on the last day of the season and end the campaign on another unusual note. After the Colonels had rallied for a 6–5 lead in the ninth, thick smoke from neighboring steel mills enveloped the field, severely reducing visibility. The game was called by umpires, and the score automatically reverted back to the eighth inning with the Pirates leading 5–2. For the Colonels, it was a disheartening finish to a dismal campaign.

September 7, 1899

After this eventful game between the Superbas and Beaneaters was completed, an article in the *Sun* proclaimed that "never before in the history of baseball in Brooklyn has such a riotous demonstration of spectators been seen." It was indeed an ugly scene as umpires Bob Emslie and Frank Dwyer set off the crowd of six thousand with controversial rulings.

Brooklyn led the third-place Bostonians by nine and a half games in the standings entering the match. It was closely contested throughout, with the Superbas nursing a 1–0 lead after seven innings. The trouble began in the eighth, when Boston catcher Marty Bergen led off with a walk but strayed too far from third after a single by Chick Stahl. A relay from rival catcher Deacon McGuire appeared to nail Bergen, but Dwyer called him safe, inspiring the crowd to display "a tremendous outburst of disapproval." Boston tied the score in the inning and plated another run in the ninth thanks to a leadoff walk to Hall of Famer Billy Hamilton. According to newspapers, the crowd was in "a frenzy" when the bottom of the ninth got under way.

After two quick outs, second baseman Tom Daly drew a walk. Bill Dahlen followed with a hit to center field. Dahlen was running on the play and had no intention of stopping at third. The throw from second baseman Bobby Lowe was high, and Bergen applied the tag to Daly's head. Emslie called Daly out to end the game, and chaos followed.

The *Sun*'s hyperbolic description of the scene was as follows: "The crowd piled out of the bleaching boards and grandstand like a human waterfall. At least half of the assemblage rushed at the umpire, who was joined immediately by his assistant, Dwyer." Brooklyn players surrounded the arbiters but could not prevent one fan from punching Emslie in the face. Emslie responded with a right to the man's chin, knocking him flat on his back. Several others flailed at Emslie while Dwyer was shoved roughly about.

Boston players began to push the crowd back led by Fred Tenney, who had armed himself with a bat. Brooklyn team president Charlie Ebbets shouted at people to disperse, but he was quickly drawn into the fray, and his words were ignored. The umpires were showered with dirt and stones as they climbed into the grandstand. A man wearing an army hat reportedly punched Emslie in the stomach. A gaggle of police officers then appeared, escorting the embattled officials to the dressing room.

Ebbets offered protection, but the umpires refused, boldly walking out the park's front entrance into an angry throng of fans. Police were forced to intervene, escorting the arbiters up the street and then drawing their clubs to allow Emslie and Dwyer access to an elevated train platform. There were more protesters waiting above as the two were safely ushered onto a train. Emslie told a reporter: "I called Daly out because he did not touch the plate. It was as I saw it and I was perfectly honest in my judgment." Brooklyn claimed the NL championship that year, with Boston finishing a distant second.

Part 2
THE DEADBALL ERA, 1900-1919

Timeline of Significant Events

1901   The American League is declared a major league.

1903   Foul balls are counted as strikes in both leagues. The first World Series pits Boston against Pittsburgh.

1904   Highlanders pitcher Jack Chesbro sets a post-1800s record for wins in a season (forty-one). Cy Young tosses the first perfect game in American League history.

1905   Vic Willis sets the all-time mark for losses in a season with twenty-nine. He'll find his way into the Hall of Fame despite this dubious feat.

1906   The Cubs establish a modern record for wins with 116. They lose the World Series to the White Sox, who hit just .230 collectively during the regular season.

1907   A committee organized by sporting goods manufacturer Al Spalding declares Abner Doubleday the inventor of baseball despite overwhelming evidence to the contrary.

1908   Ed Walsh of the White Sox hurls 464 innings—a record that will likely stand forever.

1909   Forbes Field in Pittsburgh and Shibe Park in Philadelphia open—the first all concrete and steel stadiums.

1910   Comiskey Park in Chicago opens. William Howard Taft becomes the first president to open the season with a ceremonial pitch.

1911   Cy Young records his last major league win, establishing a virtually unsurpassable lifetime mark of 511.

1912   Fenway Park in Boston opens. Owen Wilson of the Pirates sets an all-time record for triples with thirty-six.

1914   The Federal League opens for business, billing itself as a third "major" league. Napoléon Lajoie and Honus Wagner each collect career hit number three thousand.

1915   Unable to meet salary demands of many star players, the once-proud Athletics begin a run of seven consecutive last-place finishes. The Federal League closes its gates as Eddie Plank becomes the first lefty to register three hundred career wins.

1916   Pete Alexander of the Phillies tosses a record sixteen shutouts. The Giants win seventeen straight road games but still end up in fourth place.

1918   World War I brings the season to a close on September 2.

1919   Members of the White Sox conspire to throw the World Series.
           The repercussions will change the sport forever. Babe Ruth hits
           twenty-nine homers, a single-season record he will shatter the
           following year.

April 26, 1900

On their way to the Polo Grounds for a game against the Boston Beaneaters, three Giants players displayed true heroism when they hopped off a
streetcar and entered a burning building on West 144th Street to save some of
the inhabitants. Shortstop George Davis pulled out a woman who had fainted
in the extreme heat. Second baseman Kid Gleason and catcher Mike Grady
worked together to assist a woman and child down a fire escape. More than
forty families were reportedly left homeless in the tenement fire.

The trio of Gotham players continued their heroics on the field as the
Giants rallied from a 10–5 deficit in the ninth to send the game into extra
innings. Gleason scored two runs and drove in another with a sacrifice. Davis
scored once and delivered a clutch RBI triple. Grady plated a run and recorded six putouts. When Boston rallied for three runs in the tenth, the Giants
resorted to drastic measures.

With Vic Willis on the mound for Boston and darkness fast approaching,
Grady and several of his teammates began to protest loudly that the game
should be called. Umpire Tom Connolly ignored their pleas, fining them five
dollars apiece. Kip Selbach and Jack Doyle took their sweet time reporting to
the plate and then loitered outside the batter's box between pitches. Several
of the Giants' players lit scraps of paper on fire and waved them at Connolly
while fans in the bleachers followed suit. Finally, with two men out and a man
on first, the arbiter could delay the inevitable no longer. The score reverted to
a 10–10 tie as the game was called. Defending his decision to drag things out,
Connolly told a reporter, "I simply refused to call the game as long as there
was light enough for me to see the plays."

August 17, 1900

Center fielder Roy Thomas spent his best seasons with the Phillies from
1899 through 1907. Extremely lanky at five feet eleven inches and 150
pounds, the pesky leadoff man had a penchant for irritating opponents with
his keen batting eye. The slap-hitting Thomas often wore hurlers down by
fouling off pitch after pitch. According to multiple sources, Thomas once
fouled off twenty-seven offerings in a single at bat. During a lengthy plate

appearance against Brooklyn in 1900, manager Ned Hanlon shouted at him: "Have your fun now, kid, because we're going to take care of you next year!"

On August 17 of that year, the Phillies and Reds were locked in a tight match at League Park in Cincinnati. Thomas was doing his thing against right-hander Bill Phillips. The *New York Tribune* reported that Thomas had fouled off "ten balls or more" when Phillips began to protest to umpire Bob Emslie. After another foul brought a new ball into play, Phillips walked to the plate and knocked Thomas down "with a right hook on the jaw." He reportedly would have kept swinging had Emslie not stepped in front of him. Phillips claimed that Thomas had made a snide remark to him, but Emslie was having none of it, tossing the exasperated hurler out of the game. Interestingly, the altercation took place on "Ladies Day" at the stadium. Doc Newton assumed mop-up duties for Phillips as the game went into extra innings. The Reds came away with a 5–4 win in eleven frames. Thomas and Phillips reportedly shook hands after the game was over.

As predicted by Brooklyn manager Ned Hanlon, the NL adopted the foul-strike rule in 1901 to eliminate "the tediousness of seeing batsmen deliberately foul off good balls in the hope of tiring the pitcher." The new regulation hardly affected Thomas at all as he would lead the league in walks for five straight seasons, drawing more than one hundred bases on balls every year in that span. He retired with a handsome .413 on-base percentage in thirteen big league campaigns. He remains the only major league regular to score three times as many runs as he drove in, according to baseball guru Bill James.

September 19, 1900

Commenting on the game played between the Superbas and Cardinals on this date, a writer from the *Sun* offered the following words: "Baseball as controlled by the National League has received a hard knock of late but nothing so disastrous as the row that wound up the Brooklyn-St. Louis game at Washington Park yesterday afternoon."

The "row" occurred in the third inning, when Brooklyn catcher Duke Farrell opened with a double and then moved to third on a sacrifice by his battery mate, Joe McGinnity. Fielder Jones then hit a grounder to shortstop Bobby Wallace, who threw home ahead of Farrell. The ball took a bad hop in front of the plate, but Cards catcher Wilbert Robinson retrieved it in time to attempt a tag. Umpire John Gaffney called Farrell safe, after which Robinson completely lost his composure, ripping off his mask and throwing the ball at Gaffney's legs. Infuriated, Gaffney hit Robinson over the head with his mask. Players separated the two, and Robinson was ejected and fined five dollars.

Cardinals captain John McGraw rushed to the scene, calling Gaffney a "dirty robber." He was promptly put out of the game along with Robinson. McGraw then informed Gaffney that backup catcher Lou Criger had a broken rib and third-stringer Fritz Buelow was incapacitated with a bad finger. This left the Cardinals without a backstop. Mulling it over, Gaffney consulted with Brooklyn captain Joe Kelley, asking whether the hosts would be willing to allow Robinson back in the game. Kelley contended that Gaffney should stick to his original decision. The game was declared a forfeit in favor of Brooklyn just as the injured Criger was getting ready to suit up.

Gaffney's decision stirred the crowd of one thousand to clamor for refunds. Team secretary T. C. Simpson authorized the issuing of rain checks, but many patrons continued to complain loudly. Owner Charlie Ebbets finally arrived on the scene and instructed personnel at the main entrance to give out cash refunds. Gaffney told a reporter, "I am sorry for the people who paid to see a game, but it could not be helped. The St. Louis captain told me on the field that my decision was just." Robinson expressed regret for his actions and issued an indirect apology.

May 5, 1901

Even after the turn of the century, managers expected their starting pitchers to go the distance. White Sox manager Clark Griffith adhered stubbornly to this philosophy despite Roy Patterson's ineffectiveness on the above-mentioned date. Though Patterson would receive the nickname of "Boy Wonder" during his career, he was far from wonderful against the Brewers during this disastrous outing, facing a major league record of fifty-seven batters. (Bill Phillips of the Reds would set the National League record a month later, when he faced fifty-five batters in a loss to the Phillies.)

The home team batted first, a practice that was not unheard of at the time. Patterson was moderately effective through the third frame, at which point Chicago held a 4–1 lead over their hosts. But Milwaukee came storming back in the middle innings, adding seventeen runs by the end of the sixth. Patterson was not helped at all by seven White Sox errors but had no excuse for the twenty-five hits and thirty-six total bases he surrendered. Manager Clark Griffith was thrown out of Milwaukee's Lloyd Street Grounds by umpire Tom Connolly for arguing a call (perhaps he was tired of watching Patterson pitch).

Milwaukee finished dead last that year with a 48–89 record while the White Sox captured the American League pennant. Patterson won twenty games and posted a respectable 3.37 ERA (still a bit suspect for the deadball era). He completed thirty of his thirty-five starts that year.

June 4, 1901

A correspondent from the *Sun* referred to Cincinnati's Barney McFadden as "Wild Barney" after he issued eleven walks in this game against the Brooklyn Superbas. According to the same writer, McFadden was "not half as wild as [Jimmy] Sheckard, who nearly precipitated a riot by a disgusting exhibition of hot-headed rowdyism."

In the third inning, Sheckard drew a walk and then stole second base. Tom Daly followed with another walk. Shortly afterward, Sheckard got caught off the bag at second on a relay by Cincinnati catcher Heinie Pietz. Sheckard didn't believe the tag had been made in time and ended up getting tossed from the game when he directed a stream of profanity at umpire Bert Cunningham. Sheckard ignored the arbiter and took his position in left field anyway. When Cunningham insisted he sit on the bench, Sheckard ran toward home plate, shouting. After being ordered off the grounds by the arbiter, he spat in Cunningham's face and threw a handful of dust at him. Police were summoned to escort Sheckard out of the stadium as Cincinnati fans peppered him with verbal abuse. On the way out, a fan in the bleachers threw a punch at him. Lefty Davis took over in left field as the Superbas breezed to a 7–3 win.

After the game, Cunningham was credited with the following quote: "That's the limit and if any other player tries the same trick, I shall pick up a bat and use it. How do they expect an umpire to work if they get no protection?" Brooklyn manager Ned Hanlon fined Sheckard an additional fifty dollars, but no further action was taken. The National League did not renew Cunningham's contract in 1902. "Wild Barney" McFadden would issue forty walks in forty-six innings of work during the 1901 campaign yet be released from the majors after one lackluster start the following year.

July 1, 1901

The Irish-born Jack Doyle rarely backed down from a fight, receiving the nickname of "Dirty Jack" for his aggressive style of play. In the first half of the 1901 campaign, Doyle broke his hand and was out of action for quite some time. By July 1, he had recuperated sufficiently enough to be penciled into the Orphans' lineup against the Giants. Doyle had spent portions of seven seasons in New York and had been traded to Chicago during the off-season.

Perhaps seeing Doyle as a traitor or defector, numerous fans at the Polo Grounds harassed him every time he took the field. By the end of the fifth inning, Doyle's patience was wearing thin. On the way back to the Chicago dugout, he "spoke sharply" to a man in the right-field bleachers. When the man challenged Doyle to come up and settle the dispute face to face, the hot-headed first sacker gladly obliged, hopping over the railing into the stands. Doyle threw a hard left at the heckler and, according to one newspaper account, "There was a sound as if someone had slapped a couple of fat boards together." The two grappled briefly until police broke it up, and Doyle returned to the dugout.

As it turns out, the right-handed Doyle had chosen the wrong fist to lead with. When he struck the fan, he reinjured the hand that had recently healed. Manager Tom Loftus was forced to pull him from the game in the eighth inning. Doyle was hitless in the 6–4 loss as Frank Chance took over at first. Hampered by injuries that year, Doyle missed more than seventy-five games. He ended up compiling a lifetime .299 batting average in seventeen major league seasons.

August 21, 1901

A game at Washington's American League Park was marred by yet another violent incident. In the bottom of the fourth, Boileryard Clarke and Pop Foster were on base for the Senators when Bill Coughlin drew a walk off of White Sox hurler Jack Katoll. Chicago catcher Joe Sugden didn't agree with the ball four call, and after Billy Clingman followed with a bases-clearing triple, Sugden decided to get even with umpire John Haskell.

With Win Mercer at the plate, Sugden deliberately let Katoll's second pitch elude his glove and hit the umpire. The vengeance came with a price as Haskell ruled that Clingman was entitled to advance from third on the play. After the call had been made, Katoll demonstrated his frustration by throwing the ball full speed at Haskell. The besieged official promptly ejected Katoll from the game and was then assaulted by shortstop Frank Shugart, who hit Haskell in the mouth, drawing blood. Haskell tangled with Shugart briefly as the entire Chicago club converged on him.

Washington players and police rushed to the umpire's aid, and a free-for-all ensued when fans swarmed onto the field. After a considerable delay, Shugart and Katoll were arrested and escorted off the grounds. When the game resumed, Washington rolled to an 8–0 victory. Both offending players were fined by the league.

Haskell was not the only umpire to come under fire that day. Tom Connolly found himself surrounded by angry Orioles players when a close call at first went against Baltimore. According to various accounts, Hall of Fame pitcher Joe McGinnity spat in Connolly's face, and when Detroit's Kid Elberfeld stepped in, he was punched by Mike Donlin of Baltimore. A full-scale brawl erupted, and numerous players were arrested. The game was declared a forfeit in favor of Detroit.

September 5, 1901

Right-hander Roscoe Miller had an auspicious major league debut in 1901, winning twenty-three games for Detroit while posting a respectable 2.95 ERA. He had honed his craft in the Interstate League before signing with the Tigers in 1900, when they were considered a minor league club. Miller posted a 19–9 record that year. Nicknamed "Roxy" or "Rubberlegs," the slender hurler could be quite temperamental on the mound.

On September 5, Miller became aggravated for some undisclosed reason and began to sulk. The Tigers had blown a 4–3 lead in the middle innings to the A's, and Miller inexplicably decided to help the opposition. He began lobbing pitches to Philadelphia batters and then grinning when batters hit them. According to one account, he deliberately threw a bunt into the stands, allowing three runs to score. Thanks to Miller's "gift," the A's came away with an 11–9 victory. Socks Seybold, Dave Fultz, and Joe Dolan administered the most damage for Philly, with three hits apiece.

Miller would not start another game for a week, returning on September 12 to beat Cleveland, 5–4. He fell on hard times after the 1901 slate, never winning more than seven games in a season. He was gone from the majors after the 1904 campaign.

April 27, 1902

One of the most bizarre plays in history unfolded during a game between the Chicago Orphans and Pittsburgh Pirates at Chicago's West Side Grounds. Nineteen-year-old rookie Jim St. Vrain pitched brilliantly until the eighth, when a pair of singles and two hit batsmen resulted in two Pirate runs, which proved to be the difference in the Orphans' 2–0 loss. Despite St. Vrain's impressive pitching line (9 IP/5 H/2 R/1 BB), his performance was overshadowed by an embarrassing gaffe that was witnessed by more than fifteen thousand spectators.

Though St. Vrain was a left-handed pitcher, he batted from the right side. Looking to jump-start the Chicago offense that day, manager Frank Selee suggested that St. Vrain hit lefty against the right-handed Deacon Phillippe. Following instructions, the freshman hurler grounded to Honus Wagner at short but became disoriented and ran to third base. Wagner was reportedly "astonished," collecting himself in plenty of time to throw St. Vrain out at first.

Despite his handsome 2.08 ERA in twelve games, St. Vrain didn't fit into Chicago's plans, making his last big league appearance in June 1902. He finished his career in the minors. Interestingly, statistics reveal that St. Vrain was a perpetual victim of sloppy defense. In 1905, his last professional season, he posted a 2–11 record despite a miserly 0.81 ERA.

July 4, 1902

Heavy rains in Pittsburgh caused the Allegheny River to overflow, flooding Exposition Park. But the Pirates weren't about to let a little water undercut the profits of an Independence Day doubleheader. Both games were played in their entirety as twenty thousand loyal fans turned out to see the defending NL champions take two from the Brooklyn Superbas.

Accounts of playing conditions vary widely. The *Sun* reported that the river was high and the field was "wet." The *New York Tribune* described water on the field as being "ankle deep." The *Pittsburgh Press* elaborated even further, publishing the following lines: "A remarkable feature of the game was that before the morning game was over the Allegheny, which does not seem to know its place, sneaked up a sewer and entered Exposition Park. By afternoon, the outfielders were nearly knee deep in water and the way they played despite the handicap was a source of pleasure to the crowd."

The water was deepest in center field, and balls hit out there were ruled singles. On occasion, players plunged beneath the surface in pursuit of fly balls and were greeted with resounding cheers. In the first game, Jesse Tannehill was virtually unhittable for the Pirates, limiting the Superbas to three base runners in a 3–0 victory. Hall of Famer Jack Chesbro was equally effective for the Bucs in the second game, yielding just five safeties and walking none through nine frames. The result was a 4–0 win and sweep.

Heavy rain in Pittsburgh would cause problems again on the last day of the 1902 campaign. Looking to break the single-season record for wins, the Pirates were determined to play that day despite sloppy conditions. This irritated Cincinnati manager Joe Kelley, who put his players out of position in protest. According to Charlton's *Baseball Chronology*, Joe Kelley, Cy Seymour, and Mike Donlin all smoked on the field. First baseman Jake Beckley was used as a pitcher, coughing up eight runs on nine hits before being relieved by outfielder Cy Seymour. Seymour had taken the hill numerous times during his career, posting a 61–56 record in 140 games. The 1902 novelty appearance was the last of his career. He yielded three runs in three innings of work on that wet afternoon.

A correspondent from the *Pittsburgh Press* remarked that "while the Reds were acting more like monkeys than men, the champions were doing the best they knew how." With the Reds making a mockery of the proceedings, the Pirates captured their 103rd win, the most of any NL team to that point. The mark would be surpassed multiple times over the next decade. Fans who witnessed the Pirates' record-breaking win were offered refunds by team president Barney Dreyfuss, who commented, "We're not going to take money from our friends under false pretenses."

July 7, 1903

Police intervention was required in another episode of umpires and players behaving badly. This time, the setting was Hilltop Park in New York. Chicago's right fielder Danny Green made the second out of the seventh inning, and after complaining loudly to umpire Jack Sheridan, he was thrown out of the game. On his way back to the dugout, Green muttered something to the official that sounded to witnesses like an invitation to slug it out after the game.

Shortly afterward, Green called Sheridan a "bull head" from the bench. Sheridan pulled off his mask and approached the White Sox dugout as the sulking outfielder stepped up to greet him. To the complete surprise of players and spectators, Sheridan smashed Green over the head with his mask. The two clenched briefly until police broke it up. Several unruly fans had to be ushered back to their seats.

Sheridan was carted to the police station, where he was held on charges of disorderly conduct. Highlanders president Joseph Gordon reportedly posted bail. Chicago's Patsy Flaherty and New York's Monte Beville were recruited as umpires to finish the game, which lasted for ten innings. The White Sox came away with a 3–2 victory when a hard smash by George Magoon took a bad hop through the legs of third baseman Harry Howell. Jimmy Callahan scored the deciding run on the play. Magoon had four hits in the contest.

August 8, 1903

A Saturday doubleheader at Philadelphia's Baker Bowl was preempted when beams supporting an overhanging gallery in the left-field bleachers collapsed. Twelve people were killed, and more than two hundred were injured.

The tragedy occurred shortly after 5 p.m. as Boston was batting in the fourth inning of the second contest. Single-game admission was charged for the twin bill, and the crowd was reported to be roughly ten thousand. The bleachers were full, and many more fans were stationed in a gallery that projected roughly three feet beyond the left-field wall over the street. The structure was supported by a series of three-by-eight spruce timbers that were partially rotted, according to sources.

A disturbance on the street involving two drunken men and a group of children who were harassing them caught the attention of spectators. When one of the men hit a little girl, numerous patrons scrambled from their seats to join the crowd already in the gallery. The weight was too much for the decrepit support beams. According to newspaper reports, "There was a sound of rending, splintering wood and a great cry of horror and alarm from the men and boys crowded along the rail" as roughly five hundred people plunged onto Fifteenth Street some twenty feet below.

The *Pittsburgh Press* described the scene in horrifying detail. "They were piled up on the street in a mass of struggling, writhing, groaning humanity with the broken planks and beams of the gallery pressing upon those underneath and adding to their misery." In a remarkable display of altruism, people from neighboring houses and stores and from inside the park rushed quickly to the aid of the stricken. Ambulances and surgeons were dispatched from every city hospital, and police from every precinct responded. Street vendors used their carts to transport the wounded. One vendor carrying beds promptly put them to use as a kind of makeshift hospital. Neighboring houses were opened to those who could walk.

The Phillies were forced to play their remaining games at Columbia Park. Deeply dispirited, they slumped to a 4–13 record in August and a 49–86 showing overall. The team would see better days in 1915, making a World Series appearance against the Red Sox. After that, frugal owners perennially traded or sold the club's best players. As attendance began to sag, the Baker Bowl continued to fall into a state of disrepair. On May 14, 1927, portions of two sections of the lower deck extension along the right-field line collapsed during a game. Again, the mishap was caused by rotting timber supports. A sizable crowd of people who had been seeking shelter from the rain were forced to scramble to safety. According to Charlton's *Baseball Chronology*, the only death was attributed to the stampede, not the collapse.

October 3, 1903

Employees of the Huntington Avenue Grounds in Boston got more than they bargained for on the date above. With baseball's first official World Series knotted at one game apiece, eager fans mobbed the box office and quickly snatched up all the available seats. By the time ticket sales were cut off, a crowd of close to nineteen thousand had entered the park (the largest gathering ever to witness a ball game in Boston to that point). The *Sun* reported that by game time, "men stood fifteen rows deep around the diamond, the pavilion was thronged and every inch of square space on the fence surrounding the grounds was occupied." Others refused to be turned away.

Thousands of trespassers broke through a cordoned-off area and headed toward the reserve grandstand, where they tangled with Boston players and police. A number of female patrons were caught in the crush, and outfielder

Chick Stahl personally ushered two to safety. Armed with a fire hose and bats (supplied by the home team's business manager), police reinforcements were able to secure a fifty-foot stretch beyond the diamond and a thirty-foot swath behind home plate.

By the time the game got under way, the horde of spectators had swelled to roughly twenty-five thousand—more than twice the park's capacity. Special ground rules were established to compensate for the diminished playing surface. It was agreed that balls hit into the crowd (a meager one hundred fifty feet from home) would count as doubles. Tom Hughes was chased from the mound in the third inning as Cy Young carried Boston the rest of the way. A total of seven two-baggers were hit that day as the Pirates notched a 4–2 victory. Pittsburgh eventually dropped the Series in eight games.

May 7, 1904

A tight match between the Giants and Cardinals ended in controversy as a strange play unfolded in the final frame. St. Louis put up a run in the second but failed to break through for the rest of the game against right-hander Dummy Taylor and reliever Joe McGinnity. The Giants were held scoreless until the ninth, when Jack Warner started a rally with a one-out single. Player/ manager John McGraw installed himself as a pinch runner, and Roger Bresnahan, batting for Taylor, smashed a ball to left field. McGraw scored easily on the play as mass confusion set in.

By the time Bresnahan was approaching third, the Giants' players had gathered along the third baseline and were shouting. The Cardinals suffered a defensive lapse when first baseman Jake Beckley ran to third to take the cutoff from left fielder George Barclay. Backing him up were pitcher Jack Taylor (no relation to Dummy) and catcher Mike Grady, who had inexplicably left home plate unattended. With all the shouting and activity, Beckley threw home anyway, and his relay ended up near the grandstand. Bresnahan scored the deciding run.

St. Louis manager Kid Nichols protested the game, citing a rule that stated the following: "If one or more members of the team at bat stand or collect around a base for which a baserunner is trying, thereby confusing the fielding side and adding to the difficulty of making such a play, the baserunner shall be declared out for the interference of his teammate or teammates." On the surface, the argument appeared to be sound, prompting one writer to comment: "Whatever may be the merits of that case, manager Nichols of St. Louis is not one to protest unless he thinks he has a case." NL president Harry Pulliam was of a different mind-set, rejecting the protest. The game would not have meant much anyway as the Cardinals finished in fifth place with a 75–79 record.

May 21, 1904

Some days at the park are better than others. Boston Americans outfielder Bill O'Neill probably wished he was off fishing rather than subbing at shortstop for the defending world champions on the above date. Boston's manager Jimmy Collins must have been questioning his judgment when O'Neill made errors on all three balls hit to him in the first inning, helping the Browns to a 2–0 lead. In the second, O'Neill's display of incompetence continued as he botched his fourth consecutive chance. Collins left him at short anyway, and by the end of the afternoon, O'Neill had set a twentieth-century mark with six miscues in a game. His final error came in the thirteenth inning on an easy grounder. Two runs scored as St. Louis escaped with a 5–3 win. Newspapers reported that "the work of O'Neill, who played at short in place of (Freddy) Parent, who is still suffering from his injury last Thursday, was poor. Out of 9 chances, he made 6 errors and practically gave the game away."

Boston won the AL pennant that year, but not with O'Neill. He was traded to Washington in July for outfielder Kip Selbach, a former standout who was on the downside of his career. O'Neill continued his clumsy play in Washington, finishing second in outfield errors with nineteen. Demoted to the minors in 1905, he made a curtain call with the White Sox the following year. He hit .248 and fielded his outfield position several points below the league average.

June 19, 1905

Things started poorly for the Giants at Cincinnati when starter Dummy Taylor staked the Reds to five runs in the first inning. On a hot, sticky day at Cincy's Palace of the Fans, the New Yorkers committed five errors and played below their vast potential. Fans in the bleachers gave Giants first baseman Dan McGann and right fielder George Browne a rude reception as they were pursuing a wild throw from reliever Hooks Wiltse. Several beer glasses were tossed onto the field, one of them striking Browne in the leg. Play was interrupted as police tried to identify the culprits, but no arrests were made. According to Charlton's *Baseball Chronology*, Browne later filed charges against a fan that were dismissed in court due to lack of testimony.

The game continued, and Wiltse was moderately effective into the fifth, when he accidentally swallowed a large plug of tobacco and became nauseous. In the sweltering heat, he was unable to continue. Joe McGinnity, the so-called Iron Man, was useless in relief, walking two and then serving up a bases-clearing triple before being replaced by Claude Elliott. The Reds would tack on several more runs in a 17–7 blowout—the Giants' most lopsided loss of the year. New York would win the next twelve meetings against Cincinnati and finish the season with a 16–5 record against them.

August 9, 1905

The Pirates lost to the bottom-feeding Boston Beaneaters 5–3 behind southpaw Irv Young, who carried the lofty nickname "Cy Young the Second" (a moniker he never lived up to). All of Boston's runs came off of Homer Hillebrand in the first five innings. Staff ace Sam Leever took over after that as Hillebrand moved to center field to relieve Ginger Beaumont, who had been suffering from rheumatism.

Trailing 5–2 in the ninth, the Pittsburgh reserves, led by pitchers Chick Robitaille, Mike Lynch, and Charlie Case, began to heckle first-year umpire Bill Klem, mocking his animated calls. Klem grew self-conscious and irritated, throwing everyone on the bench out of the game while treating each to a ten-dollar fine. Even the team mascot was ejected. According to one newspaper account, "This did not leave an extra player for Pittsburgh and had one of the men in the game got hurt, it's hard to tell what would have happened."

What did happen was unforeseeable as Klem was forced to hide in the ladies' room after the game (puritanical newspapers referred to it as "a room in the grandstand"), when irate gamblers came looking for him. The betting odds were apparently ten to three in favor of Pittsburgh, and when the Bucs failed to make a game of it, Klem became a scapegoat. While the rookie arbiter cowered in the restroom, "about 300 tough looking fellows" reportedly milled around outside until they were run off by police.

The *Pittsburgh Press* headline read: "Both Teams Played Stupid, Dopey Ball in Yesterday's Game."

August 24, 1905

A marathon affair between the Phillies and Cubs at the Baker Bowl in Philadelphia ended in a 2–1 loss for the hosts. Twenty innings were necessary to decide the game. Incredibly, both starters went the distance and threw twelve shutout innings before yielding a run. In the twentieth inning, a tiring Tully Sparks gave up a leadoff single to Chicago's Jack McCarthy. Following a sacrifice by Doc Casey, first baseman Frank Chance singled McCarthy home. Philly failed to answer in the bottom of the frame. The twenty-inning duration had been duplicated twice before, once in each league.

In his book, *Touching Second*, Johnny Evers recounted a colorful incident from this game, which may or may not be an exaggeration of the truth. In the eighteenth inning, Cubs outfielder Jimmy Slagle allegedly reached into his pocket for some chewing tobacco. To his complete dismay, he realized that his hand was stuck just as a Philly batter cracked a hard shot in his direction. Ever the showman, Slagle reportedly made a game-saving one-handed grab and then stopped and extricated his entangled appendage. Biting off a piece of tobacco, he bowed melodramatically to the crowd.

September 18, 1905

Contrary to popular belief, St. Louis Browns' owner Bill Veeck was not the first executive to send a little person to the plate in a professional baseball game. Manager George Stallings turned the trick forty-six years earlier. Stallings, the so-called Miracle Man, who would lead the vastly underrated Braves to a surprising World Series sweep over the powerful Athletics in 1915, was managing the Buffalo Bisons of the Eastern League on the date in question. The night before, he had met an actor who was a little person named Jerry Sullivan at the team's hotel in Baltimore. The slumping Bisons were mired in fifth place, and Stallings was looking for a spark. He invited Sullivan out to the park for a game against the Orioles.

When Sullivan arrived, Stallings provided him with a specially tailored uniform to fit his slight frame. He participated in pregame practice and coached at third base for two innings. With Buffalo trailing 10–2 entering the ninth inning, Stallings made his move, sending Sullivan to the plate accompanied by clown mascot Rube Kisinger. Orioles manager Hughie Jennings lodged no complaint, so plate umpire Charley Simmer was obligated to officially announce him as a pinch hitter. Pitcher Fred Burchell was reportedly doubled over with laughter, and his first offering was high. On the second pitch, Sullivan blooped a single over third baseman Charlie Loudenslager's head. No longer laughing, Burchell tried in vain to pick Sullivan off of first. He then lost his composure, giving up two singles and a wild pitch. Sullivan scored on a headfirst slide, receiving a standing ovation from the appreciative crowd. The next day, he returned to his career as a vaudeville entertainer.

June 24, 1906

A game in Chicago between the White Sox and Tigers ended dramatically in favor of the visiting club. Newspapers reported that in the bottom of the ninth, "Schaefer batted for Donahue after two were gone and O'Leary was on first, and put a ball over the left field fence for a homer." A crowd of twelve thousand saw something far more theatrical as the scene was famously recalled by Tigers outfielder Davy Jones in Lawrence Ritter's classic work *The Glory of Their Times*.

The White Sox scattered nine hits off of Detroit starter Red Donahue that day and led 2–1 entering the final frame. Detroit had failed to get much going against southpaw Doc White. With Charley O'Leary on base, Donahue was getting settled into the batter's box when manager Bill Armour decided to send in Germany Schaefer as a pinch hitter. Donahue considered himself a decent hitter (though statistics don't back this up), and, according to Jones's account, he was "madder than a wet hen." Before stepping to the plate, Schaefer took off his cap and turned to face the crowd. "Ladies and gentlemen," he said loudly, "you are now looking at Herman Schaefer, better known as 'Herman the Great,' acknowledged by one and all to be the greatest pinch hitter in the world. I am now going to hit the ball into the left field bleachers. Thank you."

Many fans responded with raspberries since Schaefer had hit just two homers in his career to that point. But amazingly, on the second pitch, the eccentric infielder made good on his boast. Once the ball had cleared the left-field fence, Schaefer jumped high into the air and sprinted to first. He slid into each base while completing the circuit. After crossing the plate, he got up, dusted off his uniform, removed his cap again, and directly addressed fans in the grandstand: "Ladies and gentlemen, I thank you for your kind attention!" Another of Schaefer's oddball stunts is described later in this chapter.

August 7, 1906

During a 3–1 loss to the Cubs on August 6, umpire Jim Johnstone ejected Giants manager John McGraw and third baseman Art Devlin for disputing a call. Johnstone was accosted by angry fans after the game and required the protection of the police. In the wake of the incident, Giants owner John T. Brush met with local law-enforcement officials and convinced them that Johnstone's presence at the park might provoke trouble.

When Johnstone showed up at the Polo Grounds the following day, he was denied access. Standing outside the facility, he declared the game a forfeit in favor of Chicago. Assistant umpire Bob Emslie, who was inside the stadium at the time, left the premises with Johnstone after conferring with NL secretary John Heydler.

Oblivious to these events, a crowd of eleven thousand showed up for the game. After a lengthy delay, many began chanting "Play ball!" Gotham's field general, John McGraw, selected utility man Sammy Strang to serve as an umpire, but Cubs skipper Frank Chance refused to appoint one of his own. Chicago president Charles Murphy then ordered his players to leave the park, prompting Strang to award the game to the Giants. NL president Harry Pulliam later upheld Johnstone's forfeiture, commenting tersely that "I will sustain every forfeit made when an umpire is refused admittance to any park and if it doesn't suit the National League it can have my resignation at a moment's notice."

An article in the *Pittsburgh Press* accused the Giants of resorting "to anything crooked when they know their chances of winning by fair means are dim." Several examples of "trickery" on the part of John McGraw were cited, including the construction of a secret "sentry box" adjoining the players' bench at the Polo Grounds, where McGraw could continue to manage the club out of view of umpires after being tossed from a game.

While president Pulliam was sorting out affairs in New York, his attention was drawn to another irregular incident that occurred at the South End Grounds in Boston. Following a game between the Pirates and Beaneaters, Boston manager Fred Tenney approached umpire Bill Klem, complaining that the balls used in the game, which are considered property of the home team, had not been returned to him. Tenney attempted to search Klem's pockets, and an exchange of blows followed. During the brief altercation, Klem is said to have thrown one of the balls in question at Tenney's face.

September 3, 1906

It was a tough day to be an umpire at Hilltop Park in New York as the Highlanders took a pair from the visiting Athletics. Silk O'Loughlin found himself fending off irate players in both games and eventually grew tired of it, ending the second match in a forfeit. For New York, the controversial victory capped off the Highlanders' fourth consecutive doubleheader sweep, a new major league record. (They would win another twin bill at Boston the following day, raising the bar even further.)

The first game was marred by a scuffle between O'Loughlin and Highlanders shortstop Kid Elberfeld. After leading off the eighth inning with a single, Philadelphia's Topsy Hartsel moved to second on a sacrifice. He later stole third on a close play. Elberfeld, who was coming off a recent suspension caused by a temper tantrum in St. Louis, objected to the call and ended up being tossed from the game after stomping on O'Loughlin's feet. He wandered back onto the field several times and had to be restrained by police.

When Elberfeld appeared in the second game, he was booed lustily by many in the crowd of seventeen thousand. It was Philadelphia's turn to protest as another controversial play at third resulted in a pair of runs for the New Yorkers. The hosts were trailing 3–1 in the ninth with Wid Conroy at third and Willie Keeler on second when Highlanders infielder Jimmy Williams sent a chopper to third baseman John Knight. Knight stepped back to field it and collided with Keeler, knocking him flat. The ball bounced into left field, tying the score. Harry Davis and Topsy Hartsel of the A's shook their gloves in O'Loughlin's face and argued in favor of interference. Davis continued the debate for nearly ten minutes. By that time, O'Loughlin had grown tired of arguing, awarding the game to the New Yorkers by forfeit. He later insisted that it was Knight who had interfered with Keeler.

The Highlanders moved into a first-place tie with the White Sox. They would extend their winning streak to fifteen straight before ultimately finishing three games behind Chicago. Elberfeld ended up serving an eight-game suspension for his actions on September 3.

April 11, 1907

Commenting on this unusual game, the *New York Tribune* reported that "there have been some strange sights at opening games in the past, but that under the shadow of Coogan's Bluff yesterday afternoon surpassed all." Twenty thousand fans turned out at the Polo Grounds to see the Giants kick off the season against Philadelphia.

Things did not go swimmingly for the New Yorkers as they managed just one hit off of Philly right-hander Frank Corridon all afternoon. By the end of the seventh, the Giants had dug themselves a 3–0 hole, and fans began filing out of the stadium. Many began to wander onto the field on their way to the exits. According to the *New York Sun*, "There was not a policeman in the grounds when the game started, and for that matter none up to the time the spectators, being under no restraint, began rushing across the lawn."

Umpire Bill Klem was able to keep the field clear enough to complete the eighth inning, but it eventually became so challenging that he was forced to declare a forfeit in favor of the Phillies. The crowd revolted, throwing cushions from the grandstand and bleachers. Snow had blanketed the city the day before, and the snowbanks along the field's perimeter had not yet melted. A massive snowball fight broke out, ending only when fans grew bored.

The game held another curiosity as New York's Roger Bresnahan introduced a new piece of catching equipment. Though masks and chest protectors were standard by that point, leg armor had not yet come into vogue. The *New York Tribune* commented that "Bresnahan caused considerable amusement by wearing large shin guards similar to those worn by cricket players." It was an unusual sight for fans, who—according to the *New York Times*—"howled with delight when a foul tip in the fifth inning rapped the protectors sharply." Bresnahan ignored many taunts about his manliness that season as other catchers began to follow his lead.

June 18, 1907

Right-hander Andy Coakley of the Reds was known for his lively fast-ball. It was a bit livelier than usual on the above date as Coakley seriously injured two Giants batters in the same inning. First baseman Dan McGann was hit on the wrist, sustaining a break that would limit him to just eighty-one games that season. Struck behind the left ear by a Coakley pitch, Roger Bresnahan was out cold by the time he hit the dirt. His injuries were believed to be so dire that he was given last rites as he lay motionless at the plate. Perhaps responding to Coakley's erratic offerings, Reds catcher Admiral Schlei donned protective shin guards later in the game—the first Cincinnati backstop to do so. The Giants won the contest minus their two first-stringers, 4–3.

As Bresnahan slowly recovered at Seton Hospital, members of the press speculated that he would be "gun shy" on returning to action. The hypothesis was tested on July 12, when the resilient backstop strode to the plate wearing a special helmet that had been designed by the A. J. Reach Company in 1905 (it had never caught on). Referred to as a "pneumatic head protector," the device was shaped like an oven mitt and had to be inflated through a rubber tube by a teammate. As fate would have it, Bresnahan stepped in to face the same pitcher who had laid him out. Coakley's aim was much better this time as Bresnahan rapped a solid single in his first at bat. According to one report, he grinned widely at the hurler as he stood on first base. During Coakley's nine years in the majors, he hit just 26 of the 4,326 batters he faced. Bresnahan, who would develop his own batting helmet in 1908, was enshrined at Cooperstown in 1945.

June 28, 1907

Branch Rickey gained wide acclaim during his career as an executive, establishing baseball's first farm system during the 1920s and breaking the color barrier in 1947. When he was posthumously enshrined at Cooperstown in 1967, it was not on the strength of his abilities as a catcher. In fact, Rickey turned in one of the most horrific performances of all time while stationed behind the plate for the New York Highlanders on the date highlighted above.

Though suffering from a sore shoulder, Rickey was pressed into action by Gotham manager Clark Griffith because of an injury to first-stringer Red Kleinow. Lew Brockett endured one of his worst starts of the season for the New Yorkers, issuing nine walks and fifteen hits. His slow delivery encouraged Washington players to run on the lame-armed Rickey all afternoon. The *Washington Times* quipped that Rickey "could not gauge the distance of the second station, having an idea that it was either just behind the pitcher's box or out near [center fielder] Danny Hoffman." The *Sun* was equally pejorative, remarking that "Rickey threw so poorly that all a man had to do to put through a steal was to start." When the game was over, the hapless backstop had established a dubious major league record by allowing thirteen thefts.

Rickey and Brockett were not the only weak links for New York. Willie Keeler dropped a fly in the outfield. Hal Chase muffed an accurate relay to first. Third baseman Frank LaPorte committed a costly throwing error. The result was a 16–5 thrashing at the hands of the Capital City crew. For Rickey, the 1907 campaign was his last full season in the majors. Interestingly, the thirteen stolen bases against Washington were the only thefts he allowed in eleven catching assignments that year.

August 30, 1908

The *New York Sun* reported that a record-breaking crowd of twenty-one thousand was on hand at Chicago's West Side Grounds to see the Cubs face the Giants in a game with pennant implications. The two clubs had been battling for the NL lead all season and were separated by a game and a half in the standings. In a tightly contested match, the bitter rivals played errorless ball and managed a collective total of ten hits as the Cubs completed a three-game series sweep.

Fans began showing up at the ballpark as early as 7:30 in the morning. By the time the game was under way, an overflow crowd intruded on the playing surface, necessitating special ground rules. Clever tactics by Johnny Evers in the fifth prevented a potential run for the Giants. After Shad Barry had led off the frame with a single, Al Bridwell hit a ball on a line over second base. Evers made a convincing bluff, poising himself to catch a phantom pop fly near the bag. According to one source, Barry fell for the ruse, standing "owl-like and complacent on first." The ball dropped in front of right fielder Del Howard, who relayed to shortstop Joe Tinker at second for the force.

Immediately after the Cubs had secured a 2–1 victory, fans demonstrated their maturity by engaging in a massive seat-cushion battle. According to one colorful newspaper account, the melee "was one of the most animated in years, all kinds of millinery being biffed and smitten." Players departed under a barrage of projectiles, and several women were injured. The *New York World* felt it pertinent to mention that many of the wounded females had their hats destroyed.

September 4, 1908

Most baseball buffs are familiar with the infamous baserunning mis-take by Fred Merkle in 1908, which had a major impact on the pennant race that year. Few are aware that the event had been foreshadowed less than three weeks earlier.

The Pirates had the bases loaded in the bottom of the tenth against the Cubs with two outs on September 4. Playing in his rookie season, Owen Wilson delivered a clutch single to center field, chasing Fred Clarke across the plate with the game winner. Believing the contest to be finished, Bucs infielder Warren Gill (who had occupied first) stopped short of second base and headed off to the clubhouse. Johnny Evers, the clever tactician who would victimize Merkle with the same stunt on September 23, called for the ball and stepped on second. Failing to grab the attention of umpire Hank O'Day, he confronted the arbiter in front of the Pittsburgh dugout. Responding to Evers's appeal, O'Day replied simply, "Clarke has crossed the plate."

Cubs owner Charles Murphy was dissatisfied with the ruling, sending an official protest to league president Harry Pulliam by telegram. At the time, the NL still employed a single-umpire system, which had resulted in numerous blown calls over the years. Murphy told reporters: "Had there been another umpire on duty yesterday to look after the plays in the field, Gill would have been declared out and Clarke's run would never have been allowed. . . . The National game has progressed to a stage where two umpires should officiate on every occasion." Despite those poignant words, his protest was overturned. The Cubs would have their comeuppance as "Merkle's Boner" forced a one-game playoff between the Giants and Cubs at season's end. An account of that game follows.

October 8, 1908

After Johnny Evers's slick maneuver robbed the Giants of a crucial win on September 23, the two teams remained tied for first place at the close of play on October 7. A one-game playoff the following day produced pandemonium in New York. Tickets were available on a first come, first served basis, and when the gates opened, thousands were lined up. The stadium was completely sold out in a short span. Trying desperately to gain entry into the Polo Grounds, a horde of fans burned down a fence and had to be repelled by police with fire hoses. Others snuck into the park via a sewer entrance or kicked their way through the grandstand. Thousands watched from whatever vantage points they could find outside. At least one fan was killed in a fall from a pillar on an elevated subway platform.

According to multiple sources, the umpires were bribed at some point before the contest by an undisclosed party. The offer was refused and the incident reported to the league office. Umpire Bill Klem would later accuse

Joseph Creamer, Giants team physician, of the indiscretion. John McGraw sent Joe McGinnity, who was not scheduled to pitch that day, over to provoke a fight with Frank Chance, hoping that the Cubs' player/manager would get thrown out of the game. Resisting the urge to spar with McGinnity, Chance instead encouraged his players to needle opponents all afternoon.

Giants ace Christy Mathewson faltered in the third inning, when all of Chicago's four runs were scored. Mordecai "Three Finger" Brown held the New Yorkers to a pair of runs on five hits. The Cubs moved on to the World Series against the Tigers and captured the last championship in franchise history.

April 12, 1909

It was a festive atmosphere in Philadelphia as the A's opened their new stadium, a concrete and steel marvel known as Shibe Park. The first of its kind, the park featured a double-decked grandstand and an ornate French Renaissance exterior with a tower at the main entrance. The *Philadelphia Public Ledger* called it "a palace for fans, the most beautiful and capacious baseball structure in the world."

More than thirty thousand fans turned out for the grand opening, with roughly five thousand being turned away. At game time, a ring of spectators up to seven-deep lined the outfield. The A's didn't disappoint that afternoon as future Hall of Famer Eddie Plank held the Red Sox to just six hits in an 8–1 victory. The game was marred by tragedy, however, after Philly catcher Doc Powers went crashing into the wall to catch a foul pop and sustained an internal injury. By the seventh inning, he was writhing in pain in the dugout, complaining of stomach discomfort. He stayed the game but fell unconscious at its conclusion and had to be transported to Northwestern General Hospital.

According to newspaper accounts, doctors found him to be suffering from strangulation of the intestines. Some sources cited the collision during the game as the source of the problem while others blamed a tainted sandwich he had eaten. At least three operations were performed. Powers soon developed peritonitis and died as a result of postsurgical infections. The *New York Times* listed the cause of death as "gangrene poisoning." Catcher Ira Thomas assumed catching responsibilities as the A's finished in second place that year.

Interestingly, the handle of "Doc" was more than just a nickname. Powers had studied at the College of the Holy Cross and Notre Dame before ascending to the major league ranks. After passing his Pennsylvania medical boards, he had worked at St. Agnes's Hospital assisting in eye and throat procedures. During the off-season of 1907 and 1908, he had practiced surgery in his hometown of Jefferson, Pennsylvania.

August 3, 1909

Fired by the National League in 1897 for reprehensible on-field behavior, umpire Tim Hurst proved that he was too volatile for the junior circuit as well. In the first game of a doubleheader at Philadelphia, the belligerent arbiter found himself surrounded by angry fans after a close call at first base went against the home club. He was protected by a gaggle of police officers, who quickly restored order. There would be even more trouble later on as Hurst committed a shameful act that would cost him his job.

After dropping the first match 2–1, the visiting White Sox had built a 4–1 lead through six frames in the second contest. They failed to hang on as the A's tagged pitcher Doc White for five runs in the bottom of the seventh. The Philly hit parade continued in the eighth, when one of the most infamous umpire-player confrontations of all time took place.

With runners on base, Philly infielder Eddie Collins singled and moved to second, where he appeared to be safe due to a dropped throw. Hurst may not have had a good angle on the play, and he ruled Collins out. Incensed by the blown call, Collins (a future Hall of Famer and lifetime .333 hitter) hounded Hurst, using various derogatory terms such as "yellow," "blind bat," and "crook." Hurst's mercurial temperament allowed him to stand only so much. He turned and spat in Collins's face. It would prove to be his undoing as a professional umpire.

After the game, police fought to restrain fans for nearly a half hour as they flung cushions and bottles in Hurst's direction. He was suspended the following day pending a full investigation by league executives. On August 12, he was officially dismissed from his duties. Most sportswriters weren't terribly surprised by the developments. A correspondent from *Sporting Life* remarked: "Umpire Tim Hurst's excessive pugnacity has at last landed him outside the major league breastworks—as had long been expected."

August 28, 1909

Skies in Chicago were threatening at the start of a doubleheader between the White Sox and Washington Senators. Any Capital City fans in attendance would likely have been praying for rain as Dolly Gray set a new record for walks in the second inning.

Using the colorful language of the era, the *Washington Herald* reported that "eleven passes, eight coming in the second, must have tossed an awful chill into manager [Joe] Cantillon. But he blinked an eye as the White Legs scampered gaily around the sacks, counting at home with ridiculous ease." Questioning Cantillon's decision to leave Gray in the game, Thomas Rice of the *Washington Times* commented: "We have seen a manager several times actually engaged in thinking and we once saw one sprain his mind at the heavy work, but we do not recall one who thought so long and hard that he let a pitcher remain in the box until he gave up eight free passes." The situation became so comical for the Sox that Chicago manager Billy Sullivan jokingly suggested that left fielder Patsy Dougherty go to the plate without a bat.

Among the oldest rookies in the majors at thirty years of age, Gray had torn up the Pacific Coast League with thirty-two wins in 1907 and twenty-six more in 1908. Recovering from the horrors of the second frame, he surprised nearly everyone in attendance by completing one of the ugliest one-hitters in baseball history. Not a single Chicago safety was recorded after the first inning. Gray went the distance as a Washington rally fell short, resulting in a 6–4 loss. For the Nationals, it was the second in a series of eleven straight defeats. The club would drop a total of 110 games that year as Gray posted a dreadful 5–19 record. He lasted through three unsuccessful seasons in Washington, retiring with a 15–51 lifetime mark.

September 25, 1909

The New York Highlanders were well out of the running at the start of this doubleheader, trailing the first-place Tigers by twenty-three games in the standings. That didn't deter George Stallings from running a spy operation out of Hilltop Park. Stallings had been stealing signs from opposing teams all year. At the beginning of the season, he rented an apartment behind the right-field fence and planted a conspirator with a telescope to watch for catchers' signs and then signal Highlanders batters with a mirror. This didn't work well on overcast days, so Stallings devised a backup plan.

A mechanism attached to a hat advertisement in center field was used to tip off pitches. A spy later identified as Gene McCann, a former pitcher and future Yankee scout, would pilfer signs from opponents and then move a handle to flip a crossbar device situated inside the *H* in the hat billboard. A black crossbar indicated a fastball was on the way, while a white bar signified a breaking ball.

At some point during the season, Washington manager Joe Cantillon suspected that a plot was afoot and dispatched trainer Jerry Ettinger to watch for anything suspicious. On learning of the scam, Cantillon passed on the information to Detroit skipper Hughie Jennings. Jennings saw nothing out of the ordinary in the first game of the September 25 twin bill (which was won by the Tigers, 2–1), but when the Highlanders jumped on starter George Mullin in the second contest, Jennings sent his own trainer out to investigate. The operation was exposed, and Detroit personnel were dispatched to destroy the crossbar device. Jennings's crew completed a sweep with a 10–4 rout.

June 17, 1910

Giants manager John McGraw once commented that Arthur Raymond was one of the greatest pitchers he ever worked with. A spitball artist who could be quite effective when he was on his game, Raymond was a chronic alcoholic who had earned the nickname "Bugs" for his eccentric behavior on and off the field. Reminiscing about the erratic hurler years later, former teammate Rube Marquard told a writer, "Sometimes it seemed the more he drank the better he pitched."

But sometimes the opposite was true.

McGraw took on Raymond as a project in 1908, believing he could re-form him. Drunken episodes were numerous, and Raymond abruptly quit the team during the 1909 slate to work as a bartender. He returned in 1910, landing himself in hot water yet again. On June 17, Giants starter Louis Drucke was clinging to a 3–2 lead over the Pirates and growing tired. McGraw sent Raymond to the bullpen to warm up, but Raymond had other ideas. Avoiding McGraw's watchful eyes, the incorrigible hurler snuck off to a neighborhood tavern, trading a baseball for some shots of whiskey (or so the story goes). He returned in time to relieve Drucke in the ninth. He entered the game with no out and two runners on.

Apparently intoxicated, Raymond threw a first pitch that sailed over Chief Meyers's head, advancing Ed Abbaticchio to third and Bill McKechnie to second. Raymond then hit Vin Campbell to load the bases. McGraw must have breathed a sigh of relief when a ground ball by Tommy Leach resulted in a force at home, but his respite would have been short-lived as the next batter, Bobby Byrne, hit a sacrifice fly to tie the game at 3. With two outs, Honus Wagner tapped a grounder back to the mound. Raymond threw wildly to first, scoring Campbell and Leach. Making matters worse, Meyers chased down the errant throw and relayed poorly to second, advancing Wagner to third. Putting the finishing touches on an epic blown save, Raymond coughed up an RBI single to Dots Miller before hitting Ham Hyatt with a pitch. It took a slick play by Fred Merkle to retire the side.

The Giants lost the game, 6–3, and when McGraw found out where Raymond had been before his call to the bullpen, he suspended the hurler indefinitely. He later had a change of heart, reinstating the right-hander in early July. Raymond underwent alcohol treatment before the 1911 slate and was clean for a while before relapsing. By 1912, he was all washed up. He ended up playing at the semipro level. According to numerous sources, Raymond was attacked by an angry fan named Fred Criganz during a game in Chicago and took several blows to the head with a bat. He was hospitalized and released but later died at his hotel after complaining of a severe headache.

October 9, 1910

Almost everyone who played with Ty Cobb had strong opinions about him. His hard-edged style of play and ruthless desire to win earned him a legion of enemies over the years. Teammate Davy Jones commented, "He antagonized so many people that hardly anyone would speak to him, even among his own teammates."

Cobb's tremendous unpopularity came back to bite him in 1910, when members of the St. Louis Browns plotted to rob him of a batting crown. Believing he held a secure lead over Napoléon Lajoie of Cleveland, Cobb sat out the last game of the season. Chalmers Automotive, a Detroit-based company, had offered a new car to the winner, making the title especially appealing that year. With his team scheduled to face the Naps (later known as the Indians) at home in a doubleheader on October 9, Browns manager Jack O'Connor saw an opportunity to get back at baseball's most universally despised player. The game had no real impact on the standings anyway as both clubs were out of the playoff picture. O'Connor instructed rookie third baseman Red Corriden to play back near the edge of the outfield grass every time Lajoie came to bat.

Taking full advantage of the situation, Lajoie beat out numerous bunts, boosting his average considerably. Browns pitching coach Harry Howell reportedly attempted to bribe the official scorer to give Lajoie an extra hit, but the offer was refused. It appeared to be of no consequence when newspapers prematurely declared Lajoie the batting champion by less than a percentage point over Cobb.

Suspecting foul play, AL president Ban Johnson questioned O'Connor and Corriden. Though Corriden was absolved, Howell and O'Connor were blacklisted. When the *Sporting News* published the official season averages, Cobb was declared the winner by a slender margin. Chalmers Automotive gave cars to both contenders, and Lajoie later joked, "The automobile I got ran a lot better than the one they gave Ty."

May 12, 1911

Ty Cobb was a one-man wrecking crew against the New York Highlanders, running amok on the bases at Detroit's Bennett Park. The New Yorkers jumped out to a 4–0 lead in their first at bat but couldn't hang on as Cobb single-handedly turned the tide of the game. In the opening frame, "The Georgia Peach" scored all the way from first on a Sam Crawford single. In the third, he spiked Roy Hartzell in the knee while trying to advance on a grounder. Hartzell had to be carried to the clubhouse. In the sixth frame, Cobb was at it again, scoring from second on a wild pitch. He would bring the winning run home on another daring maneuver in the seventh.

With two on and two out, Cobb slashed a hard drive to left field. Birdie Cree fielded it cleanly and threw home in an attempt to cut down Donie Bush. It was a rough day for the Highlanders all around as catcher Ed Sweeney got spiked on the play, resulting in an injury that would keep him out of action for a while. Umpire Rip Egan called Bush safe, and with the score now tied, irate New York players gathered at the plate to protest. They forgot to call for time as the footloose Cobb decided to see how far he could get, moving from second to third and then heading for home. The *Sun* reported, "He tiptoed along until about 15 feet from the plate and peeked through for an opening through which he could slide." Finding one, he delivered the tie-breaking run. It would hold up in a 6–5 Tiger win. The next day, the *New York Tribune* referred to Cobb as "a meteor on the basepaths." On top of the injuries to Hartzell and Sweeney, the Highlanders' star first baseman Hal Chase came down with a case of tonsillitis.

June 27, 1911

The A's breezed to a win over the Red Sox at the Huntington Avenue Grounds in Boston, scoring in each of the first five innings. They ran up a 6–3 lead until the eighth, when they tacked on another run in bizarre fashion.

In the interest of shortening ballgames, which had begun to regularly break the dreaded two-hour mark, AL president Ban Johnson enacted a rule limiting the number of warm-up tosses used by hurlers. The rule stated that a pitcher must immediately end his warm-up routine after the first batter had stepped into the box. Fleet-footed first baseman Stuffy McInnis exploited this new regulation during the game in question.

As Boston players meandered back onto the field before the top of the eighth, pitcher Ed Karger went out to the mound and lobbed a soft toss at catcher Les Nunamaker. According to one source, at least one member of the Philly squad had not even left the field yet as Tris Speaker stood socializing with A's second baseman Eddie Collins. Several Boston regulars were still looking for their gloves, which were routinely left on the field between innings until a rule later prohibited the practice.

Karger's lollipop throw went wide of the plate as McInnis, who was slated to lead off for the A's, jumped into the box and slapped it playfully to center field. The crowd reportedly "giggled, appreciating a bit of horseplay." It was no laughing matter for the BoSox when McInnis circled the bases and umpire Rip Egan counted the run. Led by manager Patsy Donovan, Red Sox players began to sound a mass protest as the crowd roared its approval.

According to one newspaper account, "As stiff and sound as Horatio at the Bridge, Egan waved them all back, dusted off the plate and called for the next batter." The A's won by a score of 7–3 that day, and Johnson lifted the restriction on warm-up pitches soon afterward.

This may or may not be the only incident of its kind. In a possibly apocryphal account from the same era, utility man Jay Kirke of Cleveland is said to have pulled a similar stunt. According to scouting reports, Kirke hit almost exclusively to the opposite field and at some point developed a reputation for being unable to handle curveballs. As a result, he received a steady diet of them whenever he came to the plate. As he waited in the on-deck circle one day, the batter ahead of him ripped a single to center field. There was a play at home, and as a nearly perfect throw arrived, Kirke stepped in front of it and smashed a long shot to the outfield. He stood there beaming proudly as he was called out for interference. "I couldn't help it," he explained after the game. "It was the first fastball I'd seen in over a month."

August 4, 1911

Infielder Germany Schaefer was a likable character who delighted crowds with his amusing behavior on the diamond. A tactician, prankster, and incorrigible bench jockey, he was known to snack on popcorn in the coach's box and use bats as oars to "row" across the grass. One of his most famous displays of showmanship occurred while he was playing for Detroit and is described in an earlier section of this book. The following account took place while Schaefer was wearing a Senators uniform.

In the bottom of the ninth in a game against the White Sox, the Senators had runners at the corners and two out. Clyde Milan represented the winning run at third, and Schaefer was on first. Looking to break a scoreless tie, Schaefer bolted for second, hoping to draw a throw from catcher Fred Payne. Payne knew what Schaefer was up to and wisely held onto the ball. Before the next pitch, Schaefer took his lead on the right-field side of the bag. As the ball headed toward the plate, he ran back to first. Again, Payne opted not to throw as Schaefer became one of the first major league players to complete a "steal" of the initial sack. White Sox manager Hugh Duffy didn't like it and came out to argue. As he was jawing with umpire Tom Connolly, Schaefer strayed from first again and got caught in a rundown. This was exactly what he had intended as Milan headed for the plate. Unfortunately, Schaefer's gambit didn't work as Milan was thrown out. Schaefer argued that the run shouldn't count since the ChiSox had ten men on the field (including Duffy). Duffy had not been active since 1908, and Connolly rejected the appeal.

The game meandered into the eleventh inning, with Washington's Walter Johnson and Chicago's Doc White going the distance. In the bottom of the frame, the Senators loaded the bases and scored the game's only run on a grounder hit to shortstop Lee Tannehill. The *Washington Times* commented of Schaefer's ninth-inning ruse: "Such a play will not be duplicated in a cycle of baseball." After 1920 it certainly would not, as a new rule prohibited running the bases backward "for the purpose of confusing the defense or making a travesty on the field." Schaefer is often given credit for this change.

October 7, 1911

One of the most fascinating tales of the deadball era is the saga of Charles "Victory" Faust. Born in Marion, Kansas, Faust had virtually no athletic ability and was suffering from some form of mental illness. In the summer of 1911, he introduced himself to New York Giants manager John McGraw. He told McGraw that a fortuneteller had predicted he would pitch the Giants to a championship. McGraw, who was somewhat superstitious, offered Faust a tryout, but it was clear that the right-hander was not major league material. When Faust kept showing up at the ballpark anyway, McGraw allowed him to participate in pregame activities. The Giants responded positively to his presence, and Faust was officially adopted as a team mascot.

What impressed McGraw most was Faust's self-proclaimed ability to jinx opposing teams. There may have been something to it as the Giants compiled an astonishing 36–2 record with Faust in uniform. McGraw often let him warm up in the bullpen, where his quirky windmill delivery delighted fans. Faust eventually became so popular that he was signed to a limited vaudeville engagement.

Determined to fulfill the fortuneteller's prophecy, Faust pestered McGraw constantly to let him pitch. The Giants' skipper finally conceded after the club had clinched the 1911 pennant. The simple-minded hurler made his major league debut on October 7, giving up a hit and a run in an inning of work. The *Sun* reported that "Faust, who takes himself seriously, gave a judicious exhibition of the boxman's art. He wound himself into knots and hurled up slow, dinky curves in a way that convulsed players and spectators." McGraw sent Faust to bat in the ninth after the side had been retired, telling him there were only two outs. The thirty-year-old "rookie" tapped a grounder back to the mound and circled the bases as Boston players deliberately threw wildly. Completing the circuit in dramatic fashion, he slid headfirst into home and was called out.

On October 12, Faust appeared in relief again versus the Dodgers. This time, a correspondent from the *Sun* wrote that "his swing was a revelation to those who had not seen him before and his posture just before his windup, followed by sweeping convulsions of his arms, tearing the air into geometric tatters, so dismayed the Brooklyn batters that they failed to score in the inning that they faced the sunflower phenom." Outfielder Jud Daley swung so hard at one of Faust's bloopers that he fell flat on his back. Umpire William Brennan reportedly covered his face with his hand and laughed. Faust was intentionally hit by a pitch in his first official trip to the plate. He stole second and third and later "scored" on a squeeze play.

During the 1911 World Series, Faust's jinxing powers were no match for the A's mascot, a hunchbacked young man named Louis Van Zelst. The Giants lost the affair in six games. In 1912, Faust continued to insist that he was a bona fide pitcher. McGraw grew tired of his frequent requests to take the hill and eventually dismissed him. In the end, it took some deception on the part of Giants players to get Faust to return home. As soon as he was gone, the club went into a tailspin. Fortunately, the Giants had built a comfortable lead in the NL and took the pennant anyway. They lost the Fall Classic to the Red Sox that year.

Faust spent the rest of his days trying to find his way back to the big leagues. In 1914, he walked from Seattle to Portland on a quest to "save" the Giants from the upstart Boston Braves. He was picked up by police and sent to an institution, where he was diagnosed with "dementia." He eventually returned to Seattle and was committed to another state hospital. He died in June 1915 from tuberculosis.

May 8, 1912

A sloppy game in St. Louis between the Giants and Cardinals prompted one scribe to remark: "The contest proved exciting at times, but for the better part of nine innings the playing of both teams was of worse than minor league caliber." The Giants built up a 9–1 lead after three innings and then barely hung on for an 11–8 win as the New York defense committed four costly errors. Right-hander Jeff Tesreau (who would post the lowest ERA in the circuit that year) walked nine batters and was lifted for staff ace Christy Mathewson in the ninth. "Matty" promptly slammed the door on the St. Louis rally.

Two innings earlier, the game had been delayed by a pair of injuries. The first mishap occurred when Giants backup catcher Art Wilson was sliding into third after a dropped fly by error-prone outfielder Rebel Oakes. Wilson hurt his foot on the play and was replaced by third-string backstop Grover Hartley. Shortly afterward, Tesreau hit a grounder to shortstop Wally Smith. Smith fielded the ball efficiently and then relayed to first, but the throw never reached its target, instead hitting umpire Brick Owens in the back of the head. According to newspaper accounts, "The field judge dropped like a log." Owens's wife was in attendance, and when she saw him hit the ground, she followed suit, passing out in her seat. Both were revived shortly afterward.

Home-plate umpire Bill Brennan then made an unusual call, sending Tesreau back to the plate to hit again since (technically) there had been no official presiding over the play. Hartley returned to third base as Tesreau popped out to end the New York threat. One beat writer referred to the sequence as "the queerest of all plays."

May 15, 1912

Proving that no one was exempt from his violent temper, Ty Cobb climbed twelve rows into the stands at New York's Hilltop Park and assaulted a fan. According to numerous sources, the unruly patron had been making disparaging personal remarks to Cobb for several innings. A reporter from the *New York Tribune* supported Cobb's actions, commenting that "a noisy fan in the left field stands at yesterday's game heaped abuse and vilification on Ty Cobb until the outraged player was provoked into administering a well deserved beating." Cobb also defended his actions, telling journalists that "a ballplayer should not be expected to take everything as we have some self-respect and we cannot endure more than human nature will stand for."

Either of those remarks might have held some water had the incident in the stands been a fair fight. But the target of Cobb's fury was a disabled man named Claude Leuker, who reportedly had only three fingers as a result of an unfortunate industrial accident. One New York newspaper reported colorfully: "Though there was no official decision in the Cobb vs. Spectator fight, the unanimous verdict was that Cobb won. There could not have been any other verdict because Cobb did all the punching."

AL president Ban Johnson, who was in attendance, was asked whether Cobb would draw a suspension. "I can't see any justification for a player climbing up in the stand and fighting a spectator," he said. "If a spectator is abusive, a player has the recourse of notifying the umpires and the man can be removed." Cobb had indeed spoken to umpire Silk O'Loughlin before the incident, and Leuker had reportedly been warned to "keep still." But the insults continued until the bottom of the fourth inning, when Cobb finally decided to handle the situation himself.

"The Georgia Peach" was suspended indefinitely as Detroit players went on strike. Tigers manager Hughie Jennings was forced to send a unit composed mainly of college players into action against the Philadelphia Athletics. The result was a 24–2 blowout. Regular players were reinstated soon afterward as Cobb's suspension was eventually reduced to ten days.

May 3, 1913

A wild game in St. Louis was referred to as "a burlesque which kept the spectators in roars of laughter." A total of seven different hurlers took the hill, combining for eleven walks, five hit batsmen, a pair of wild pitches, and a balk. Each team committed three errors in the Browns' 11–8 loss to the Naps. Umpire Charlie Ferguson found the "burlesque" less than amusing when he was spat on by St. Louis player/manager George Stovall.

The disturbance took place in the sixth inning, during which the Naps overcame a 5–3 deficit by scoring seven runs. Stovall objected to Ferguson's calls and, during a heated debate, snatched the umpire's cap and threw it on the ground. (According to Charlton's *Baseball Chronology,* he spat on it as well.) Following his subsequent ejection, Stovall loitered on the field looking for his glove, and when Ferguson told him to hurry up, he hawked a wad of tobacco in the official's face. Teammate Jimmy Austin later recalled, "It was an awful mess. It was terrible. George always did chew an uncommonly large wad, you know."

League president Ban Johnson suspended Stovall indefinitely and rebuked his attempts at arranging a face-to-face meeting. But on May 22, Johnson had a change of heart, reinstating the St. Louis skipper on the condition that he draft an apology letter to Ferguson and pay a relatively small fine.

Described by one writer as "outspoken but amicable," Stovall was no stranger to controversy. In 1907, he had thrown a chair at manager Napoléon Lajoie after Lajoie fined him $100. In 1911, Stovall had defied Ban Johnson by refusing to play on the day of Addie Joss's funeral. Joss, one of Cleveland's top pitchers for many seasons, had died unexpectedly of tubercular meningitis at the age of thirty-one. Johnson wanted the Naps to play, but Stovall informed him that the team was going "on strike" in order to attend services.

July 12, 1913

A's right-hander Boardwalk Brown had difficulty finding the plate, setting a new record for free passes allowed in a nine-inning game. Two different beat writers referred to this contest as a "travesty." It featured a total of twenty-eight hits, seven errors, and twenty-four walks.

Fifteen of those passes were issued by Brown, who somehow managed to win the game by a 16–9 margin. He was so wild that he walked every man in the Tiger lineup at least once and handed out three base on balls in two different innings. Remarkably, none of the walked batters scored a run until the eighth as the Philadelphians played errorless ball and turned three double plays.

When Brown finally got in a serious jam after working seven and two-thirds innings, Connie Mack sent future Hall of Famer Eddie Plank to the hill. Plank was hit hard during his short stint as Detroit plated eight runs in the last two frames. It was a rough day all around for future Cooperstown inductees. Returning to the lineup after missing a week with a knee injury, Ty Cobb fared poorly in his only career assignment at second base. "The Georgia Peach" botched three of four chances at the keystone sack. Two of his errors led to Philadelphia runs. The Tigers auditioned several men at second base that year, including Ossie Vitt, Baldy Louden, and Paddy Bauman.

The game's central figure, Boardwalk Brown, walked more batters than he struck out in three of his four full seasons in the majors. He averaged nearly four free passes per nine innings during his short career. His dubious record would be broken on June 23, 1915, when Bruno Haas walked sixteen men in a complete game loss to the Yankees. It was Haas's only career decision.

August 30, 1913

A game between the Giants and Phillies at the Baker Bowl ended in utter chaos as the Giants came away with a victory by forfeit. The Giants had built up a 6–0 lead at one point before the Phillies came storming back with eight runs off of staff ace Christy Mathewson. The score stood at 8–6 in the ninth when manager John McGraw complained that fans in the bleachers were distracting his hitters.

His complaint was well founded as a crowd of several hundred fans in center field had moved into a direct line with home plate. They had taken off their coats and were waving straw hats in an attempt to fluster the Giants' batters. Umpire Bill Brennan made a request for the group to move from the area, but the appeal was met with jeers. Newspapers reported that a record crowd was on hand to see the second-place Phillies attempt a series sweep.

McGraw refused to continue the game, and during a conference at home plate, he was asked to play under protest. When he again refused, Brennan awarded the match to the visitors. It was an unpopular decision, and fans rushed onto the field. Projectiles were hurled and scattered, punches were thrown, but no injuries were reported.

Outside the stadium gates, an angry crowd awaited New York players. Police escorted Giants personnel several blocks up the street to a train station. At one point, a brick was thrown and officers drew their guns to disperse the disorderly throng. Later that evening, Philly manager Red Dooin referred to Brennan's decision as an "outrage" and filed an official protest with NL president Thomas J. Lynch. The appeal was upheld, inspiring McGraw to lodge a protest of his own. In the end, the game was replayed from the point at which it had been stopped. On October 2 at the Polo Grounds, the Phillies completed the 8–6 win. They finished in second place anyway, more than ten games behind the Giants.

July 17, 1914

The longest game in National League history (to that point) took place at Forbes Field in Pittsburgh. Rube Marquard of the Giants and Babe Adams of the Pirates both went the distance, setting a pair of records in the process. For Marquard, the 3–1 New York victory was the lengthiest win ever recorded in the National League. Adams set a new mark for consecutive innings pitched without yielding a walk. But both accomplishments were overshadowed by an unusual play in the sixth inning that resulted in an official protest by the Pirates.

Honus Wagner was on first when Pittsburgh's Jim Viox singled, chasing "The Flying Dutchman" around second. Giants center fielder Bob Bescher made a timely throw to Milt Stock at third, but the ball disappeared. As Stock searched frantically for the missing sphere, Wagner ambled home. As he did, the ball dropped out of his jersey. It had bounced up into his sleeve and he had kept it pinned there as he dashed for the plate. Umpire Bill Byron called Wagner out for interference, and Bucs manager Fred Clarke was ejected after an angry tirade. The Pirates believed that Wagner should have been sent back to third and lodged an official protest with league president John K. Tener.

The rest of the game proved to be one of the hardest-fought pitching duels in history. Adams surrendered just twelve hits through twenty-one frames. According to the *New York Tribune*, Marquard yielded fifteen safeties while walking two. Adams was finally sunk in the twenty-first frame when Bob Bescher singled with two outs. Larry Doyle followed with a well-struck ball to center field. Accounts of the play vary. One scribe reported that Doyle's hit was a "clean single" that was mishandled by Joe Kelly. Another correspondent begged to differ, remarking that the ball came off Doyle's bat "like a meteor" and was not touched until it reached the outfield fence. In either case, both runners scored.

As the story of this game was passed down through the years, an urban legend became attached to it. According to popular myth, Giants outfielder Red Murray was struck by a bolt of lightning while catching the final out. This is actually an exaggeration of something that happened five years earlier in another tight match between the two clubs. According to multiple accounts, Murray preserved a 2–2 tie for the Giants during a torrential downpour on

August 16, 1909. With two on and two out in the eighth and mound master Christy Mathewson on the hill, Pirates second baseman Dots Miller sent a hard smash into the angry skies. Murray sprinted after the ball and made a spectacular bare-handed grab as a bolt of lightning illuminated the field—rendering the catch all the more dramatic to witnesses. Bill Klem called the game on account of inclement weather shortly afterward.

Together, the two contests make one fascinating amalgam.

July 30, 1914

A showdown between the Tigers and Senators at Navin Field in Detroit was marred by a near riot during the ninth inning. Before then, fans had been enjoying a well-played stalemate between the two clubs. After tagging Detroit starter Harry Coveleski for two runs in the first, the Senators wouldn't get a man across the plate for the rest of the afternoon. The Tigers answered with a pair of their own in the third on a two-out triple by Sam Crawford. The score remained tied until the bottom of the tenth.

The game almost didn't get that far. In the top of the ninth, Washington's Ray Morgan appeared to be safe on a grounder after sliding into first. Umpire John Sheridan disagreed, calling Morgan out on the play. In frustration, Morgan got up and threw a handful of dirt at Sheridan's feet. Sheridan took exception to the gesture and punched Morgan in the face. George Burns of Detroit and Clark Griffith of Washington rushed to the scene, separating the two, but the fight was far from over.

Senators backup catcher Eddie Ainsworth charged out of the dugout along with several teammates, landing a retaliatory blow to Sheridan. He was ejected, but on his way out, a fan in a box-seat section peppered him with verbal abuse. The hot-headed backstop jumped into the stands and started swinging. He was followed by Morgan and Washington's first-string catcher, John Henry. Henry was hit in the back with a chair, prompting several Detroit players to get involved. Oscar Stanage, Donie Bush, Marty Kavanagh, and several others fought valiantly to break things up before a group of police officers arrived on the scene. The altercation lasted for roughly fifteen minutes before cooler heads prevailed.

The game ended in the tenth, when Shaw made a wild throw to third that brought George Moriarty across the plate with the winning run for Detroit. Morgan and Ainsworth were both suspended and fined. League president Ban Johnson told reporters that the actions of Ainsworth in particular were "cowardly and uncalled for." Henry escaped suspension, but he was kept out of action for a while with a swollen hand and a laceration on his back.

July 14, 1915

Connie Mack was an exploiter of rules dating all the way back to his days as a catcher. They didn't call him the "Tall Tactician" for nothing. While working behind the dish for the Pirates and Nationals during the 1800s, he was known to deliberately drop pop flies in the interest of turning force plays or wander up the first baseline and signal for pitches before scrambling behind the plate just in time to catch them. The latter ruse was allegedly used to strike out the unsuspecting (and completely flabbergasted) Cap Anson one afternoon. When he signed on to manage the A's in 1901, Mack still had plenty of tricks up his sleeve.

On the date in question, dark clouds had gathered above Comiskey Park in Chicago. With rain imminent and his team trailing the White Sox 4–2 in the bottom of the fourth, Mack ordered his players to resort to stalling tactics. He was hoping to prompt a rainout call from umpire Bobby Wallace.

Following instructions, Philly pitcher "Bullet Joe" Bush deliberately plunked opposing moundsman Red Faber. The ultracompetitive Faber tried to speed things up with a half-hearted steal of second, but the A's made only a perfunctory attempt to retire him. Around the bases he went, stealing third and home due to defensive indifference. The three thefts he collected that day represented nearly half of his lifetime totals.

With the A's now trailing by three runs, something completely unexpected happened—or didn't happen. The rain never came, and the game ended up being played in its entirety. Faber's steal of home proved to be the deciding run in a 6–4 White Sox victory. Though he would later be credited with the gentlemanly quote "You can't win them all," this was almost certainly one of those games that Connie Mack wished he could have had back.

August 7, 1915

Brooklyn hurler Ed Appleton committed one of the most bone-headed plays in baseball history during a game against the Cardinals. A correspondent from the *New York Tribune* compared Appleton to John Anderson, who attempted a steal of second with the bases loaded one day, and Clyde Engle, who had once suggested a sacrifice fly with two outs. Appleton was less of a numskull and more the victim of a clever tactic employed by St. Louis player and manager Miller Huggins.

Playing in his first major league season, Appleton had been summoned from the bullpen after Brooklyn starter Wheezer Dell staked the Cardinals to three runs in the first inning. The rookie right-hander was highly effective until the seventh, when Huggins took advantage of his inexperience. With the bases loaded, Huggins shouted from the coach's box behind third base: "Hey Appleton, lemme see that ball! I think it's a 'rabbit' they rung in on you." ("Rabbit" is slang for a lively baseball.) Incredibly, Appleton fell for it, tossing the ball in Huggins's direction. The conniving field general stepped aside as the throw bounced into foul territory, bringing Dots Miller home with the tie-breaking run. Even Robins manager Wilbert Robinson couldn't help laughing at the play, although he pulled Appleton from the game after an RBI groundout put the Cardinals ahead, 6–4. "Take him out of there before I kill him!" said "Uncle Robbie" to his pitching coach.

Though he never fell for the same ruse again, Appleton struggled to a lifetime mark of 5–12 during two seasons in the majors. Huggins would enjoy his most successful years as manager of the Yankees, guiding one of the greatest collections of players ever to six pennants and three World Series titles between 1921 and 1928.

May 30, 1916

The Baker Bowl in Philadelphia was the setting for an all-too-familiar scene as players and fans dramatically demonstrated their displeasure with an umpire. This time, the victim was Pete Harrison. During the evening half of a doubleheader, Harrison was showered with garbage and cushions as an army of police armed with nightsticks fought to clear a path for him out of the stadium. He had reportedly sought refuge in the clubhouse before making his exit.

The day began peacefully enough as the Phillies snapped a seventeen-game Giants winning streak with a dramatic five-run outburst in their last at bat against New York's staff ace Pol Perritt. But the second contest was marred by a series of ugly disputes. The trouble began in the fifth inning, when Quakers catcher Bill Killefer was ejected for arguing balls and strikes. He smeared dust on Harrison's uniform during the squabble. In the eighth, backup receiver Eddie Burns reportedly "made a nuisance of himself" while Bill Rariden was hitting for the Giants. He was tossed from the game, putting Philly manager Pat Moran in a tough spot. With third-stringer Bert Adams nursing a hand injury, Moran was forced to install veteran third baseman Bobby Byrne behind the plate. According to the original box score, Byrne was credited with two putouts and an assist, though those statistics are not recognized by Retrosheet or Baseball-Reference.com.

In the bottom of the eighth, Dode Paskert became irritated with Harrison's calls and hit the arbiter's whisk broom with his bat, knocking it clear across the field. Fans were on edge anyway as the Giants had battered Philly ace Pete

Alexander for seven runs on ten hits. After Paskert's ejection, the field was littered with pop bottles. According to multiple newspaper reports, Harrison stood facing center field with his arms folded sternly and never flinched, even when one of the projectiles grazed his leg. It took police five full minutes to restore order. The Giants prevailed, 10–2. The rain of bottles began anew at the game's conclusion, and several spectators sustained minor injuries.

July 18, 1916

The Cubs threw away a game at Weeghman Park in Chicago when umpire Bill Byron grew tired of their protests and awarded the match to the Brooklyn Robins. The score was tied at 4 in the top of the tenth with southpaw Hippo Vaughn on the mound for Chicago. The Robins had runners at second and third when Vaughn suddenly refused to pitch, repeatedly shaking off signs from catcher Bill Fischer. Byron grew impatient and ordered the big hurler to get to work or leave the field. When Vaughn refused to comply, Byron called a ball on Ollie O'Mara. This brought Tinker out of the Chicago dugout.

During a lengthy debate that grew more intense as it progressed, Tinker insisted that the Robins had been stealing signs and using them to an unfair advantage. Tinker refused to leave the field as players from both teams congregated around home plate. Byron pulled out his watch and declared the game a forfeit in favor of Brooklyn after three full minutes of squabbling. He tacked on an additional $1,000 fine to the Cubs. After the game, Tinker accused Byron of abusing his power and told reporters he intended to file an official protest with baseball's National Commission. Byron's decision was upheld.

May 11, 1917

In one of many dramatic encounters between the game's most iconic players, Babe Ruth got the best of Ty Cobb at Navin Field in Detroit. Ruth notched his seventh straight win of the season, holding the Tigers to just one run on five hits. The *Boston Globe* reported, "Ruth made Tyrus look cheap. . . . The Red Sox bench warmers gave Tyrus a great riding, getting what they were after—his goat."

Cobb got more than a verbal jab in the ninth, when he led off with a bunt single and then daringly tried to advance to third on a groundout. Covering the bag, Ruth treated Cobb to a taste of his own medicine, tagging "The Georgia Peach" so hard that he was unable to get up for two full minutes. The double play eliminated Detroit's late-inning threat as the Sox came away with a 2–1 victory.

The viciousness of Ty Cobb is well documented. The ferocity of Ruth is often buried beneath his more pleasing attributes. Several weeks after the previously mentioned incident, the Babe put on a flagrant display of hooliganism in a game against the Senators. While facing Washington's leadoff hitter Ray Morgan on June 23, Ruth became exasperated with the calls of Brick Owens. After Owens issued ball four, Ruth confronted the umpire. According to the *Boston Globe*, the dialogue was as follows:

"Open your eyes and keep them open!" barked Ruth.

"Get in and pitch or I'll run you out of there," Owens retorted.

"You run me out and I'll come in and bust your nose," the Babe threatened.

When Owens ejected him, Ruth rushed to the plate. Catcher Pinch Thomas tried to restrain Ruth, but a blow was landed behind the arbiter's left ear.

The entire Boston battery was replaced with Ernie Shore taking the hill and Sam Agnew assuming catching responsibilities. Ray Morgan was promptly thrown out stealing second as Shore went on to retire all twenty-six batters he faced. For several decades, Shore was credited with a perfect game, but in 1991, stricter definitions were established. His feat was reduced to a combined no-hitter. And so, despite creating an ugly disturbance during the game, Ruth still managed to find his way into the record books in a positive light. He did, however, receive a fine and suspension for his actions.

June 8, 1917

Frustrations ran high for the Giants as retired Gotham great Christy Mathewson, now serving as manager of the Reds, led his new squad to a 2–1 win over the New Yorkers in Cincinnati. The *New York Tribune* reported that "the Giants seemed to have left their wallop at the hotel" as they scattered four hits off of Cincy southpaw Clarence Mitchell. The loss knocked the Giants off the top of the NL perch as the Phillies moved into first place temporarily.

A major disturbance took place in the sixth inning, when Heinie Groh doubled and scored on consecutive sacrifices by Larry Kopf and Edd Roush. Giants field general John McGraw felt that Groh had left the bag too early and argued passionately with assistant umpire Ernest Quigley. After being tossed from the game, McGraw reportedly went after Quigley but ended up punching crew chief Bill Byron instead. As a member of the groundskeeping staff moved in to separate the two, Giants catcher Bill Rariden attacked the man from behind. No injuries were reported.

McGraw received a $500 fine—the largest ever imposed on a manager to that point. While serving a lengthy suspension, he bad-mouthed NL president

John K. Tener, charging that he was out to sabotage the Giants. Forced to explain himself to league magnates, McGraw later retracted the statement. He was strapped with an additional $1,000 fine—an unheard-of sum for an individual in those days.

September 1, 1917

Hall of Fame outfielder Tris Speaker didn't carry the nickname "Blood and Guts," but he should have. In the bottom of the first, Speaker was on third base for the Indians as teammate Joe Evans was batting against Detroit's Hooks Dauss. Getting the green light from manager Lee Fohl, Speaker was off and running with a pitch as Evans smashed a liner up the third baseline. The drive hit Speaker in the face at relatively close range, opening a nasty wound.

During the deadball era and beyond, teams were allowed to use "courtesy" runners or fielders to replace players who were injured and temporarily unable to continue. The selections had to be approved by opposing managers, so in many cases the substitutions were of the inferior variety. The player being replaced was allowed to return to his spot in the lineup if and when he was able. Current rules prohibit the practice.

With Speaker's face oozing blood, Detroit manager Hughie Jennings approved the use of Elmer Smith in center field during the second inning. Proving he was a true warrior, Speaker had his face stitched up and then returned to his post in the third. It was a rough day all around as he was hit by a Dauss pitch as well. The Indians won the game, 3–2.

October 7, 1917

Referring to himself as "the Modern Voltaire," sportswriter Ring Lardner facetiously penned a World Series game account in French. The English version that ran in the *New York Tribune* was provided by Grantland Rice. It contained the headline "Crushed and Humiliated Polo Grounders Fleeing toward Coogan's Bluff."

It was White Sox pitcher Red Faber who was humiliated in game 2 of the 1917 Fall Classic, when he committed an inexplicable baserunning gaffe during the fifth inning. After singling and advancing to second on a throw to third, Faber apparently forgot that Buck Weaver was ahead of him on the base paths. On the next pitch, he took off for third with reckless abandon. "It was a clean steal," Grantland Rice reported. "The only drawback was the annoying presence of another Sox mate in charge of the same spot." Giants infielder Heinie Zimmerman tagged both men, and Faber was called out. The embarrassed hurler was protected from the role of a goat by his teammates, who had staked him to a five-run lead.

A total of twenty-two hits were recorded that afternoon—all of them singles. After the 7–2 loss, Giants manager John McGraw commented optimistically, "We had bad breaks in both the games played in Chicago. The Series is not ended yet. The advantage will be with the Giants in the coming games." He was right, as New York took the next two contests at the Polo Grounds. But McGraw's luck ran out in Chicago as the Sox captured their second championship in franchise history.

April 29, 1918

An odd play in the eighth inning helped Cincinnati to a 4–3 win over the Cardinals at Redland Field. St. Louis had a 3–0 lead until the bottom of the sixth, when Heinie Groh and Edd Roush of the Reds scored on a triple by Sherry Magee. Tommy Griffith followed with a single, tying the game. The score stood at 3 apiece until the top of the eighth, when Bert Niehoff doubled and Doug Baird drew a free pass. Reds starter Mike Regan was replaced by Hod Eller, who walked the dangerous Rogers Hornsby to load the bases. Walton Cruise then lifted a one-out fly to Edd Roush in center field. Roush juggled the ball and eventually made a shoestring catch as Niehoff crossed the plate. Niehoff was called out since he had left third base early, ending the St. Louis threat. After Cincinnati plated the winning run in the bottom of the ninth, the Cardinals lodged an official protest, claiming that Roush had deliberately bobbled the ball. The appeal was upheld, and records from the game were expunged. The contest would have a dramatic effect on the National League batting race that year.

On June 23, the Cardinals played in their second protested match of the season. The game went twelve innings and was won by St. Louis, 15–12, though it wouldn't count in the standings. The Brooklyn Robins were leading 11–9 in the top of the sixth when Walton Cruise hit a sinking liner to center field that was trapped by Brooklyn's Jim Hickman. Believing the ball to be caught, Doug Baird beat a hasty retreat back to second base. He progressed about twenty feet from third before hanging a sharp right turn and cutting across the diamond on his way home. In a travesty of justice, umpire Cy Rigler counted the run, ruling that Baird was not compelled to retouch third base. Brooklyn shortstop Ivy Olson was ejected for arguing, and Brooklyn manager Wilbert Robinson announced that the game was being played under protest. The appeal was accepted, and game records were erased.

Both contests became meaningful when Zack Wheat of Brooklyn narrowly beat out Edd Roush of Cincinnati for the batting title. Things would have turned out differently had either of the eradicated games counted. Wheat's 0-for-5 performance on June 23 would have dropped his average from .335 to .331. In that case, Edd Roush would have claimed the crown anyway with his .333 mark, but his 2-for-3 showing on April 29 would have given him more breathing room.

August 6, 1918

The temperature at game time was one hundred degrees as the Phillies and Pirates opened a four-game set at the Baker Bowl. Newspapers reported that it was the hottest day in Philadelphia in nearly twenty years. The *Pittsburgh Press* referred to the meeting of the two Pennsylvania clubs as a "dull game." But the contest was far from dull for multiple individuals affected by the heat.

Catcher Walter Schmidt was the first to succumb as Bucs manager Hugo Bezdek ordered his replacement before the start of the sixth. His substitute, Red Smith, collapsed and had to be revived with ice. Umpire Hank O'Day, who reportedly sought shade every chance he got, became wobbly in the late innings and required attention. Additionally, Dave Bancroft of the Phillies was removed from the game when he grew light-headed after the sixth frame. Both O'Day and Smith were able to complete their duties as the Pirates romped to a 10–2 win.

A similar scene would unfold in St. Louis on July 25, 1935, when Giants hurler Hal Schumacher collapsed on the mound in ninety-five-degree heat. He had pitched brilliantly to that point, allowing just one run on four hits through six innings. When a team trainer got to him, he was allegedly without a heartbeat. Fortunately, he was packed in ice and revived.

May 15, 1919

The number thirteen has long been associated with ill omens and bad luck. Brooklyn Robins pitcher Al Mamaux was left with little reason to doubt this superstition after the thirteenth inning proved to be a chamber of horrors for him on the date in question. Before then, the game had been a tight pitching duel between Mamaux and Reds hurler Hod Eller. Eller, who had tossed a no-hitter in his previous start, picked up right where he left off, holding the Robins scoreless through twelve frames. Mamaux had matched him all the way, limiting the potent Cincinnati offense to just five hits.

With one out in the bottom of the tenth, Greasy Neale made a spectacular diving catch in right field that preserved the game for the Reds. He reportedly slid across the grass on his face after making a one-handed grab. The game remained deadlocked until Mamaux suffered a complete meltdown in the thirteenth.

One can only speculate what manager Wilbert Robinson was thinking as he stood idly by and watched the Reds go through their entire batting order, victimizing Mamaux for ten runs on eight hits and a walk. Six of those runs came with two outs as the Brooklyn defense unraveled with three costly errors in the frame. Newspapers reported that a fourth error should have been charged to left fielder Zack Wheat, but the official scorer "was very kind."

Eller shut down the Robins in their last at bat, completing a string of twenty-two consecutive scoreless innings. He finished the season with a 19–9 record. He would emerge victorious twice more in the World Series that year, though his postseason statistics should be considered cautiously since eight members of the White Sox conspired to throw the Series.

May 31, 1919

The last game of a Memorial Day series (known then as Decoration Day) at Philadelphia was soured by an incident between Red Sox pitcher Carl Mays and unruly fans. The Sox jumped out to a 2–0 lead in the second inning off of right-hander Jing Johnson. But the A's answered with three runs in the bottom of the frame off of Bill James, who had been acquired from the Tigers a week earlier. A sizable Saturday crowd grew excited, and some fans began pounding on the roof of the Red Sox dugout. Ornery Boston hurler Carl Mays became aggravated by their behavior and came off the bench to confront the group. He fired a fastball into the stands, hitting a fan named Bryan Hayes. Not content to let the matter rest, Hayes sought out police, and a warrant was issued for Mays's arrest. Mays reportedly skipped town before he could be taken into custody. He would be forced to avoid appearances in Philadelphia for over a year. According to Charlton's *Baseball Chronology*, A's manager Connie Mack arranged a meeting between the two parties in July 1920. Mays grudgingly apologized to Hayes, who subsequently dropped the charges.

Trouble would find Mays again on July 13 of the 1919 slate. During a game against the White Sox at Comiskey Park, he got roughed up on the mound, allowing four runs on five hits in a two-inning stint. He had been griping about various issues all year, including poor run support. When a throw to second base from catcher Wally Schang hit Mays in the head, he stalked off the field and refused to pitch. With several more road games scheduled, Mays defiantly took a train back to Boston and demanded a trade. He would end up with the Yankees after a series of troubled negotiations.

June 28, 1919

Several newspapers were content to focus on an injury to Cubs shortstop Charlie Hollocher, who was slated to return to the Chicago lineup after injuring his thumb. During batting practice, he was knocked unconscious after being hit in the mouth with a ball. He remained out of action with a split lip and would miss a total of twenty-five games that year. According to Retrosheet, another unusual event occurred in the ninth inning of this game, which took place at Weeghman Park in Chicago.

When Cardinals manager Branch Rickey submitted his lineup to umpire Bill Klem, he had Doc Lavan batting seventh and Frank Snyder hitting eighth. Klem apparently wasn't paying attention when Snyder appeared in Lavan's spot during the second inning. In that frame, St. Louis scored two runs that should not have counted. Lavan and Snyder continued to hit out of order until the ninth, when Lavan suddenly came to bat in the seventh slot. The Cubs protested despite the fact that Lavan was actually hitting correctly for the first time all afternoon. Chicago ended up winning anyway, 6–5, staving off a major controversy.

August 24, 1919

A game between the Indians and Athletics at Dunn Field in Cleveland featured one of the most bizarre finishes in baseball history. Released by the Red Sox three weeks before, Ray Caldwell was making his mound debut for the Tribe and pitching a gem. Through eight and two-thirds innings, he had yielded just one run on four hits. The sky darkened suddenly, and to the complete astonishment of players and spectators, a bolt of lightning descended to the field, knocking the hurler flat on his back. He lay there for a full minute before getting up and polishing off a 2–1 victory.

Caldwell was not the only one affected. The bolt knocked off catcher Steve O'Neill's mask, along with the cap of Philly's third-base coach, Harry Davis. Numerous other players were jostled by the impact but were not injured. Davis received a second jolt when A's catcher Cy Perkins came over to see whether he was okay. The lightning had charged Davis's hair with electricity, and his whole body reportedly tingled after Perkins touched him.

Speaking to reporters after the game, Caldwell said: "It felt just like somebody came up with a board and hit me on top of the head and knocked me down. Then I looked around to see if anybody was hurt." The veteran moundsman theorized that the bolt had struck the button on his cap and then moved through his body before exiting via his metal spikes. He was left with a minor burn on his chest.

Caldwell had been roughed up in three straight outings before being dumped by the BoSox. He pitched six games for Cleveland in 1919, notching a 5–1 record and 1.71 ERA. He would win twenty games during Cleveland's championship run of 1920.

Part 3
THE LIVELY BALL YEARS, 1920-1945

Timeline of Significant Events

1920   The story of the White Sox scandal breaks. Eight team members are suspended, later to be banned for life. The spitball and other similar pitches are banned. The Negro National League is founded.

1921   The first radio broadcast of a baseball game airs on August 5. With the so-called lively ball in full swing, the Tigers compile an astonishing .316 team batting average. The first of three consecutive Subway Series is played in New York. The Yankees and Giants share a home for the first two.

1922   White Sox hurler Charlie Robertson tosses the last perfect game in the majors until 1956.

1923   Yankee Stadium opens. Fittingly, Babe Ruth seals a victory over Boston with a three-run homer in the inaugural game. Tris Speaker sets the modern record for doubles with fifty-nine—a record soon to be broken.

1924   Rogers Hornsby compiles the highest BA of the twentieth century with a .424 mark. The Senators claim their first and only World Series title.

1925   Yankee infielder Everett Scott ends a streak of 1,307 consecutive games played. Lou Gehrig begins his assault on that record.

1926   Firpo Marberry of the Senators records an unprecedented twenty-two saves. George Burns of the Indians clubs sixty-four doubles, breaking the standard set by Tris Speaker in 1923.

1927   Babe Ruth smashes sixty homers—a feat that will not be surpassed until 1961. Ty Cobb gets his four thousandth career hit. Detroit's Harry Heilmann wins his fourth batting title. He has the unusual distinction of having claimed the crown in every odd year over the past eight seasons.

1929   The Giants begin using a public address system at the Polo Grounds—the first major league team to do so. Yankee manager Miller Huggins resigns due to illness near the end of the season. He dies five days later.

1930   Chicago's Hack Wilson sets the all-time single-season record for RBIs with 190 (that number would later be increased by one). Wally Berger of the Braves raises the bar for rookies, slugging 38 homers and driving in 119 runs.

1931   Earl Webb of the Red Sox breaks the major league record for doubles in a season with sixty-seven.

1932   Lou Gehrig hits four home runs in a game—the first twentieth-century player to turn the trick.

1933   Babe Ruth pitches the last game of his career, a 6–5 win over the Red Sox. The annual All-Star Game makes its debut at Comiskey Park in Chicago. The AL prevails, 4–2.

1934   Babe Ruth hits his seven hundredth career homer. Burleigh Grimes becomes the last legal spitballer to record a victory.

1935   The first night game in history is played at Crosley Field in Cincinnati.

1936   Baseball writers vote for the inaugural Cooperstown class. Ty Cobb, Babe Ruth, Honus Wagner, Christy Mathewson, and Walter Johnson are among those selected.

1937   Joe Medwick of the Cardinals becomes the last National Leaguer to win a triple crown during the twentieth century.

1938   Johnny Vander Meer of the Reds pitches back-to-back no-hitters. The Yankees become the first team to win three straight World Series. Lou Gehrig hits his twenty-third career grand slam, setting the all-time mark.

1939   The first major league game to be televised pits the Dodgers against the Reds at Ebbets Field. Lou Gehrig is diagnosed with amyotrophic lateral sclerosis.

1941   Ted Williams becomes the last twentieth-century player to top the .400 mark. Joe DiMaggio upstages him with a fifty-six-game hitting streak. Lou Gehrig dies.

1943   A demand for rubber overseas results in the introduction of a newly designed baseball. After several consecutive games without a homer, the old balls are reintroduced.

1944   Joe Nuxhall of the Reds becomes the youngest player to appear in a major league game at the age of fifteen. The Browns finally make the postseason.

1945   The All-Star Game is canceled due to wartime restrictions. The Browns keep a one-armed outfielder named Pete Gray on their roster for the entire season. The Senators hit just one homer in their spacious ballpark all year. Not surprisingly, it's an inside-the-parker.

May 1, 1920

The longest game in major league history (in regard to innings played) ended in a 1–1 tie at Braves Field in Boston. Brooklyn Robins starter Leon Cadore and Braves hurler Joe Oeschger each twirled twenty-six frames that afternoon, a record that still stands. The stadium was filled to less than half its capacity; only fifteen thousand fans were on hand to witness a piece of baseball history.

The Robins' only run came in the fifth on a single by shortstop Ivy Olson. Boston knotted the score an inning later and nearly took the lead when Rabbit Maranville's double to center brought Tony Boeckel around third. Brooklyn outfielder Wally Hood made a strong relay to Cadore, who fired home in time to nail Boeckel at the plate.

The Braves threatened again in the ninth, loading the bases with one out, but the Robins turned a timely double play. In the seventeenth inning, it was Brooklyn's turn to load the bases with one down. Catcher Rowdy Elliott grounded back to the mound and Zack Wheat was forced at the plate, but Braves backstop Hank Gowdy nearly blew the game when he made a poor throw to first that was bobbled by Walter Holke. Brooklyn's Ed Konetchy came racing home as Holke made a desperate peg to the plate. His throw was offline, and Gowdy made a spectacular diving tag, which he applied to Konetchy's spikes with his bare hand. The game remained relatively quiet after that until it was called on account of darkness by umpire Barry McCormick.

Brooklyn managed just nine hits in the game. Cadore did nothing to help his own cause with a bat, going 0 for 10. Boston's Charlie Pick fared even worse with an 0-for-11 performance. The time of the game was three hours and fifty minutes—fairly brisk, considering the number of innings played.

May 27, 1920

As baseball entered a new decade, rowdyism on the diamond was still commonplace. In a game between the Yankees and Red Sox at Fenway Park, umpire George Hildebrand was obligated to defend himself when hurler Bob Shawkey took a swing at him. The scrape was precipitated by a series of calls in the fourth inning that resulted in a bases-loaded walk to Wally Schang. As the Red Sox plated their only run of the afternoon, Shawkey proceeded to fuss and fume, deliberately taking five full minutes to tie his shoe. After striking out opposing moundsman Harry Harper to end the inning, Shawkey doffed his cap and bowed to Hildebrand mockingly. An argument led to fisticuffs, and both benches emptied. Shawkey was injured when the arbiter swatted him over the head with his mask. The wound required stitches, and Carl Mays was called on to finish the game.

Babe Ruth hit a pair of solo homers in the contest, giving him five in his past five games. He would go on to break the single-season homer record he had set the previous year (twenty-nine), finishing the season with fifty-four circuit blasts. Shawkey was credited with a win—his fifth of the year. He would later be fined and suspended.

August 16, 1920

The most infamous scene in baseball history unfolded at the Polo Grounds in New York. The Indians had arrived in the Big Apple tied for first place with the White Sox and leading the Yankees by a half game in the standings. Hitless in two trips to the plate, Cleveland's shortstop Ray Chapman stepped into the box against Carl Mays. The twenty-nine-year-old Chapman was primarily a singles hitter with above-average speed. He was just coming into his prime offensively, having hit .300 in 1919. He carried a .304 average into this game.

The right-handed Mays used a submarine delivery to keep hitters on their heels. He had a good rising fastball and could make the ball sink or curve, depending on his arm angle at the time of release. Chapman crouched slightly and crowded the plate as Mays wound and fired. The day was damp and overcast. Camouflaged in a wet, hazy background, it's doubtful that Chapman even saw the pitch, which struck him squarely in the left temple. There was an audible crack.

Accounts of what happened next vary to some extent. According to one newspaper report, the ball bounced toward Mays, who picked it up and threw it to Wally Pipp at first base. Pipp stepped on the bag, making the apparent out, as Chapman staggered out of the box and then collapsed. At some point, the Cleveland infielder regained consciousness and was helped to his feet. He tried to walk but fell again before being transported to St. Lawrence Hospital. Several hours later, he was dead. Having already established a reputation as one of the most disagreeable men in the majors, Mays became even more of a pariah.

Numerous players and coaches clamored for Mays's permanent banishment. By some reports, the Indians threatened to boycott the series if he played. Manager Miller Huggins kept him out of action for a week. The beleaguered hurler returned to the mound on August 23, spinning a complete game shutout over the Tigers. Despite all the negative attention, he managed to win twenty-six games that year and twenty-seven more the following season. He never escaped the enduring stigma of the fatal pitch.

In the wake of the Chapman incident and the 1919 World Series scandal, emphasis was put on fair play. Spitballs and foreign substances were banned, along with deceptive deliveries. Umpires were encouraged to put fresh balls into play more often. Balls had previously been used until they were lopsided and soggy. The result was an offensive explosion that led to a virtual abandonment of the old "small ball" strategy.

October 10, 1920

Baseball's seventeenth official World Series featured several fabulous firsts, including the postseason debut of the Cleveland Indians. Three different milestones were reached in game 5, beginning in the first inning. With surly Hall of Famer Burleigh Grimes leering at batters from the mound and serving up a steady diet of spitballs, the Indians managed to send their first four batters all the way around the bases. Charlie Jamieson, Bill Wambsganss, and Tris Speaker all singled, setting the table for right fielder Elmer Smith, who became the first player in World Series history to launch a grand slam.

Cleveland's Doc Johnston led off the fourth with a single and then moved to third on a passed ball and a groundout. Grimes intentionally walked Steve O'Neill to get to staff ace Jim Bagby, a thirty-year-old right-hander who had won thirty-one games that year. Bagby was a fair hitter (for a pitcher) but had never demonstrated much power. In six big league seasons, he had collected just two long balls. On this day, he added a third and final career dinger to his resume with a three-run shot that led to Grimes's early exit. It was the first World Series homer by a pitcher.

The game's most remarkable turn of events occurred in the fifth inning. Brooklyn's Pete Kilduff singled to left, and Otto Miller followed with another hit to center. Clarence Mitchell, who had replaced Grimes, slashed a hard liner to Indians second baseman Bill Wambsganss. A correspondent from the *New York Tribune* provided the following account: "It sounded like a hit and looked like a hit. Everybody started to travel. Wamby made a desperate stab and held the ball. A cool person is this man of many consonants. He stepped over (second base), doubling Kilduff. In the meantime, Miller continued to flounder toward second. Wamby reached out and tagged him. The suddenness of it all dazed the multitude for a second. They saw the Indians start to trot in from the field. Then they realized what they had seen, a play that comes once in a lifetime and then is only seen by a few." This is not an exaggeration. To date, Wambsganss's heads-up play remains the only unassisted triple play in World Series history.

The Series had been sullied to an extent the previous day, when Brooklyn pitching star Rube Marquard (enshrined at Cooperstown many years later) was taken into custody by a Cleveland undercover cop at the team's hotel after attempting to scalp several box-seat tickets for an exorbitant sum. By some accounts, the hurler was asking $350 for eight tickets that carried a face value of $52.80. Marquard told the detective that his offer had been a joke, but a municipal court judge was skeptical, fining Marquard one dollar plus court fees. The veteran left-hander made a relief appearance on the day of his arrest (October 9), but it would turn out to be his last assignment of the Series. Incensed by the occurrence, Brooklyn owner Charlie Ebbets benched Marquard after game 4 and traded him to Cincinnati later that year.

May 28, 1921

Dolf Luque was one of the most irritable moundsmen ever to take the hill. The Cuban-born hurler once threw an ice pick at a teammate who had directed an ethnic slur at him. On another occasion, he was removed from a game after charging into the Giants' dugout and punching Casey Stengel in the mouth. On the date above, his temper cost Cincinnati a game.

The Pirates and Reds were engaged in a tight battle at Forbes Field in Pittsburgh. Both clubs had put up a pair of tallies in the fourth. In the top of the eighth, Cincinnati scratched out a run off of starter Whitey Glazner, giving Luque a little breathing room. The fiery hurler got into a jam in the bottom of the frame and briefly took leave of his senses.

Enraged by a safe call at the plate by umpire Bill Brennan, Luque impulsively fired the ball into his own dugout. Acting on the advice of Pittsburgh manager George Gibson (who was reportedly coaching third base), infielder Clyde Barnhart took off running on the play. The ball was retrieved in time to tag him at third base, and Gibson emphatically argued the call, insisting that the ball should have been ruled dead immediately on entering the Cincinnati dugout. The argument fell on deaf ears. After the Reds won in extra innings, Gibson took his complaint to a higher authority. NL president John Heydler upheld the protest and ordered the game replayed from the point at which it had been disrupted. The Pirates won the rematch on June 30, 4–3. Luque collected seventeen wins against nineteen losses that year.

August 17, 1921

A horrific scene unfolded at Dunn Field in Cleveland on the one-year anniversary of Ray Chapman's death. Honoring the fallen shortstop, YWCA volunteers handed out rosebuds to fans as they entered the park. A crowd of six thousand collectively held its breath as a scene eerily reminiscent of the Chapman incident took place during the bottom of the first inning. Cleveland outfielder Charlie Jamieson hit a rope to first base that struck Johnny Walker of the A's on the right side of the head. He was instantly knocked unconscious and lay on the ground unmoving for roughly a minute. He came to, but he remained in a semiconscious state for the next hour and later remembered nothing of what had happened to him.

The infielder was transported to Lakeside Hospital, where doctors found no evidence of any fractures but diagnosed him with a severe concussion. Official word from the hospital was that Walker was "resting easily" but expected to be out for at least ten days. Finishing off a dreary afternoon in

Cleveland, a poorly pitched match ended in favor of the Indians, 15–8. The second game of this ill-fated doubleheader was postponed due to rain.

August 25, 1921

Trailing the first-place Yankees by just a half game in the standings, the Cleveland Indians pummeled New York pitching for seventeen hits. With the visiting Bombers behind 11–1 in the eighth, manager Miller Huggins summoned southpaw Harry Harper, who hadn't pitched since May because of a thumb injury. Harper was the third Yankee hurler to take the mound. Rust was evident as he hit Charlie Jamieson, Larry Gardner, and Steve O'Neill. Believing the beanings to be intentional, O'Neill picked up the ball and fired it at Harper's head. A first-string catcher, O'Neill had a strong, accurate arm, and his throw was nearly on the mark. The benches cleared, and in the brief scuffle that followed, O'Neill reportedly landed a blow to Harper's jaw. He was ejected along with Bronx moundsman Bill Piercy. Displeased with O'Neill's banishment, fans confronted umpires Ollie Chill and George Moriarty after the game.

Cleveland nudged the Yankees out of first place with a 15–1 pasting. The game held another point of interest as Yankee fly chaser Bob Meusel nearly tied the record for errors in a game by an outfielder (set by Kip Selbach of the Orioles in 1902). "Long Bob" committed four miscues, two of which led to Cleveland runs. He would collect 135 RBIs for the Yankees that year but prove to be among the club's least reliable fielders with twenty muffs—the highest annual total of his career while manning the outer perimeter.

May 5, 1922

Ty Cobb couldn't stand to lose. With Browns left-hander Bill Bayne staked to a 6–0 lead and carrying a no-hitter into the ninth at Navin Field in Detroit, most managers would have acted in a sportsmanlike manner. But Cobb wasn't like most managers.

In an effort to break up Bayne's gem, the ultracompetitive Tiger player/manager sent a gaggle of pinch hitters to the plate. Stories still circulate widely that Cobb made five straight hitting substitutions, but box scores and original game accounts do not support this claim. A verifiable fact is that outfielder Ira Flagstead hit for pitcher Howard Ehmke in the eighth. Larry Woodall, a backup catcher, broke up the no-hitter in the ninth while hitting in place of infielder Dan Clark. Clark had been installed as a replacement for regular second baseman George Cutshaw. With the no-hitter ruined, Cobb then benched himself and sent rookie outfielder Bob Fothergill to the plate. Fothergill, a short, stout man who would be referred to as "Fats," proceeded to fly out. He is believed to be the only man in history to pinch-hit for Cobb. Bobby Veach followed with a single, and Harry Heilmann lifted a sacrifice fly to spoil Bayne's shutout bid. The Browns won the contest, 6–1.

Cobb may not have used five straight pinch hitters, but his actions were no less objectionable considering the size of the St. Louis lead and the fact that the Tigers were mired in last place at the time. Bayne had an unremarkable career, finishing with a 31–32 record and 4.84 ERA in nine major league seasons. His 1981 obituary made reference to the 1922 no-hit bid.

May 25, 1922

In the fall of 1921, Babe Ruth, Bob Meusel, and pitcher Bill Piercy went on an All-Star barnstorming tour against the wishes of Commissioner Kenesaw Mountain Landis. On December 5, Landis showed his disapproval by suspending all three Yankee players until May 20—roughly seven weeks into the 1922 campaign. Surprisingly, the Bombers did fine without them, hanging onto first place through May 19.

Ruth returned to much fanfare, receiving the honorary title of team captain. He would serve in that capacity only briefly. The layoff hadn't done him any good, and he now felt pressure to deliver. Through the first five games, he was hitting .095 with one homer. The boo birds began showing up every day, the first time in Ruth's career that he was subjected to such abuse on a regular basis. On May 25, he hit a single in the third inning and was tagged out trying to stretch it into a double. Exasperated with the call, he got up and threw dirt on umpire George Hildebrand. Hildebrand promptly tossed him out of the game.

A chorus of jeers greeted Ruth on his way back to the dugout, and he tipped his cap sarcastically. He might have exited without further incident had he not been subjected to a barrage of objectionable comments from two Pullman conductors in the stands. The Babe leaped over the wall into the seats and went after one of them. The man backed away, drawing Ruth further into the crowd. Frustrated and angry, Ruth hopped up on the dugout roof and openly challenged anyone in the stands to a fight. There were no takers.

It was a long walk to the clubhouse at the Polo Grounds, and Ruth was jeered all the way. He later said that he didn't mind when fans booed him but took exception to degrading personal remarks. "This fellow today, whoever he was, called me a 'low-down bum' and other names that got me mad," he told reporters. The Bambino got off with a warning and a small fine, but Miller Huggins stripped him of his honorary title. He was replaced as captain by infielder Everett Scott. In 110 games, Ruth still managed to hit 35 homers and gather 99 RBIs.

May 30, 1922

There have been some highly unusual trades in baseball history. In 1890, Cy Young was sold by a minor league club in Canton, Ohio, for $250 and a new suit of clothes. First baseman Jack Fenton was sent packing by a San Francisco League club for a box of prunes. Hall of Famer Lefty Grove was peddled by the Martinsburg Mountaineers in 1920 for the cost of a new fence. The trade between the Cubs and Cardinals on May 30, 1922, was not quite as bizarre in comparison, but it was by no means an ordinary event.

Between games of a doubleheader, Chicago and St. Louis swapped players. Max Flack of the Cubs learned he had been traded to the Cardinals for fellow outfielder Cliff Heathcote after returning from lunch. Both players appeared in their new uniforms for the second contest and adjusted fairly well. Flack had played right field and batted fifth in the opener, going hitless for the Cubs. In the second game, he remained in right field and assumed leadoff duties, going 1 for 4 as a Cardinal. Heathcote had been 0 for 3 out of the seventh slot while playing center field for St. Louis. Shifted to right field by Cubs skipper Bill Killefer, he appeared fifth in the Chicago batting order and had a 2-for-4 day at the plate. The Cubs swept the twin bill, 4–1 and 3–1.

Years later, a similar scene would play out for New York outfielder Joel Youngblood. On August 4, 1982, Youngblood played in an afternoon game for the Mets at Chicago and then flew to Philadelphia to play that night after being traded to the Expos. Youngblood left his glove at Wrigley Field and almost missed his flight when he went back to get it. He became the first player in major league history to get a hit in two different cities for two different teams off of two Hall of Fame pitchers (Fergie Jenkins and Steve Carlton) in the same day. Twenty-five years after the fact, Youngblood remembered it being "a very, very long day."

August 25, 1922

The highest-scoring game in baseball history was played on June 8, 1869, between the Universities of Columbia and Niagara. Niagara thrashed their opponents by an inconceivable score of 209–10. Every player in the winning club scored at least twenty runs. Incredibly, Columbia used just one pitcher that day, a fellow named Mack, who (not surprisingly) never went on to a major league career. Mack coughed up forty runs in the first, twenty-six in the seventh, and fifty-eight in the eighth. SABR researcher Arthur O. Schott estimated that Niagara batters ran roughly fourteen miles on the bases that day.

The highest-scoring game in major league history took place on August 25, 1922, between the Phillies and the Cubs at Chicago. Both managers had the sense to call on their bullpens as a total of seven pitchers were used that day—five by the hosts. Pitching could not be blamed entirely for the game's farcical outcome as a total of nine errors—four committed by outfielders—led to nineteen unearned runs. Jimmy Ring of the Phillies was hurt the most by his club's defense (or lack thereof) as ten of the sixteen runs scored off of him were the direct result of misplays.

A number of records were set during the slugfest, including most runs (forty-nine) and hits (fifty-one). Additionally, Cliff Heathcote of the Cubs reached base seven times (a franchise record later tied by Eric Young in 2000). The Cubs jumped out to a 25–6 lead after four frames, but the Phillies outscored them 17–1 the rest of the way. The end result was a sloppy 26–23 Chicago victory. In one of the game's defining moments, Hack Miller of the Cubs smashed an impressive three-run homer in the second inning that reached the center-field scoreboard. By some reports, it was only the second homer ever hit to that vicinity of Cubs Park.

October 5, 1922

Game 2 of the World Series ended on a highly unsatisfactory note as umpires George Hildebrand and Bill Klem declared the contest a tie on account of darkness. It was exactly 4:40 p.m. according to the center-field clock at the Polo Grounds when the arbiters made their decision. By then, the Giants and Yankees had just completed the tenth inning, and the score was knotted at 3 apiece. According to numerous accounts, there was not a cloud in the sky and the sun was still shining, though there was a haze hanging over the field. Many sportswriters believed that another inning should have been played. Grantland Rice of the *New York Tribune* commented: "Due to the immense amount of money paid in and the great amount of gossip that baseball has drawn in the past few years, it would have been wiser to let the game run out at least another chapter to effectually stifle any shrill voice of indignant protest, fair or otherwise."

The crowd of thirty-eight thousand voiced a thunderous roar of disapproval at the outcome, and an angry mob surrounded Commissioner Landis's box. He was escorted by police out of the stadium as a riot was narrowly avoided. Rumors persisted after the game that the teams had allowed the tie to happen in the interest of increasing gate receipts. These murmurs were quickly squelched when Landis announced that the proceeds, totalling more than $120,000, would be donated to disabled war veterans and other charities. According to multiple sources, the commissioner was unhappy with the ruling himself and had confronted Hildebrand.

"Why in Sam Hill did you call the game?" he demanded.

"There was a temporary haze on the field," the arbiter replied.

After game 2, momentum shifted in favor of the Giants. They won the next three meetings by a combined score of 12–6 to claim their second straight world championship. The ill-fated second match was the last tie in Series history. Two others had occurred, in 1907 and 1912. After the 1922 slate, a rule was established requiring all tied games to be resumed at a later date. This happened in 2008, when game 5 of the Fall Classic between the Rays and Phillies was suspended in the sixth inning due to rain.

July 4, 1923

The opener of an Independence Day doubleheader in Cleveland was played to an exciting finish. With the score tied at 7 in the tenth, Tigers catcher Larry Woodall was ejected by umpire Pants Rowland for arguing over a force play at second. This put player/manager Ty Cobb in a predicament. Cobb was known to overmanage at times. In this game, he used four pitchers and two catchers. He had sent his third-string backstop in to pinch-hit for hurler Syl Johnson. In desperation, he instructed one of his coaches, Fred Carisch, to suit up for the bottom of the tenth. Carisch was forty-one years old and hadn't been a playing member of a major league roster since 1914. When active, he had never caught more than seventy-nine games in any season. Nevertheless, Cobb had slipped him into the lineup a couple of months earlier during a 16–1 pasting of the Browns at Sportsman's Park. No one on the St. Louis bench had complained since the game was so far out of hand.

With a lot more at stake, however, Cleveland manager Tris Speaker objected to Cobb's substitution, drawing umpire Billy Evans's attention to the fact that Carisch was not on the "eligible list." The arbiter ignored Speaker's overtures and allowed Carisch to get behind the dish. The rest of the game was played under protest. Speaker opted not to pursue the matter any further after pinch hitter Glenn Myatt drilled a towering three-run homer over the center-field wall, which was located roughly 460 feet from home plate. Cleveland fans had less reason to celebrate during the second game, in which Detroit romped to a 15–3 win.

August 20, 1923

Babe Ruth was known for his showboating and clowning. During the bottom of the ninth inning of this 16–5 laugher at Comiskey Park, a small dog wandered into left field, where Ruth was stationed. According to *New York Daily News* correspondent Paul Gallico, the Babe got down on all fours and began following the animal around. He then took off his glove and threw it at the canine, prompting the dog to fetch. When Ruth's new pet took off with his mitt, he was forced to catch a fly ball hit by rookie pitcher Paul Castner bare-handed. This delighted many in the crowd of 8,500.

The White Sox battered Hall of Famer Herb Pennock for fourteen hits that day—four of them by fellow Cooperstown inductee Harry Hooper. Chicago hitters consistently failed in the clutch, however, stranding eight runners in the loss. In addition to his ninth-inning "show," Ruth was one of the offensive stars of the game, with two runs scored and three more driven in.

September 7, 1923

Baseball is a fickle sport. Howard Ehmke would have attested to that fact. The Red Sox staff ace had a no-hitter going in the late innings at Shibe Park in Philadelphia when opposing moundsman Slim Harriss hit the ball all the way to the wall. Harriss was a weak hitter unaccustomed to legging out extra base hits (he had just one double in more than two hundred plate appearances at that point in his career). While rounding first, he missed the bag and was called out, erasing the hit. A bit later, Philly outfielder Frank Welch belted a liner that was mishandled. Initially ruled a hit, the official scorer changed his mind before the inning was over. And so, with a little help from outside sources, Ehmke ended up with a no-hitter. It would be the last one thrown by a Red Sox pitcher for more than thirty years and one of only nine in the majors during the decade of the 1920s.

Ehmke came close to duplicating the feat during his next start against the Yankees on September 11. Whitey Witt led off the bottom of the first with a bouncer up the third baseline. The ball hit BoSox third sacker Howard Shanks in the chest, and he didn't recover in time to throw to first. It looked like an error to eighteen thousand fans in attendance, but scorer Fred Lieb (who would later become a prominent baseball historian) believed that Witt would have beat it out anyway. There was no public address system, and after Ehmke retired the next twenty-seven Yankees in order, he was mobbed by jubilant Red Sox teammates. Even the New York crowd reportedly cheered for him. Lieb was pressured to change his ruling but refused. "Had the same play occurred in the eighth inning, I must admit I might have been tempted to rule it an error, but once I made my decision, I stuck to it," he later recalled. Ehmke missed being the first pitcher in history to twirl consecutive no-hitters. Johnny Vander Meer of the Reds would turn the trick in 1938. Years later, Lieb would deprive Giants hurler Sam Jones of a no-hitter with a similar ruling.

May 28, 1924

Jake Daubert of the Reds had a lot going for him. A slick-fielding first baseman, he drew frequent comparisons to Hal Chase, who was generally considered to be the top defensive first sacker of the era. Daubert held his own offensively as well, winning consecutive batting titles in 1913–1914. Respected and admired by peers, he was appointed vice president of the Baseball Players Fraternity. Popular with fans, he was nominated to run for alderman of Brooklyn (though he did not capture enough votes to win the election). When he died unexpectedly on October 9, 1924, the loss was felt by many.

The trouble began on May 28, when he was beaned by Allen Sothoron of the Cardinals in the first game of a doubleheader at St. Louis. Daubert had homered against the same club the previous day, and it was rumored that the act was retaliatory. He left the game in the first inning, walking without assistance to the dugout. X-rays later showed no evidence of a fracture.

Daubert returned to action after a brief layoff, though he suffered from headaches and insomnia. He missed more than fifty games that year, still managing a respectable .281 batting average. Near the end of the season, he grew weak and was rehospitalized. Doctors attributed his condition to either appendicitis or gallstones, and an operation was performed. Daubert died a week later, prompting one of the attending physicians to list the secondary cause of death as "a concussion resulting from a pitched ball." According to Charlton's *Baseball Chronology*, this allowed Daubert's widow to file a lawsuit against the Reds.

Years later, Daubert's son would develop a spleen condition common to several family members and contend that the same ailment had killed his father. Daubert's death was the second tragedy to strike Cincinnati in 1924. On March 7, manager Pat Moran had died of Bright's disease.

September 7, 1924

The 1924 pennant race between the New York Giants and Brooklyn Robins was among the most dramatic of the decade. The Robins were led by Hall of Fame moundsmen Burleigh Grimes and Dazzy Vance, who would win fifty games between them that year. The Giants' roster featured seven future Cooperstown greats, among them first baseman George Kelly, second baseman Frankie Frisch, and shortstop Travis Jackson.

At the close of play on August 9, the Robins stood thirteen games behind the first-place Giants. Within a month, they had clawed their way to within a half game of the NL lead. A showdown between the two clubs at Ebbets Field on September 7 was the hottest ticket in town. The park was completely sold out before game time, and thousands of latecomers were determined to get in. A mob of disorderly fans worked together to batter down the left-field exit gate with a telephone pole, allowing roughly seven thousand unauthorized customers access to the park. It took an army of 150 police officers to restore order.

A standing-room-only crowd saw the Giants prevail in an 8–7 slugfest that featured thirty-three hits—eleven of them for extra bases. The visitors broke a 3–3 tie in the eighth with a five-run outburst. Brooklyn nearly tied the game with a dramatic three-run rally in the bottom of the ninth. The Giants would wait until the second-to-last day of the season to clinch the pennant, ultimately leaving the Robins a game and a half behind.

October 10, 1924

The 1924 World Series was one of the strangest ever. Shortly before the opening game, Phillies shortstop Heinie Sand reported to Commissioner Landis that Giants outfielder Jimmy O'Connell had offered him a bribe to throw a September 27 match between the two clubs. O'Connell admitted his indiscretion and implicated New York coach Cozy Dolan along with three other players. Pirates owner Barney Dreyfuss then fueled the fire by alleging that Dolan had additionally tried to talk his star third baseman, Pie Traynor, into holding out for more money during the spring. He insinuated that Giants skipper John McGraw may have been involved. McGraw's longtime nemesis, AL president Ban Johnson, threw his hat into the ring, clamoring for Landis's resignation and McGraw's banishment. Neither event took place, but O'Connell and Dolan were run out of baseball.

Another minor scandal broke when rumors surfaced that more than 30 percent of the World Series tickets had fallen into the hands of scalpers, who were charging exorbitant prices. The Series was not expected to go seven games, and on the eve of the final match in Washington, tickets had not even been printed yet. Fans camped outside Griffith Stadium all night, and when the box offices opened on October 10, there was mass confusion.

Fittingly, game 7 featured one of the most bizarre conclusions in history. President Calvin Coolidge and his wife were on hand to witness a marathon twelve-inning encounter that was decided on the last play. With one out in the bottom of the twelfth and the game tied at 3, Giants reliever Jack Bentley induced a pop-up near home plate off the bat of Muddy Ruel. The sure-handed Hank Gowdy settled under it but accidentally stepped on his discarded mask. It stuck to his shoe and, despite frantic attempts, he could not shake it loose. The distraction allowed the ball to drop harmlessly into foul territory. Given new life, Ruel drilled a double to left field. The game quickly unraveled for the Giants as the aging Walter Johnson, who had pitched four scoreless innings in relief on less than two days' rest, reached on an error by shortstop Travis Jackson. Earl McNeely then hit a potential double-play ball to Fred Lindstrom at third. The ball took a weird hop and bounded over the Hall of Famer's head. Ruel scored the winning run, lifting the Senators to their first world championship.

June 1925

The summer of 1925 kicked off with a bang as a slew of uncommon events occurred within the month of June.

On June 2, Jim Bottomley of the Cardinals had a banner day at the plate, blasting a pair of homers off of Reds right-hander Neal Brady. This included a two-out grand slam in the fifth inning that proved to be the game's deciding blow. One of Bottomley's drives struck a fan named Irwin Hayes in the face, causing minor injury. The event seemed inconsequential until Hayes filed a $7,500 lawsuit. According to a report in the *St. Louis Star*, Hayes's laughable petition charged that Bottomley "deliberately and with the intention to create a situation known as a home run, struck and drove a baseball which hit the plaintiff's nose, causing severe nervous damage."

Things looked bleak for the A's on June 15 as five different hurlers staked the Indians to a 15–4 lead through seven innings at Shibe Park. Believing the outcome to be a foregone conclusion, many fans began filing toward the exits. Had they stuck around, they would have witnessed one of the most dramatic comebacks in history. Four different hurlers took the mound for Cleveland in the eighth as the A's went through their batting order twice, scoring thirteen runs—a franchise record for the frame. Southpaw Carl Yowell and right-hander By Speece faced a cumulative total of six batters, allowing six runs without recording an out. Staff ace George Uhle finally put out the fire after coughing up four runs of his own, including a dramatic two-out, three-run homer to slugger Al Simmons. There were forty-three hits in the game, which was won by Philly, 17–15.

Another unusual scene played out in St. Louis the following day. In the sixth inning of a game between the Phillies and Cardinals, visiting pitcher

Jimmy Ring requested permission from umpire Cy Pfirman to change his undershirt, which was apparently soaked with perspiration. When the appeal was denied, catcher Jimmie Wilson became irate and was ejected for arguing. His replacement, Butch Henline, continued the debate and was tossed out as well. Things began to heat up even further as manager Art Fletcher came storming out of the Philly dugout to take up the cause. Feeling left out, Cardinals skipper Rogers Hornsby joined the dispute and exchanged heated words with Fletcher. Both men were thrown out as Hornsby decked the elder manager. While the commotion was taking place, Ring slipped off and changed his shirt without permission. He was pulled from the game after giving up a pair of runs, and the Philly bullpen promptly blew a 4–2 lead as St. Louis prevailed, 6–4. Both Fletcher and Hornsby were fined for their part in the fracas.

On June 17, the Tigers embarrassed the Yankees by scoring thirteen runs in the top of the sixth off of Alex Ferguson, Walter Beall, and Hank Johnson (who combined for a 49.50 ERA in a two-inning span). Lasting nearly an hour, the disastrous inning featured six hits and seven walks. The biggest blow was a grand slam by Ty Cobb as eleven runners crossed the plate before a single out was recorded. The Yankees got their only run on a homer by Lou Gehrig in the 19–1 blowout. It would be nearly eighty years before a visiting team again scored that many runs at Yankee Stadium.

Putting the exclamation point on a wild month for baseball, Pirates second baseman Eddie Moore escaped being retired twice in the same at bat on June 22. In the top of the first inning at Sportsman's Park in St. Louis, Moore was facing Johnny Stewart of the Cardinals. Stewart had come on in relief of an ineffective Flint Rhem, who would be charged with six earned runs in the frame. Moore flied out to left fielder Ray Blades, apparently ending the inning, but the play was nullified when home-plate umpire Monroe Sweeney called a balk. Moore stepped back into the box and hit a catchable fly in foul territory that was dropped by Blades. Few players in history have been given a third chance to make good, and Moore did just that, lifting a single to center field that plated two more runs. Pirates center fielder Max Carey became the first player to have two multiple-hit innings in the same game as he collected a pair of singles in the first and another pair in the eighth. Pittsburgh breezed to a 24–6 win, moving within a game and a half of the NL lead. They would capture the pennant and the World Series that year.

October 10, 1925

Senators outfielder Sam Rice knew how to keep secrets. When he was in his early twenties, a tornado ripped through his family's Illinois home, killing everyone inside, including his wife, children, parents, and sisters. For years, he kept details of the tragedy to himself. Even his second wife, Mary, didn't know about it until a man from Rice's hometown recognized the marquee ballplayer in a restaurant one day and offered condolences about the "storm." Only then did Sam relay the story to Mary.

Among the greatest right fielders of the lively ball era, Rice helped guide the Senators to their only world championship in 1924. He hit .364 in the Series the following year and was involved in one of the most controversial plays in postseason history. The truth about the play was another secret, one he would carry to the grave.

The Pirates and Senators split the first two games at Pittsburgh, and the Series moved to Washington. In the seventh inning of game 3, the Sens scratched out a pair of runs off of Pirates hurler Ray Kremer to take a 4–3 lead. Washington's player/manager Bucky Harris made a defensive shift in the top of the eighth, moving Rice to right field from center to accommodate Earl McNeely, who had been inserted as a pinch runner in the previous frame. It would prove to be a fortunate move as Bucs catcher Earl Smith hit a long drive to the deep recesses of the park. Rice tracked the ball at full speed all the way to the temporary bleachers that had been installed. He lunged for it, flipped into the stands, and disappeared out of view of the umpires. For ten full seconds, he was unaccounted for. When McNeely hauled Rice to his feet, he had the ball in his possession. Umpire Cy Rigler ruled it a catch, and Smith was stripped of a game-tying homer. A hot debate ensued, but the umpiring crew upheld the decision. Commissioner Landis asked Rice after the game whether he had made the catch, and the enigmatic outfielder replied, "Judge, the umpire said I did."

The Senators lost the Series in seven games, but members of the print media hounded Rice about the "catch" for years. He could have made a pretty penny by selling his story but refused, insisting that the mystery was "more fun." At the request of historian Lee Allen, Rice drafted a letter telling his story in July 1965 with the understanding that it would not be read until after his death. The letter was opened by Hall of Fame president Paul S. Kerr in 1974. In his own words, Rice contended, "At no time did I lose possession of the ball."

August 15, 1926

Babe Herman's *New York Times* obituary stated that despite his tremendous hitting, he became widely known for a handful of mistakes as a fielder and base runner. The gangly slugger enjoyed his peak offensive seasons between 1928 and 1932, topping the .300 mark every year and reaching a high of .393 in 1930. He hit for the cycle twice in the same season (1931)—a feat that would be unmatched for more than eighty years.

At the same time, Herman earned the nickname "the Headless Horseman of Ebbets Field" for his misadventures on the bases. Twice in 1930 he stopped to admire the home runs of teammates and was passed on the base paths. The victims, Del Bissonette and Glenn Wright, had their long balls reduced to singles. Herman committed his most infamous baserunning gaffe during his rookie season of 1926. For years, rumors persisted that Herman had tripled into a triple play, but as Herman himself said, "There was one out on the play, so how could I do that?" Here is what really happened (more or less):

On August 15, Herman was batting against George Mogridge of the Braves with one out. The bases were loaded with Brooklynites—Hank De-Berry was on third, Dazzy Vance was on second, and Chick Fewster was on first. Mogridge hung a curveball to the lefty-swinging Herman, who hammered a shot to the top of the wall in right field. DeBerry scored easily, but as Herman was rounding second, he was instructed to go back since Fewster had not yet turned the corner at third. Dazzy Vance misunderstood the coach's instructions and returned to the bag. Fewster got hung up, and Herman, ignoring the advice altogether, kept running with his head down. Umpire Beans Reardon remembered the play as follows: "Now I've got three men on third and every one of them is being tagged. . . . Finally I said, 'The bag belongs to Vance, so Fewster you're out and so are you (Herman) for passing a runner on the baselines.'" Herman remembered Fewster being tagged in the outfield. Apparently, the flustered second baseman had wandered off to pick up his glove, assuming that the inning was already over. The incident inspired a long-running joke in Brooklyn that went as follows:

"The Dodgers have three men on base!"

"Oh, yeah? Which base?"

May 17, 1927

The Cubs and Braves engaged in an epic battle at Boston that went twenty-two frames and set a new record for innings played between two clubs in consecutive games (forty). The first of the two marathon encounters took place on May 14 at Braves Field. Chicago's Guy Bush and Boston's Charlie Robertson (author of a perfect game for the White Sox in 1922) dueled to a 2–2 tie through seventeen rounds. Player/manager Dave Bancroft may have pushed a bit too hard when he sent Robertson back to the hill in the eighteenth. The tiring right-hander faced five batters, yielding two runs on four hits before getting the hook. His relief, a former Dartmouth College hurler named Foster Edwards, issued an intentional walk and a wild pitch before giving up two straight singles to make the score 7–2 in favor of Chicago. That's how the game ended.

On May 17, the second chapter of the grueling showdown was written. After the Braves knotted the score at 3 in the bottom of the seventh, neither club would break through for another fourteen innings. Boston's durable workhorse, Bob Smith, lost a heartbreaker after issuing a leadoff walk to slugger Hack Wilson in the top of the twenty-second frame. Riggs Stephenson sacrificed Wilson to second, and Charlie Grimm came through with a clutch single, breaking the tie. The Braves were completely shut down by swingman Bob Osborn, who tossed fourteen scoreless innings in relief. Smith's twenty-two-inning stint would be unequaled for the remainder of the century. In an age of pitch counts and relief specialists, it seems likely that no hurler will ever last that long again.

September 27, 1928

When he arrived in the majors, Lefty Grove had just three pitches in his arsenal: fast, faster, and fastest. As one sportswriter colorfully put it, Grove "could throw a lamb chop past a wolf." With his fiery temperament and perpetual scowl, he was a dominant presence on the hill. During the 1928 slate, the ornery left-hander showed just how dominant he could be, throwing two "immaculate innings."

The first one came on August 23 against the Indians. It happened in the second frame before a sparse crowd at Philadelphia's Shibe Park. Three men came to the plate against Grove in that round—first baseman Eddie Morgan, center fielder Luther Harvel, and catcher Chick Autry. Each of them struck out on three pitches. Grove's graphic display of efficiency had been duplicated only six times in history to that point (twice in the American League and four times in the senior circuit).

On September 27, Grove would set himself apart from this elite group by turning the trick again against the White Sox at Comiskey Park. This time, the victims were catcher Moe Berg, pitcher Tommy Thomas, and center fielder Johnny Mostil. At the time, Grove was the only hurler in history to throw two "immaculate innings." Though he would later be joined by illustrious fireballers Sandy Koufax and Nolan Ryan, he remains the only hurler to do it twice in the same season. After 1928, the event would not be seen in the majors for another twenty-five years.

May 19, 1929

Tragedy struck at Yankee Stadium when a sudden cloudburst sent fans scrambling for shelter in right field. Two people died and scores were injured.

Rain began falling in the fourth inning, but many fans remained in their seats with Ruth and Gehrig due to bat in the bottom of the fifth. Both men had gone deep in the third. A huge crowd was on hand for what was slated to be a Sunday doubleheader against the Red Sox. One section of the right-field bleachers, known as "Ruthville," where many of Babe Ruth's home runs landed, was particularly crowded with younger fans.

When the much-anticipated half of the frame arrived, soggy spectators saw Boston's pitcher, Jack Russell, induce a harmless grounder off the bat of Ruth. Gehrig was just heading to the plate when the skies opened up. The right-field exit in the "Ruthville" section was located down a long flight of steps below the seats. Seeking shelter from the downpour, a mass of fans made a mad dash. The Associated Press described the scene as follows: "As the pressure of the crowding fans increased, those first on the stairs were toppled down and those behind them fell on them. In a few seconds, the stairway was a mass of screaming, fighting, panic-stricken humanity while those in the rear, unaware of the crush in the stairway, pressed forward to push others into the human heap."

Eleanor Price, a seventeen-year-old college student, and Joseph Carter, a sixty-year-old truck driver, were killed, and more than sixty others were injured. The game was declared official with two outs in the fifth and the Yankees ahead, 3–0.

It was alleged that the other right-field exits were either closed or malfunctioning that day. Rumors also surfaced that the game was not immediately called because Yankee officials did not want to honor rain checks. An investigation by the local district attorney on May 20 absolved the organization of any wrongdoing. Ruth personally visited young victims in Lincoln Hospital, shaking hands, handing out baseballs, and promising to hit home runs. The Babe delivered the goods on May 23 and May 26 with homers off of Milt Gaston and Ed Carroll of the Red Sox.

July 4, 1929

Hack Wilson was one of the most oddly proportioned players in history, at five-foot-six and 190 pounds. He had an eighteen-inch neck, a barrel-shaped torso, short legs, and extremely small feet (size six). He was also among the most powerful sluggers of the lively ball era, winning four home-run crowns between 1926 and 1930. His story is one of personal tragedy—chronic alcoholism led to his rapid decline after a record-setting season of 191 RBIs in 1930.

In an effort to curb Wilson's heavy drinking, Cubs manager Joe Mc-Carthy allegedly approached him one day before a game and said, "If I drop a worm in a glass of water, it swims around. If I drop it in a glass of whiskey, the worm dies. What does that prove?"

"If you drink whiskey, you'll never get worms," the slugger reportedly fired back.

Near the end of his career in 1933, Wilson was summoned to pinch-hit by Brooklyn manager Max Carey with runners on base and two outs in the ninth. Teammate Joe Judge found Wilson in the locker room amid a pile of empty beer bottles. Despite being in an obvious state of intoxication, Wilson delivered a walk-off homer. Judge disposed of the evidence while Wilson was at bat.

Not all of Wilson's on-field exploits ended triumphantly. During the second game of a July 4 doubleheader against the Reds in 1929, the hard-drinking outfielder (then with the Cubs) delivered a fifth-inning single—his third of the day. As he reached first base, he was treated to "a barrage of criticism" from Cincinnati hurler Ray Kolp, who was sitting on the bench. Kolp dared Wilson to come into the dugout, and, woefully short on self-restraint, Wilson abruptly left the bag without calling for time. According to multiple newspaper accounts, Kolp ended up with a black eye after Wilson struck him repeatedly. Wilson was called out at first and ejected from the game.

Later that day, the incorrigible Cubs slugger got into another altercation as players from both clubs were boarding the same train. Wilson confronted Cincinnati pitcher Pete Donahue, announcing his intention of demanding an apology from Kolp. Donahue suggested that Wilson might not make it off the train alive if he did so. Wilson landed a roundhouse blow to Donahue's chin, knocking him down, and then followed with another clout to the hurler's mouth. The volatile fly chaser ended up being suspended for the incident at the ballpark. In a stern reprimand, NL president John Heydler asserted that Wilson's actions "might easily have started a riot."

October 5, 1929

For the Phillies, who had not been to the World Series in over a decade and had placed sixth or lower in the standings for eleven straight seasons, the 1929 home finale could not have been more eventful. Quaker City hero Chuck Klein, playing in his first full season, was tied with Giants slugger Mel Ott for the NL home-run lead at forty-two. Determined to salvage something good out of yet another lackluster season, Philly manager Burt Shotton and his pitching staff conspired to steal the homer crown away from Ott during a doubleheader against the Giants on this date.

The right-field wall at the Baker Bowl in Philadelphia, located a mere 280 feet from home plate and topped by a 60-foot wall and screen barrier, made an inviting target to both lefty sluggers. But Ott would scarcely get to swing his club after Klein homered in the fifth inning of the first match. Ott was walked by right-hander Les Sweetland in his next at bat and would get virtually nothing to hit for the rest of the afternoon.

In the second game, Ott delivered a single in his first plate appearance. After that, Philly moundsmen worked conspicuously around him, issuing five consecutive semi-intentional walks. Before the last free pass, Ott ran up a 3-2 count before Phil Collins walked him with the bases loaded. Klein would go on to claim three more home-run titles over the next four seasons. Ott would lead the league in circuit blasts six times during his illustrious career.

Neither team was in the pennant race, but the showdown between Ott and Klein drew an above-average number to the park. In another newsworthy event for the hometown faithful, Philly outfielder Lefty O'Doul rapped out his 251st hit of the season, a new NL record. He would add three more that afternoon, running his batting average up to a league-leading .398. Unfortunately for the Phillies, their opponents generated even more offense than they did. Fifteen different Philadelphia hurlers combined for a miserable 6.13 team ERA in 1929 as the club finished eleven games below the .500 mark.

August 29, 1930

A bit of vaudeville on the bases in Philadelphia delighted a small crowd at the Baker Bowl. The moment of comic relief was provided by Braves shortstop Rabbit Maranville and Phillies second baseman Fresco Thompson. Neither player was new to the performing arts. Thompson was a notorious bench jockey and wisecracker. Asked by pitcher Waite Hoyt one day why he gargled so much before games, the cheeky infielder replied that he was getting in shape. His wry sarcasm would eventually cost him his job in New York when Giants skipper Bill Terry asked him to pinch-run one afternoon. Thompson declined, joking that he had just shined his shoes. Terry was not amused, sending him to Montreal of the International League. Maranville was an incorrigible prankster who was known to sit on runners after tagging them out, striking the pose of Auguste Rodin's famous sculpture *The Thinker*. On the way to second base one day, he deliberately crawled through the legs of an umpire.

Thompson and Maranville's slapstick routine took place in the top of the fourth inning when Maranville was thrown out trying to steal second for the third out of the frame. Maranville didn't like the call and stood arguing the play with umpire Michael Donohue. The debate continued for quite some time, with Maranville making a lively show of it. Growing anxious for the dispute to end, Thompson, a waif of a player at five feet eight inches and 150 pounds, picked up the even smaller Maranville (five-foot-five) and carried him to his shortstop position while fans hooted with laughter. The Braves would have the last chuckle that afternoon, coming away with a 9–8 win in eleven innings. Thompson and Maranville put on an offensive show as well, collectively going 7 for 11 at the plate with three runs scored and an RBI.

April 26, 1931

The weather was foul in Washington at the start of this game at Griffith Stadium. After a fifteen-minute delay, the Senators and Yankees squared off with high winds wreaking havoc on the field. Earle Combs opened with a groundout off of right-hander Firpo Marberry. Lyn Lary drew a walk, and Dusty Cooke struck out, bringing Yankee cleanup man Lou Gehrig to the plate. "The Iron Horse" belted a massive drive to the cavernous expanse of center field. The ball sailed into the bleachers and bounced back onto the field, where it was caught by Senators outfielder Harry Rice. Believing it to be a legal catch, Lary headed off to the dugout after reaching third. Gehrig continued to circle the bases and was called out for passing Lary. His homer was reduced to a triple with no RBIs. The repercussions of the play were vast.

The two runs proved critical after the Yankees lost, 9–7. Manager Joe McCarthy, who was coaching at third on the play, knew he had been negligent and removed himself from further coaching responsibilities that year. The loss of the round tripper cost Gehrig sole possession of the AL homer crown. He ended up tied with Babe Ruth at forty-six. Furthermore, the erasure of the two RBIs would forever alter an all-time record. Gehrig finished the season with 184 ribbies—a single-season high for the American League and a mark that still stands.

In 2012, SABR researcher Herm Krabbenhoft determined that there were six games during the 1931 slate in which Gehrig's RBI totals were incorrectly recorded, resulting in a net gain of one. If MLB ever acknowledges that research, Gehrig's AL single-season mark will be increased to 185. Considering the two ribbies that Gehrig lost during that windy afternoon in Washington, that number should be even higher.

It's amazing how one little play can cause so many ripples!

July 12, 1931

The Cardinals, defending NL champs, were sitting in first place before this doubleheader at home against the Cubs. Interest in baseball was reaching a fever pitch in St. Louis, and the organization's refusal to turn fans away resulted in the skewing of two offensive records. The Associated Press reported that a crowd of 45,715 was on hand to see the Red Birds take on Chicago—the largest gathering ever to see a game at Sportsman's Park. Roughly eight thousand spectators were allowed to stand on the field, necessitating special ground rules. Balls hit into the encroaching crowd were counted as doubles, and this led to some irregular results.

Each team sent three pitchers to the mound in the first game, which featured twelve runs, twenty-three hits, and nine doubles. The second game was much wilder; nine hurlers allowed a total of thirty runs on thirty-seven hits. Twenty-three of those safeties were doubles, shattering the previous single-game mark of seventeen set by Chicago and Buffalo back in 1883. The thirty-two two-baggers in both games established a new mark for a doubleheader. Ripper Collins of St. Louis had four doubles on the day while nine other players had at least a pair. The unusual twin bill ended in a split as Chicago took the first match, 7–5, and St. Louis prevailed, 17–13, in the second game.

As time marched on, the practice of allowing overflow crowds on the field was gradually abandoned. By then, baseball history had been irrevocably altered on several occasions.

May 30, 1932

Cleveland bats were on fire during a doubleheader at home against the White Sox. The Tribe took the first game handily, 12–6, and then rallied for four runs in the final frame of the second contest to complete a sweep by a narrow 12–11 margin. There were more fireworks after the game when four angry Chicago players confronted umpire George Moriarty.

Disgusted with Moriarty's calls, catcher Charlie Berry challenged the official to a fight under the stands. A gaggle of Sox players was there for backup: catcher Frank Grube, pitcher Milt Gaston, and player/manager Lou Fonseca. Never one to shy away from a challenge, Moriarty told Berry he "would fight them all, one after another." Gaston stepped forward, saying, "You might as well start with me."

Moriarty landed a combination to Gaston's jaw, breaking his hand while reportedly knocking the hurler out cold. The fight was broken up by several White Sox players. One columnist later quipped: "Moriarty must be slipping. I remember when he used to take on whole ball clubs as a warm-up." Defending his actions, Fonseca told reporters that the umpire had "deliberately brought on the dispute by sneering at the Chicago players all afternoon."

Gaston was fined $500 by AL president William Harridge and suspended for ten days. The rest of the Chicago combatants were fined as well.

Additionally, White Sox coach Johnny Butler was suspended five days for his involvement. Moriarty received a stern reprimand but escaped punishment.

July 10, 1932

Connie Mack never forgot the lean years. After piloting the A's to five World Series appearances between 1905 and 1914, his club languished in the AL basement for seven straight seasons. By 1932, the Athletics were the defending junior circuit champs for three years running. Mack remained cost-conscious nevertheless, and on July 10, his frugality led to disaster.

To save train fare for a single-game makeup appearance at Cleveland, Mack sent just two pitchers to the Forest City—twenty-year-old farmhand Lew Krausse and aging knuckleballer Eddie Rommel. He overestimated the abilities of both hurlers as the game turned into one of the most grueling slugfests in history.

When Krausse proved ineffective in the first inning, Rommel was called on to pitch. He turned in a gutsy but horrific performance, staking the Indians to twelve runs in his first eight innings of work. The A's had the guns to back him up, rallying from a 14–13 deficit in the ninth to send the game into extra frames. Rommel and opposing hurler Wes Ferrell settled down for awhile, matching zeroes for six straight innings before the A's emerged with an 18–17 victory in eighteen rounds. Jimmie Foxx was a one-man wrecking crew for Philadelphia with eight RBIs and six hits—three of them homers. Cleveland committed five errors and stranded twenty-four runners, a new AL record.

For Rommel, the win was the last of his career and the ugliest by far. In seventeen innings of work, he yielded twenty-nine hits—another AL record. Years later, Rommel still remembered the game. "I was thirty-four at the time and had worked two previous days," he told a writer. "It never occurred to me that I'd have to go more than a couple of innings if any. It was the end of me as a pitcher." He would not pitch again for more than a month, and when he did, he was unreliable. Mack released him after the season was over. Rommel later became an American League umpire, serving for more than twenty years in that capacity.

October 1, 1932

Babe Ruth's "called shot" is one of the most debated topics in baseball history. Questions still remain as to what happened on the field that day: Did the Babe point to center field and forecast his fifth-inning homer off of

Cubs hurler Charlie Root? And how many shots did he call that day—was it one or possibly two?

By 1932, age was catching up with Ruth. The thirty-seven-year-old slugger was suffering from gimpy knees that required regular attention. He had put up solid offensive numbers during the regular season but conceded the AL homer crown to Jimmie Foxx. He would never lead the league in any major statistical category again (aside from walks in 1933).

The Yankees were still a powerhouse club, with three Hall of Famers on their pitching staff and six other Cooperstown greats in the daily lineup. With Ruth and Gehrig leading the way, they knocked off Connie Mack's powerful A's for the first time in four years, advancing to the World Series against the Cubs.

Former Yankee shortstop Mark Koenig, who played on three pennant-winning squads in New York, was a major contributor to the Cubs' success in 1932, hitting .353 from August through September. Since he had played in only thirty-three games, the Cubs decided to give him a half share of the postseason proceeds. This irritated Ruth, who mouthed off to the press. The Cubs responded with numerous statements unfit to print.

After the Yankees had taken the first two games by a combined score of 17–8, the Series moved to Chicago. Before Ruth's first plate appearance in game 3, he was standing outside the batter's box jawing with Cubs players, who were heckling him relentlessly. Charlie Root was in an early jam with two runners on and nobody out. According to multiple reports, Ruth abruptly stopped shouting and began pointing toward the right-field seats. He deposited a home run there shortly afterward. Could this have been the first of two called shots that day? No one will ever know for certain.

The most iconic moment of Ruth's career occurred during the fifth inning. At that point, the score was knotted at 4 and Root was still on the mound. The crowd had joined in the harassment of the Babe, and one unruly fan threw a lemon at him as he stepped to the plate with the bases empty. The first pitch was a called strike, and the crowd cheered wildly. Ruth held up one finger as if to say, "That's only one." Root fell behind in the count, 2-1, before getting another called strike. There was a cacophony of noise as the Bambino held up two fingers, acknowledging that he still had one strike left. He pointed to the outfield again and, according to Lou Gehrig (who was in the on-deck circle), shouted at Root: "I'm going to knock the next one down your goddamn throat." He followed with a majestic solo homer to center field. The Yankees ended up sweeping the Series.

Only one article written on game day mentioned Ruth pointing to the outfield in the fifth inning. But reporter Joe Williams never actually referred to the homer as a "called shot." The story morphed into an urban legend on its own, and Ruth did nothing to debunk it. When questioned about it on one particular occasion, he responded: "Well, it was in the newspapers." According to some reports, he finally refuted the tale on his deathbed.

An amateur film taken by Matt Miller Kandle surfaced fifty years after the fact, but it didn't help resolve the matter. The grainy black-and-white 16mm footage shows Ruth pointing at something before his fifth-inning blast, but it's impossible to tell precisely what. The film also captures Ruth making a waving gesture in the direction of the Cubs dugout while rounding the bases and twice making a pushing motion between second and third base.

Charlie Root was one of the toughest competitors of the era. Questioned about the incident in later years, he commented brusquely: "If [Ruth] had pointed to the bleachers, I would have put one in his ear and knocked him on his ass." Though Ruth's own daughter came forward in 2009 and discredited the myth of the called shot, there are some who still choose to believe otherwise.

August 17, 1933

Lou Gehrig played in his 1,308th consecutive game on this date, breaking the previous major league endurance record set by Yankee shortstop Everett Scott. In recognition of the accomplishment, "The Iron Horse" received a silver trophy from AL president William Harridge. He would add more than eight hundred games to the streak before he was sidelined in 1939 with amyotrophic lateral sclerosis, a crippling disease that would come to bear his name.

Though the August 17 meeting between the Yankees and Browns at Sportsman's Park would be remembered mainly for Gehrig's feat, it featured another remarkable deed by a future Hall of Famer. Rogers Hornsby was not accustomed to being the underdog. During his twenty-three years in the majors, he hit .358 (second all-time to Ty Cobb) while accruing one of the highest on-base percentages in history at .434. By August 1933, his skills had eroded, and he was serving primarily as a manager. While Gehrig was enjoying his moment in the sun, Hornsby was being treated to an incessant barrage of harassment from the Yankee dugout. The 1933 squad included some of the most notorious goat getters ever to adorn a bench, among them outfielder Ben Chapman and third-base coach Art Fletcher. Hornsby grew tired of the razzing and decided to do something about it.

The Browns were trailing by a score of 6–5 in the ninth when "Rajah" inserted himself as pinch hitter for pitcher George Blaeholder. He blasted a game-tying homer off of staff ace Lefty Gomez, at least temporarily quieting the Yankee bench jockeys. Herb Pennock and Wilcy Moore couldn't hold the lead for New York in the tenth as the Browns walked away with a 7–6 win.

June 30, 1934

Gee Walker played fifteen years in the majors, becoming tremendously popular with fans in Detroit. He hit at the .300 level for five straight seasons, reaching a high of .353 in 1936. Before then, he helped the Tigers to two straight World Series appearances. A line-drive hitter, Walker was known for his remarkable speed on the bases. But his impulsiveness landed him in hot water with manager Mickey Cochrane during the 1934 slate.

Not only was Walker thrown out while trying to steal during an intentional walk one day, but he was picked off base twice in the same inning on June 30. After Hank Greenberg had singled against Browns hurler Jack Knott, Walker reached base on an error. Edging too far off the bag, he got hung up when catcher Rollie Hemsley made a snap throw to first. Greenberg did his best to disrupt the play by taking off for third but ended up being thrown out. Walker moved to second. Moments later, the impetuous outfielder provoked the ire of Cochrane by meandering dangerously off base again. He froze when Knott executed a timely pickoff throw to shortstop Alan Strange, who applied the tag. The play made a difference in the game as the Tigers lost, 4–3. Cochrane reportedly fined Walker twenty dollars and suspended him for ten days.

White Sox shortstop Luke Appling remembered Walker's exploits that season vividly, sharing the following incident with a *Chicago Daily News* reporter: "We were in Detroit one day. It seemed that Mickey Cochrane had just informed the erratic base running Walker that the next time he got caught it would cost him $50. Halfway through the game, Gee was footloose again. There was a peg to second base and Walker knew he was a goner. 'Drop it!' he yelled at the Sox infielder. 'Drop it and I'll give you twenty five bucks!'"

Despite hitting at an even .300 clip in 1934, Walker was limited to just ninety-eight games during the regular season. When the Tigers claimed the AL pennant and moved on to the World Series against the Cardinals, Cochrane used the reckless fly chaser exclusively as a pinch hitter. Even in a diminished role, Walker managed to get himself into trouble. After delivering a game-tying single in the ninth inning of game 2, he was picked off by pitcher Bill Walker (no relation) while engaged in a shouting match with St. Louis bench jockeys. He would make just one more appearance in the remaining five games.

October 9, 1934

Leo Durocher, not exactly a nice guy himself, once remarked that Joe Medwick was one of the "meanest, roughest" players he had ever known.

Over the course of his seventeen-year major league tour, Medwick did little to disprove that statement, sparring with opponents, teammates, and anyone who got in his way. One of the most infamous incidents of his career occurred during game 7 of the 1934 World Series.

The Cardinals were leading the Tigers by a score of 7–0 in the sixth inning when Pepper Martin led off with a single. Detroit's Goose Goslin misplayed the ball, and Martin ended up on second. After two fly-ball outs, Medwick hit a long shot to the right-field wall. Martin scored easily, and Medwick, running hard despite his team's comfortable lead, opted to leg out a triple. At third, Marv Owen stepped on Medwick's leg (whether intentionally or not has never been conclusively determined). This infuriated Medwick, who retaliated by kicking Owen in the stomach with both of his spikes. The two scrapped briefly and were separated by umpires. Medwick later scored on a Ripper Collins single, and the Cardinals carried a 9–0 lead into the bottom of the frame.

When Medwick assumed his defensive station in left field, Detroit fans jeered at him and tossed garbage, mostly fruit, onto the field. (He later ruminated over why fans had brought fruit to the stadium in the first place.) Inciting the crowd, Medwick and his teammates began playing catch with some of the fruit. This invited a fresh rain of debris. Umpires halted play three times and called for order, but the fans would not stop. The game was delayed for nearly twenty minutes.

Finally, after a conference with Commissioner Kenesaw Mountain Landis, Medwick was removed from the game. He required a police escort off the field. An Associated Press correspondent commented that Medwick's expulsion completed "the wild picture of the psychopathic series." With Medwick out of action, the Cardinals tacked on two more runs to claim the world championship. Landis later stood by his decision, commenting, "I saw what Medwick did and I couldn't blame the crowd for what it did."

May 25, 1935

By the end of the 1934 slate, Yankees owner Jacob Ruppert was facing a dilemma. Babe Ruth was no longer the offensive juggernaut of his early days, but his tremendous popularity entitled him to a large salary. Ruppert didn't want to pay it, so he accepted an offer from Braves owner Judge Emil Fuchs. Ruth's return to Boston delighted fans, but after transforming the Braves' spring training camp into a three-ring circus, Ruth proceeded to play poorly in April. He had caught a cold and could not shake it. By May 5, he had failed to hit safely in six straight appearances. He was batting just .222 with a measly two homers and four RBIs.

With the defending champion Cardinals in town, thirty thousand fans turned out at Braves Field. Most of them were there to see the much-hyped showdown between Ruth and Dizzy Dean, who was scheduled to start that day. Dean pitched around Ruth in his first plate appearance, but after St. Louis had broken through for six runs in the second inning, the cocky hurler decided to have a little fun. With the count at 1-2 in Ruth's second at bat, Diz grinned mischievously and waved his fielders back toward the outfield fence. He then grooved a fastball straight down the heart of the plate. Ruth, forty years old and out of shape, swung right through it. He was replaced by outfielder Joe Mowry after grounding out in his next trip to the dish. The Cardinals won handily, 7–0.

Ruth had one last extraordinary performance left in him, and it came three weeks later, on May 25. With the Braves mired in last place, they traveled to Forbes Field to take on the Pirates. In his greatest offensive showing of the season, Ruth went deep three times and drove in six runs. The first homer came off of right-hander Red Lucas on the first pitch. It ended up in the right-field stands. Ruth's former teammate Waite Hoyt had warned Lucas that the Babe was still a dangerous hitter. "Should have pitched behind him," Hoyt muttered to teammates as Ruth circled the bases.

Lucas never made it out of the first inning, and Guy Bush was called on to clean up the mess. Nicknamed "The Mississippi Mudcat," Bush prided himself on the fact that he could warm up very quickly. He knew about Ruth's prolific power, having witnessed the "called shot" incident in the 1932 Series from the Chicago bench. He bragged to teammates that he had effectively handled Ruth with sinkers. When Bush threw Ruth a sinker in the third inning, the Babe crushed it for a two-run homer. From that point on, it was nothing but fastballs.

In the seventh inning, Bush blew a heater by Ruth then made a mistake on the second pitch, getting too much of the plate. Ruth launched it over the right-field grandstand. By some estimates, the ball traveled close to six hundred feet. The hurler tipped his cap at Ruth as he hobbled around the bases. "I never saw a ball hit so hard before or since," Bush commented years later. The homer was number 714, the last of Ruth's career. Despite his heroics, the Braves lost, 11–7. A contract dispute would prompt Ruth to quit the team on June 2. In twenty-eight games with Boston, he had hit a paltry .181 with six homers and twelve RBIs.

July 31, 1935

Major league game attendance was dramatically affected by the Great Depression. During the 1930s, nearly ten million fewer fans passed through major league turnstiles than in the previous decade. Perhaps wary of this statistic, Reds owner Powel Crosley and general manager Larry MacPhail allowed an overflow crowd to gather in Cincinnati on the date in question. Fans were lined up several rows deep in foul territory and, according to Reds left fielder Babe Herman, "You couldn't see the game from the dugout." In the bottom of the eighth inning, those with unobstructed views witnessed a historic (well, sort of) event.

A burlesque dancer named Kitty Burke had been heckling players throughout the game, and when Cardinals outfielder Joe Medwick yelled back at her, she decided to show him up. Clad in a provocative red dress, Burke slipped through the crowd of thirty thousand and approached Herman in the on-deck circle. The good-natured slugger kindly lent her his bat for the occasion. As she strode to the plate, umpire Bill Stewart allowed the intrusion, shouting, "Play ball!"

St. Louis hurler Paul "Daffy" Dean (Dizzy's brother) was on the mound. As a rookie the previous year, he had helped the Cardinals to a world championship with nineteen wins in the regular season and two more in the World Series. He had entered this game with a record of 11–8. Dean was ambivalent about pitching to Burke until she called him a "hick" and told him to go back to the farm and milk some cows. Amused by the insult, he lobbed a soft toss to the plate, which she grounded back to the mound. Dean fielded it and waited for Burke at first base, but she ducked back into the crowd. "If he wanted me, he'd have to chase me," she later commented. Interviewed after the game, Herman quipped: "That's the first time a broad ever pinch-hit for me."

Cardinals manager Frankie Frisch tried to exploit the incident, arguing that Burke's groundout should count as the third out of the inning. Stewart refuted his logic, reminding him that Burke was not on the Cincinnati roster. When play resumed, Babe Herman sparked a two-run Reds rally with a double. Cincinnati won in extra innings, 4–3. According to numerous sources, Burke was later given a Reds uniform, which she incorporated into her act. She toured the burlesque circuit, touting herself as the first woman to bat in a major league game. Her claim is technically true, though the statistic is not recognized by any official sources.

September 7, 1935

In the first game of a doubleheader between the Indians and Red Sox at Fenway Park, Cleveland's ham-fisted third baseman, Odell Hale, would be credited for using his head—literally. There was nothing much at stake that afternoon with the Indians in third place, the Red Sox in fifth, and the Tigers running away with the AL pennant. But fans in attendance witnessed something remarkable in the bottom of the ninth inning.

Trailing 5–3, the Sox appeared to have a rally going with the bases loaded and nobody out. The dangerous Joe Cronin was at the plate, facing reliever Oral Hildebrand. Boston's hard-hitting player/manager hammered the first pitch to Hale at third. Hale was a capable batsman who had been shifted around the infield due to his questionable defensive abilities. The Indians decided he might do less damage at the hot corner and installed him there in 1935. Hale's reaction time was a bit slow, and Cronin's liner hit him squarely in the forehead. The ball took a fortuitous carom straight into the glove of shortstop Bill Knickerbocker. Knickerbocker alertly relayed to teammate Roy Hughes at second, catching Boston's Bill Werber off the bag. Hughes then threw to Hal Trosky at first, nailing a surprised Mel Almada for a game-ending triple play.

Hale would lead the AL third basemen in errors during the 1935 slate with thirty-one. He would finish second to Buddy Lewis of Washington the next year with twenty-eight. Of the forty-nine triple plays turned during the 1930s, the one Hale participated in at Fenway was undoubtedly among the most unusual.

Hale's substandard fielding would lead to interesting results again on August 6, 1937. The Indians were leading the Yankees by a score of 6–5 in the tenth inning at New York. Bob Feller had departed after giving up a leadoff single to Myril Hoag. Indians reliever Joe Heving was in a two-out jam, with Hoag at third and Jack Saltzgaver at second. Joe DiMaggio smashed a hard liner that deflected off of Hale's stone glove at third and bounced into foul territory. Left fielder Moose Solters failed to react since the ball had been ruled foul by plate umpire Charlie Johnston. Both runners came around to score anyway. The Yankees argued the call, and after a conference with third-base arbiter George Moriarty, Johnston's foul decision was reversed. The Indians lodged a formal protest, and it was upheld by president William Harridge. The game was declared a no-decision game.

September 25, 1936

With only three games left and the team mired in sixth place, the Red Sox were playing out the string at Griffith Stadium. Rookie Jim Henry was on the mound for Boston. Though he compiled a 5–1 record in twenty-one appearances that year, his suspect ERA (4.60) and lack of composure would doom him to a career in the minors. The Senators had runners at the corners with nobody out in the bottom of the third inning. Obviously rattled, Henry walked behind the mound and picked up the rosin bag. He should have paid attention to the runners as they executed a double steal. The flustered moundsman didn't know which way to turn when Joe Kuhel took off from third and John Stone broke for second. In one of the strangest sequences in major league history, Henry spun and threw the rosin bag to second base instead of the ball. Both runners were safe.

Showing no mercy, Stone then swiped third as Henry went into his windup on the next pitch. Boston skipper Joe Cronin had seen enough at that point and pulled Henry from the game. The embattled hurler was charged with four runs in the frame. Washington tacked on five more off of reliever Jack Wilson, beating the Sox, 9–3. Henry wouldn't have much chance to redeem himself, appearing in just three games the following season before being released. He would get one more call-up from the A's in 1939, accruing a 5.09 ERA in twenty-three innings of work.

June 15, 1938

On June 11 of the 1938 campaign, Reds hurler Johnny Vander Meer no-hit the Boston Bees. It was a feat that had been accomplished more than sixty times since 1901. Though the performance earned the slender southpaw a few headlines, most fans outside of Cincinnati wouldn't even have recognized Vander Meer on the streets.

Vander Meer had spent a large portion of his rookie season (1937) in the minors working on control issues. He averaged seven walks per nine frames in his debut but returned to claim a regular spot in the Reds rotation in 1938. The no-hitter was his fifth straight win of the season against two losses. Though most reasonably informed baseball fans know what happened in the hurler's next start, many don't realize how close it came to not happening.

On June 15, Vander Meer took the hill against the Dodgers in the first night game in the metropolitan New York area. Few fans were thinking seriously about the possibility of a second no-hitter, least of all Vander Meer himself. The erratic southpaw had two knockout pitches in his arsenal—a lively, tailing fastball and a sharp-breaking curve. When he could control them, he was tough to beat. More than forty thousand fans piled into Ebbets Field, a majority of them lured by the prospect of watching a game under the lights. Roughly five hundred people from Johnny's New Jersey neighborhood made the jaunt to Brooklyn that evening.

Vander Meer was not as sharp in this game, running the count full on many Dodger batters. In the seventh, he issued free passes to Cookie Lavagetto and Dolph Camilli but worked his way out of the jam. By the ninth, he was running out of gas. After Buddy Hassett grounded out to open the frame, the fading left-hander completely lost the plate, walking the bases loaded. Manager Bill McKechnie came out to settle him down as Leo Durocher, recently acquired by Brooklyn in a trade, strolled toward the batter's box.

With the count even at 1-1, Durocher slammed a hard foul into the right-field upper deck. The tension in the park was palpable as the next pitch caught the outside corner for a strike. That's what Vander Meer and catcher Ernie Lombardi believed anyway. But home-plate umpire Bill Stewart, who was apparently having trouble seeing around the big backstop, ruled it a ball. (He later admitted that he blew the call.) Having caught a break, Durocher lofted the 2-2 offering to center field, where Harry Craft put it away for the final out of the game. Despite issuing eight walks, Vander Meer had achieved the impossible, spinning his second consecutive no-hitter—a feat that has not been duplicated since.

President Franklin D. Roosevelt sent congratulations. Newspapers and magazines sang his praises for weeks afterward. In his next start against Boston on June 20, he pitched three more hitless frames. Bees manager Casey Stengel reportedly passed Vander Meer on his way to the coaching box and said: "John, we're not trying to beat you. We're just trying to get a base hit." The comment did the trick as Vander Meer coughed up a single to Debs Garms, ending a skein of 21.2 hitless innings. It came as a relief to the southpaw. "I could have kissed him," Vander Meer said. "The tension was eating me up."

July 6, 1938

The All-Star Game was held at Crosley Field in Cincinnati. It was baseball's sixth Midsummer Classic. The Junior Circuit held a decisive edge, having won four of five showdowns. In all, twenty-two eventual Hall of Famers were listed on the rosters, fourteen of whom saw action that day.

Despite the cavalcade of all-time greats, the game was somewhat sloppy as the American League practically gave the game away. Slick-fielding Red Sox shortstop Joe Cronin allowed a roller by Billy Herman to pass through his legs in the first inning. Stan Hack, who had opened with a single, moved to third and later scored on a sacrifice fly by Cardinals slugger Joe Medwick. Several innings later, one of the most astonishing series of miscues in All-Star history took place.

Lefty Grove, thirty-eight years old and nearing the end of his career, was summoned to pitch the seventh inning. Jimmie Foxx had been shifted to third base to make room for Lou Gehrig at first. Frank McCormick, one of four Cincinnati players who saw action that day, led off with a single. Leo Durocher came to the plate with instructions to lay down a sacrifice. He ended up with much more, recording the only "bunt homer" in All-Star play.

The light-hitting Durocher pushed a sacrifice down the third baseline. Gehrig was playing shallow, and second baseman Charlie Gehringer apparently fell asleep on the play, failing to cover first. Foxx fielded the ball and made a serviceable throw to the uncovered bag. It sailed into right field. Not the fleetest of runners, McCormick chugged home as Joe DiMaggio chased down the wayward toss. Durocher was approaching third as "Joltin' Joe," playing in his third major league season, unleashed another errant throw far beyond the reach of Bill Dickey at home. As legend has it, the ball ended up in the National League dugout, where coach Casey Stengel dropped it in a bucket of water and said: "That's too hot to handle." Durocher scored and the National League prevailed, 4–1.

United Press scribe George Kirksey commented dramatically, "The National League emerged from the shadows of defeat and subjugation and, at least until World Series time, does not have to take the taunts of the American League concerning its superiority." The triumph would be short-lived as the American Leaguers won four of the next five All-Star Games.

April 6, 1939

The weather refused to cooperate in Florence, South Carolina, where the Cincinnati Reds and Boston Red Sox met in a spring-training game. Gale-force winds in excess of forty miles per hour blew out of control for more than forty minutes, rendering conditions nearly unplayable. The United Press reported that the wind kicked up swirling clouds of dust and "made pitchers ineffective to say the least." Boston hurlers Denny Galehouse, Jim Bagby, Emerson Dickman, and Bill Kerksieck surrendered eighteen runs between them. Jim Weaver, Wes Livengood, and Red Barrett yielded the same number of tallies for Cincinnati.

The infield had recently been laid out, and there was not a blade of grass to be found on it. Helped by the inhospitable weather conditions and an extremely hard diamond surface, the Red Sox plated seven runs in the third inning and seven more in the fourth. Cincinnati scored fifteen times in the first five frames. According to a game account in the *Cincinnati Enquirer*, grounders were literally blown into the air and over the outfield fence. The contest was called in the top of the ninth inning after the entire supply of balls was exhausted. At least four dozen ended up in the stands. According to Charlton's *Baseball Chronology*, a total of fifty-four balls were kept as souvenirs on that windy afternoon.

September 3, 1939

The Red Sox continued their dominance of the Yankees, winning the first game of a doubleheader at Fenway Park, 12–11. It was their seventh straight victory over the defending world champs. In more bad news for the Bombers,

Joe DiMaggio left the game early with a presumed injury to his right knee. It was a false alarm. DiMaggio would return for the nightcap, helping the Yanks end their skid against the BoSox with a 3-for-4 performance at the plate.

When the New Yorkers came to bat in the eighth, there were just fifteen minutes to go before the 6:30 Sunday curfew (a remnant of the oppressive "blue law" era). Joe McCarthy's men pushed two quick runs across and then began deliberately sacrificing themselves to speed things up. One Yankee runner stood directly in front of Boston catcher Johnny Peacock in a flagrant effort to be put out. Peacock refused to apply the tag, and plate umpire Cal Hubbard called the runner out anyway. This incited many in the crowd of twenty-seven thousand to begin rioting.

Disgruntled fans threw soda bottles, hats, cushions, and newspapers. There was no time to clear the field, so Hubbard declared the game a tie. Having avoided their eighth consecutive defeat at the hands of the Bostonians, the Yankees won four of the next five meetings, finishing the season with an 8–11 overall record against the Hub Men. They would move on to an efficient World Series sweep of the Reds that season.

October 8, 1939

Reds catcher Ernie Lombardi was one of the biggest targets in the majors. Listed at six feet three inches and 230 pounds, some say he weighed closer to 300 near the end of his career. He was nicknamed "Schnozz" on account of his enormous nose, which actually protruded beyond the wires of his protective mask, taking the brunt of foul tips from time to time. Named NL MVP in 1938, Lombardi was one of the greatest offensive backstops in history, winning two batting titles and hitting .306 over seventeen seasons. During the 1939 Fall Classic, his name would be unfairly dragged through the mud.

Most experts agree that the 1939 World Series was a mismatch. The Yankees had scored more runs, hit more homers, and posted a higher cumulative batting average during the regular season. They also had the arms to match Cincinnati's one-two punch of Paul Derringer and Bucky Walters, who had claimed fifty-two victories between them. Manager Bill McKechnie admitted after the Reds dropped the Series in four games, "They were too good for us." Someone had to take the fall for the loss, and Lombardi became the scapegoat.

There was very little drama in the first three games as the Bombers outscored the Reds by a collective 13–4 margin. Looking to stay alive, McKechnie's troops fought valiantly in game 4 at Crosley Field. The Yanks jumped out to a 2–0 lead in the top of the seventh on solo homers by Bill Dickey and Charlie Keller. Refusing to lie down, the Reds came storming back with three runs in the bottom of the frame. Outfielder Ival Goodman doubled off of reliever Johnny Murphy in the eighth, and Lombardi drove him home to put the Reds up, 4–2. With the dependable Bucky Walters on the mound, the game appeared to be in the bag. But the Yankees would not go away as Keller, DiMaggio, and Joe Gordon all singled in the ninth to even the score at four apiece.

Columnist Joe Williams commented after the Series that "the light regard in which the Yankees held the Reds was demonstrated several times. They took chances against the Reds they wouldn't take against most clubs in their own league." The tenth inning of game 4 was no exception. With Walters still on the mound, Frank Crosetti drew a leadoff walk. Red Rolfe sacrificed him to second. Charlie Keller followed with a grounder to shortstop Billy Myers, who botched the play. With runners on the corners, Joe DiMaggio lofted a single to right field. Crosetti galloped home as Ival Goodman mishandled the ball, prompting Yankee third-base coach Art Fletcher to give Keller the green light. The throw home was late, and there was contact between Keller and Lombardi.

Accounts of the play vary widely. Some say that Lombardi took a knee to the head. Others attest that it was a blow to the groin. Keller himself reported that he ran right by Lombardi without touching him, but films of the play suggest there was impact. The big backstop explained afterward that it was a sweltering day in Cincinnati and he was "feeling dizzy." The force of the collision spun him around, and he lay motionless at the plate with the ball resting nearby. As DiMaggio brazenly circled the bases, Lombardi eventually recovered. The play at the plate was close, but "Joltin' Joe" eluded Lombardi's tag with a hook slide. The Reds failed to score in the bottom half of the tenth as the Yankees clinched the Series.

Though DiMaggio's run was inconsequential to the game's outcome, journalists painted Lombardi in an unfavorable light. To this day, the play is still identified as Lombardi's "Snooze," "Swan Dive," "Swoon," or "Sit-Down Strike." Bucky Walters later admitted that only one run would have scored had he been properly backing up the play. One has to wonder where he was while Lombardi was cementing an undeserved reputation as a goat.

The Summer of 1940

The 1940 National League pennant race would be marred by the so-called beanball wars. The Dodgers remained in the thick of things until July 7, when a doubleheader loss at Boston dropped them into second place for good. By the end of the month, they had fallen eight games behind the defending NL champion Reds. Ultimately finishing twelve games out, the Dodgers would not go quietly. In fact, some would say that they went down kicking and screaming.

Brooklyn had a tough-as-nails pitching staff that year, anchored by right-handers Hugh Casey and Whit Wyatt, neither of whom were shy about throwing at hitters. Casey had led the league in beanings the year before with eleven. Wyatt would post the highest totals of his career in that department during the early 1940s. In all, the Dodgers ended up plunking thirty-one batters in 1940—third highest in the majors behind the Pirates and Bees, who at least could blame their high totals on ineffective pitching staffs. As the Dodgers began to fall further out of the race, the ugliness escalated.

The tone had been set early on, when Brooklyn's rookie shortstop, Pee Wee Reese, was beaned by Jake Mooty in a twelve-inning loss to the Cubs on June 1. Seriously injured, Reese was hospitalized for eighteen days and remained out of action for three weeks. Another unsavory incident occurred two weeks later at Ebbets Field. After spending portions of nine seasons in St. Louis, slugger Joe Medwick was traded to the Dodgers on June 12. When the Cardinals came to town on June 17, Medwick got into an argument with former teammate Bob Bowman in a hotel elevator. Bowman vowed that he would get back at Medwick and player/manager Leo Durocher (who was also involved in the spat) when the teams met the next day. Making good on the threat, Bowman hit Medwick in the head with a pitch, sending him to the hospital. Questioned by league officials, Bowman insisted the pitch had sailed on him and that his threat had not been literal.

In addition to the injuries incurred by Reese and Medwick, Giants shortstop Billy Jurges was plunked by Reds hurler Bucky Walters on June 23. He was carted off the field on a stretcher and would be sidelined until July 13. In response to the rash of beanings, Spalding offered a specially designed helmet with ear flaps. It generated very little interest.

As the season progressed, the Dodgers became less the victims and more the aggressors. In a game at Wrigley Field on July 19, Hugh Casey hit Cubs pitcher Claude Passeau in the back with a pitch. Passeau threw his bat at Casey, and the benches emptied. Passeau ended up being ejected and fined after mixing it up with Dodger outfielder Joe Gallagher (reportedly getting the worst of it). Interestingly, Casey was making his first appearance since getting beaned by a Class D hurler in an exhibition game at Johnstown, Pennsylvania, on July 10.

It was the Reds' turn to feel the wrath of the Dodgers at Ebbets Field on July 23. When Cincinnati's Lonnie Frey went into second base with spikes high to break up a double play, Brooklyn infielder Pete Coscarart started swinging. A free-for-all ensued, with Whit Wyatt landing a few blows on Frey with his glove. Apparently, Wyatt was nursing a grudge from the previous season, when he had injured his knee in a collision with Frey. Reds pitcher

Gene Thompson was badly spiked and had to leave the game. Cincy's third sacker, Bill Werber, ended up with a black eye. The Dodgers took a pounding in the standings as the Reds completed a doubleheader sweep, increasing their NL lead to seven games.

The grand finale took place on September 16 at Brooklyn. The Dodgers carried a 3–2 lead over the Reds into the ninth but couldn't hold it. With one out in the top of the tenth, Mike McCormick doubled, and Ival Goodman walked. Frank McCormick hit a double-play ball to short, but Brooklyn's Pete Coscarart dropped Johnny Hudson's relay as he was pivoting to first. Umpire Bill Stewart called Goodman out at second but appealed to crewmate George Magerkurth when Reds skipper Bill McKechnie argued the call. Magerkurth overturned Stewart's ruling, and Dodger pilot Leo Durocher went ballistic, getting tossed from the game. When play resumed, Cincy catcher Bill Baker hit a liner to left, scoring what would hold up as the winning run.

After the Dodgers failed to score in their half of the frame, hundreds in the crowd of 6,782 stormed onto the field. Magerkurth was assaulted by a twenty-year-old fan named Frank Germano, who was out on parole from the New York State Vocational Institution at West Coxsackie. Germano knocked the much larger man to the ground and began pummeling him with both fists. A famous photo captured the moment. Bill Stewart rushed to Magerkurth's aid but ended up being kicked in the head by another unruly fan. Durocher would later be suspended and fined for "inciting a riot." A 5–0 loss to the Cardinals on September 17 effectively ended the Dodgers' pennant hopes. When the 1941 season began, Brooklyn players were ordered to wear protective cap liners by GM Larry MacPhail.

October 5, 1941

A correspondent from the *Pittsburgh Post Gazette* aptly commented that "Brooklyn can beef loud and long against the cruelty of the baseball imps who today reached a new low in torturing a club on the brink of a World Series victory." The setting was Ebbets Field in Brooklyn. The Yankees held a 2–1 Series edge over the Dodgers. Brooklyn was clinging stubbornly to a 4–3 lead in the top of the ninth and appeared to have game 4 wrapped up with two outs and two strikes on Yankee right fielder Tommy Henrich. Flatbush closer Hugh Casey threw a low curve that Henrich feebly waved at.

Game over.

Or was it?

As soon as Henrich swung, police began to rush onto the field. They hadn't seen the ball pass under the glove of catcher Mickey Owen and bounce toward the backstop. Even Henrich thought he was out. He had to be prompted to run to first by coach Earle Combs. Plate umpire Larry Goetz waved the officers away as Owen scrambled after the ball. The pitch was out of the strike zone, and if Henrich had only held his swing, he would have drawn a walk.

The rest of the inning was a nightmare for Casey. DiMaggio singled to left field, sending Henrich to second. Charlie Keller blasted a double, scoring both runners. Bill Dickey walked. Joe Gordon then doubled, pushing two more runs across. Casey, who had completely unraveled at that point, issued another free pass to Phil Rizzuto before retiring Johnny Murphy on a ground-out. The Dodgers went down in order in the bottom of the ninth.

Interviewed after the game, Henrich felt some sympathy for Owen. "That was a tough break for Mickey to get," he said. "I bet he feels like a nickel's worth of dog food." Henrich's words were on the mark. According to an Associated Press reporter, Owen was on the verge of tears in the Dodgers' dressing room. He assumed full responsibility for the heartbreaking loss, stating that he was late getting his glove down. Hugh Casey commented, "I guess I've lost 'em just about every way now."

The momentum shifted in favor of the Yanks, who wrapped up the series the following day. Ironically, Owen had set a major league record for most consecutive chances by a catcher without an error during the 1941 slate.

May 31, 1942

A strange play unfolded at Ebbets Field in the first game of a double-header between the Braves and Dodgers. With five runs already in, Brooklyn was threatening again in the fourth. Boston's Johnny Sain was in a serious jam with Pee Wee Reese on third, Arky Vaughan on second, and Pete Reiser on first. Cleanup man Dixie Walker hammered one of Sain's offerings down the right-field line. Aging superstar Paul Waner, who had been released by the Dodgers the previous year, gave chase but couldn't locate the ball. No longer nimble at thirty-nine years of age, Waner took forever to find the ball under the bullpen bench. By the time he did, everyone had crossed the plate. The four runs were not charged to Sain, though Walker was credited with a grand slam. Brooklyn won easily, 10–2, and then swept the doubleheader with a 3–1 win in the nightcap.

A similar play occurred on June 19 at Comiskey Park in Chicago. Eddie Smith became the tough-luck loser when his shutout bid ended in the eighth inning on a "freak homer" by Red Sox center fielder Dom DiMaggio. DiMaggio deposited a pitch into the Red Sox bullpen, and the ball nestled under the bench. This time, the flustered outfielder was Wally Moses. Moses couldn't get his hands on the ball in time, and the speedy DiMaggio circled the bases.

The official scorer counted the run as earned. It was the only run of the game. Smith's record dropped to 1–11 on the year despite a serviceable 3.57 ERA. He would lead the league in losses with twenty that season as the hapless White Sox finished sixteen games under .500.

July 10, 1943

Brooklyn's Ebbets Field was the site of yet another odd occurrence. This time, the events prior to the game were just as anomalous as the ones on the field. Manager Leo Durocher had recently issued a three-day suspension to the outspoken hurler Bobo Newsom for insubordination. Arky Vaughan, who despised Durocher, organized a mass boycott, turning in his uniform minutes before game time. Durocher appealed to the dissenting players, but only Curt Davis and Bobby Bragan offered their services. GM Branch Rickey stepped in, convincing players to suit up and take the field.

It was "Kitchen Fat Day" in Brooklyn, with free tickets being handed out to each woman who brought a pound of fat to the game. The fat was used to make explosives, and more than five thousand pounds were reportedly collected for the war effort that day. Despite the pregame rebellion, the Dodgers trounced the Pirates, 23–6. Second baseman Billy Herman led the charge with three hits and seven RBIs. Vaughan was not in the lineup that day and would never patch up his differences with Durocher. He quit the team after the 1943 slate and waited until "Leo the Lip" had left to stage a comeback. He missed three full seasons.

June 10, 1944

There wasn't much for Reds fans to get excited about at Crosley Field as the Cardinals throttled Cincinnati, 18–0. But the ninth inning held at least one item of interest as Reds manager Bill McKechnie sent a fifteen-year-old kid named Joe Nuxhall out to the mound. Nuxhall, a left-hander, had been discovered while the Reds were scouting his father, Orville. Desperate to fill the roster deficits created by the US involvement in World War II, the younger Nuxhall had been offered a contract at $175 per month.

The jittery high-schooler retired two batters but came unglued after seeing Stan Musial in the batting circle. "Probably two weeks prior to that, I was pitching against seventh, eighth, ninth graders, kids thirteen and fourteen years old," he reminisced years later. "All of a sudden I look up and there's Stan Musial." He issued five walks and two hits before being relieved by Jake Eisenhart, who never appeared in another major league game.

Nuxhall kicked around the Cincinnati farm system until 1952, when he became a full-fledged member of the Reds staff at twenty-three years of age. He remained at the big league level for fifteen full seasons, winning 135 games. Nuxhall is widely credited as the youngest player ever to appear in a major league game, though Billy Geer's name has sometimes been thrown into the mix. Various sources have alleged that Geer was slightly under fifteen years of age when he played in two games for the New York Mutuals in 1874.

June 19, 1945

White Sox manager Jimmy Dykes once remarked that "a silent ball club is a dead ball club." Standing by those words, he hired a young man named Karl Scheel to serve as a batting practice instructor. Scheel's real job (at Dykes's behest) was to harass opposing players from the bench. The twenty-four-year-old former marine had a high, strident voice and was so effective at his job that he inspired members of the St. Louis Browns to administer a severe beating on the date in question.

The Browns were trailing 5–4 in the late innings of a losing cause when Scheel's incessant needling prompted reliever George Caster to angrily fire a ball into the ChiSox dugout. Dykes came out to argue and, when catcher Frank Mancuso began griping about Scheel, Dykes dared St. Louis players to do something about it. Two of them did. Tough guys Sig Jakucki and Ellis Clary marched into the Chicago dugout and pounded Scheel senseless. A full-scale brawl erupted. Scraped and battered in the aftermath, Scheel required first aid.

Dykes later commented that the beating Scheel received was one of the "most brutal" he had ever witnessed. He sent a telegram to AL president William Harridge accusing Browns manager Luke Sewell of instigating the donnybrook. Scheel told a United Press reporter, "I just razz the players to keep the game going. I never use profanity, nor do I get personal."

Part 4

THE GOLDEN YEARS, 1946-1959

Timeline of Significant Events

1946   On August 9, all scheduled major league games take place at night for the first time in history.

1947   Jackie Robinson and Larry Doby break the color barrier in their respective leagues.

1948   Satchel Paige becomes the oldest rookie to debut in the majors. The Negro National League folds. Thousands view the body of Babe Ruth as it lies in state at Yankee Stadium.

1949   Vern Stephens of the Red Sox collects 159 RBIs—a record for shortstops.

1950   Jim Konstanty of the Phillies becomes the first reliever to receive an MVP award. Connie Mack retires after fifty years as the Athletics' manager.

1951   Yankee moundsman Allie Reynolds tosses two no-hitters: one in July and one in September.

1952   Virgil Trucks pitches two no-hitters for a miserable Tiger club. He posts a 5–19 record overall. Ralph Kiner wins his seventh consecutive NL homer crown.

1953   Roy Campanella sets a major league homer record for catchers with forty. Bobo Holloman of the Browns becomes the only twentieth-century hurler to toss a no-hitter in his big league debut. The Yankees set an all-time mark with their fifth consecutive World Series victory.

1954   Joe DiMaggio and Marilyn Monroe are married. The couple will split nine months later. The Browns move to Baltimore—the first franchise shift in decades.

1955   The A's move to Kansas City. Cleveland's Herb Score sets a rookie record for strikeouts with 245. Honus Wagner dies.

1956   The first Cy Young Award goes to Don Newcombe of the Dodgers. Dale Long of the Pirates hits homers in a record eight consecutive games. Don Larsen throws the only perfect game in World Series history.

1957   The Giants and Dodgers play their last games in New York. The first annual Gold Glove Awards are distributed. Recipients include Willie Mays, Al Kaline, and Nellie Fox.

1958   Roy Campanella is forced to retire after an auto accident leaves him paralyzed.

1959   The Red Sox become the last team to break the color barrier, pro-
          moting infielder Pumpsie Green. Sandy Koufax is the first NL
          pitcher to record eighteen strikeouts in a game. Pirate hurler
          Harvey Haddix pitches twelve perfect innings in a game he loses
          to the Braves.

July 9, 1946

Rip Sewell overcame a career-threatening injury to become one of the
most successful hurlers of the World War II era. After leading the Pittsburgh
staff with sixteen wins in 1940, he lost part of his foot in a hunting mishap
during the off-season. He had less momentum when pushing off the rubber
and was forced to alter his mechanics. In an effort to prolong his career, he
developed the mother of all junk pitches.

Teammate Maurice Van Robays nicknamed Sewell's novelty offering the
"eephus," which some say is derived from a Hebrew word meaning "nothing." The pitch was little more than a soft toss with backspin that sailed in an
extremely high arc (twenty-five feet according to some estimates) to the plate.
Accounts vary as to exactly when Sewell unleashed his first eephus in regular
season play, but it turned his career around as he fashioned consecutive twen-
ty-win seasons in 1943 and 1944.

In addition to being highly effective for a short while, the "eephus"
was comical to watch. One can only imagine the reaction from batters accustomed to seeing fastballs in the ninety-mile-per-hour range when faced
with Sewell's blooper. On one particular occasion, outfielder Dick Wakefield
allegedly swung twice at it before nearly falling on his face. No one had ever
hit it out of the park until Ted Williams came along.

Sewell was named to his fourth consecutive All-Star team in 1946. Williams, who had never faced an "eephus" before, approached the good-natured
right-hander before the game and asked: "You're not going to throw me that
pitch, are you?" (The Boston outfielder, never known for his charming demeanor, may actually have used an expletive somewhere in that sentence.)
Sewell assured him that if the situation arose, he would.

The slender right-hander kept his promise when Williams came to bat
in the eighth inning with two runners on. Normally, Sewell would not have
used the "eephus" with the bases occupied (since runners could easily steal),
but the fans were on their feet clamoring for it. Williams fouled off the first
"eephus" and then took a fastball for a called strike. The next offering was
another blooper. Williams took two steps toward it before depositing it deep
into the right-field bullpen for a three-run homer. As the Red Sox slugger
laughed all the way around the bases, Sewell shook his head in amazement.

"That's the first homer ever hit off that pitch," he said after the game, "and I still don't believe it."

The 1946 Midsummer Classic was the first one to take place at Fenway Park. The American League romped to a 12–0 victory. Sewell's "eephus" had clearly lost its effectiveness as he finished the season with an 8–12 record and a 3.68 ERA. By 1947, the resourceful hurler was forty years old and being used almost exclusively in relief. As most of the regular players returned from military service, he faded quietly into the background. He compiled a 70–45 record during America's prime war years (1942–1945), providing entertainment to fans who desperately needed an escape.

July 19, 1946

In the third inning of a game at Fenway Park, White Sox pitcher Joe Haynes issued a brushback pitch to slugger Ted Williams. Williams ended up in the dirt, and umpire Red Jones warned the hurler about throwing at hitters. This provoked a stream of verbal abuse from the Chicago bench. Jones was in no mood for such nonsense, ejecting four players he believed were responsible. To exit the field, the foursome had to walk past home plate. As they did, one of the exiled men reportedly offered the arbiter a pair of glasses. Unaffected by Haynes's dusting, Williams stepped back into the box and lined a single.

By the next inning, Boston was leading 5–0, and Haynes had been replaced by left-hander Al Hollingsworth. Chicago players continued to yammer at Jones from the dugout, and the umpire decided to settle the matter once and for all. He thumbed ten more players from the game for a grand total of fourteen. As they paraded off the field, the White Sox were left with only three men on the bench: manager Ted Lyons, coach Mule Haas, and a trainer. Fortunately, there was at least one player left in the bullpen as Ralph Hamner was summoned to pitch in the eighth. Boston won, 9–2.

April 27, 1947

In one of the most glaring examples of baserunning ineptitude the game has ever seen, the St. Louis Browns were victims of an embarrassing triple play in front of fifteen thousand of their own fans at Sportsman's Park. The Brownies had Jerry Witte on third base and Walt Judnich on first when Johnny Berardino rapped a grounder to White Sox third sacker Floyd Baker. Baker threw home to catcher George Dickey, who rifled the ball to shortstop Jack Wallaesa in time to tag the lead runner between third and home. In the meantime, Judnich broke for third and was erased when Wallaesa alertly relayed to second baseman Cass Michaels. Completing a highly improbable triple killing, Berardino strayed too far off first and got trapped between the bags. Michaels threw to first baseman Jake Jones, who ended up with an assist after Wallaesa applied the tag to Berardino. The Browns at least partially redeemed themselves, completing a doubleheader sweep with a 4–3 win.

The uncommon all-tag triple play would not stand as the most anomalous event of the season for St. Louis. During a May 17 contest at Fenway Park, a seagull flew over the mound and dropped a three-pound smelt that narrowly missed pitcher Ellis Kinder. According to one source, the Browns' hurler was "dumbfounded." Regaining his composure, he reportedly picked up the fish by the tail, carried it off the field, and finished up a 4–2 win over the Red Sox. He would later join the Boston pitching staff, becoming their premier closer.

July 20, 1947

More weirdness at Ebbets Field. With the Cardinals leading the Dodgers by a 2–0 margin in the top of the ninth, St. Louis outfielder Ron Northey hit a towering fly ball off the top of the wall. Northey thought he saw third-base umpire Beans Reardon signal for a home run and began jogging the bases. When he reached the plate, he found catcher Bruce Edwards waiting for him with the ball. Apparently first base ump Larry Goetz had declared the ball in play as Northey was in the midst of his home-run trot. Northey was tagged out, and Cardinals skipper Eddie Dyer announced that the game was being played under protest.

Dyer would have a legitimate beef as Brooklyn rallied for three runs in the bottom of the ninth. The Cardinals' protest later found its way to the office of NL president Ford Frick, who counted Northey's blast as an inside-the-park homer and declared the game a tie even though the Cardinals technically never recorded three outs in the ninth. The contest would not directly affect the pennant race as St. Louis finished in second place, five games behind Brooklyn.

May 6, 1948

Tempers flared between the Red Sox and Tigers at Fenway Park. The Sox had knocked Hall of Famer Hal Newhouser out of the game in the first inning, but the Tigers rallied to tie the score at 3 in the top of the fourth. Sam Vico was on third, and Hal White was hitting for Detroit when manager Steve O'Neill called for a squeeze play. White tried to bunt but missed the pitch, and Vico, who was off and running, came barreling into the plate at full steam. He plowed into catcher Birdie Tebbetts and was tagged out. This instigated a nasty fight.

Vico later claimed that Tebbetts had hit him in the head during the play. Tebbetts insisted that Vico's head had hit his shin guard. After the tag had been applied, Vico punched Tebbetts's mask. Tebbetts flung it aside, and the two went at it. The benches emptied as the combatants were separated by umps and ejected from the game.

Fenway Park had been constructed with a single runway leading to the home and visitors' clubhouses, so players from opposing teams had to use the same exit to leave the field. Round 2 of the Vico/Tebbetts bout took place in that runway. As both men started swinging again, players from both sides rushed to the scene. Police were summoned to break up the brawl, and the game was delayed for fifteen minutes. When the fight was over, Tebbetts had a bloody nose and Vico had a black eye. Both players attributed their injuries to the involvement of other players.

July 4, 1949

For years, Red Sox followers have talked about a "Babe Ruth curse"— how the team was doomed to failure after the Babe was traded from Boston in December 1919. Perhaps it was the ghost of Ruth that disrupted the first game of an Independence Day doubleheader at Yankee Stadium.

The Yankees were leading 3–2 in the ninth, and starter Vic Raschi, who had entered the game with a 12–2 record, was getting tired. With one out, Johnny Pesky hit safely, and Ted Williams sent him to third with a single to right. Vern Stephens then drew a walk. According to multiple sources, a dark cloud suddenly obscured the sun, and heavy winds lashed the field, obscuring the views of the base runners. The game continued nevertheless as Boston's Al Zarilla stroked a single to right. Pesky, who couldn't see the ball, stayed on third just long enough to be thrown out at the plate by Cliff Mapes. The Sox had one more chance, but Bobby Doerr lined out to Mapes to end the game. Despite the freak weather disturbance, the United Press referred to Pesky as a goat.

April 18, 1950

Fenway Park has always been a hitter's paradise with its lack of foul territory (the smallest of any current stadium) and shorter-than-average outfield fences. All ballparks built after the 1950s are required to have foul lines of at least 320 feet. Constructed in 1912, Fenway is a relic from a bygone era, with a 302-foot right-field corner and a 37-foot wall in left field (known as the "Green Monster") located a mere 315 feet from home plate. According to one source, the absence of foul territory adds five to seven points to Red Sox batting averages every year. Compelling evidence of this claim is the fact that Boston players have captured eighteen batting titles since World War II.

1950 was a banner year for offense in Beantown. On June 8, the Red Sox shattered seven records in one game, beating up on the lowly Browns, 29–4. Carl Lundquist of the United Press referred to the game as a "massacre" and commented that fans should pity the Browns for having one game left to play in this series. Bobby Doerr had three homers and eight RBIs for Boston. Ted Williams and Walt Dropo had two dingers apiece. Four members of Boston's wrecking squad had at least four hits, tying an American League mark. Coupled with the 20–4 thrashing they administered St. Louis on the day before, several new all-time records were set. They included the following:

Twenty-nine runs were the most by any team in the twentieth century.
All twenty-nine runs resulted in RBIs—a feat never before accomplished.
Two-day totals of 49 runs, 59 hits, and 102 bases were also listed as all-time highs.

The Red Sox scored an incredible total of 104 runs at Fenway over a seven-day span from June 2 through June 8. They would go on to lead the majors with a total of 1,027 tallies in 1950. Additionally, their .302 team batting average topped both leagues. Unfortunately, their pitching staff fared rather poorly that year, yielding an average of nearly five runs per game. They finished in third place, one game behind the Tigers.

July 4, 1950

The picnic-like atmosphere of a doubleheader at the Polo Grounds was shattered by a senseless tragedy. Bernard Doyle, an unemployed freight sorter and former boxing manager, was treating his neighbor's thirteen-year-old son to an afternoon of baseball. The two had settled into their upper-deck seats to watch batting practice when a gunshot rang out. Doyle slumped in his chair with blood running from his head.

The incident took place about an hour before game time. Many spectators were unaware of the death—some eyewitnesses believed that perhaps Doyle had merely fainted and was in need of medical attention. Players didn't even get word of the incident until shortly before the second game. Roughly fifty thousand people attended the showdown between the Giants and Dodgers.

A glaring example of folks behaving ghoulishly, the *New York Daily News* reported that several people in the standing-room-only crowd fought for Doyle's seat after his body was removed.

Police believed that Doyle may have been the victim of a juvenile sharpshooting gang. Eighty detectives worked on the case, and at least 1,200 people were questioned. The mystery was solved when a fourteen-year-old boy named Robert Mario Peebles admitted to randomly firing a pistol from a nearby rooftop.

In his midfifties (reports of his age are conflicting), Doyle had at one time managed former heavyweight champion James Braddock. His death remains one of the most strange and irrational ever to occur at a ballpark.

August 9, 1950

In his famous "nice guys finish last" quote, manager Leo Durocher was referring to Mel Ott and Eddie Stanky. When a journalist commented about Durocher's prickly personality one day, the fiery Brooklyn skipper pointed across the field to rival Giants manager Mel Ott and remarked that there wasn't a nicer guy in the game. "But look where [the Giants] are," Durocher said, "seventh place. That's where nice guys end up." He then pointed to the Dodgers' scrappy second baseman and said: "Now look at [Stanky]. He can't hit, can't run, can't field. He's no nice guy, but all the little SOB can do is win."

Stanky was a lot more gifted than Durocher gave him credit for that afternoon, though many would agree he got by more on hustle than on raw talent. Frequently hitting at the top of the batting order, Stanky used any means necessary to get on base. This included leaning into pitches and crouching so low that his strike zone became virtually nonexistent. He was known to get creative on defense as well, especially during the 1950 campaign.

On August 9, Stanky's Giants were playing the Braves at Boston. Slugger Bob Elliot was a thorn in the side of New York hurlers that day, blasting two doubles, one of which drove in the tying run in a 3–2 Braves victory. Taking matters into his own hands, Stanky stood near second base and tried to distract Elliot by waving his arms as reliever Dave Koslo delivered. Home-plate umpire Lon Warneke opted to do nothing about it since the Braves lodged no formal complaint. Warneke would be forced to act several days later.

On August 11, the Giants were visiting Philadelphia. Stanky performed a variation of his previous routine while Andy Seminick of the Phillies was at bat. This time, Stanky stood directly behind pitcher Sal Maglie and imitated Maglie's windup. Seminick complained to umpire Al Barlick, but Barlick insisted that Stanky wasn't violating any rules.

Before the next day's game, the umpiring crew (which included Lon Warneke at second base) approached Durocher, warning him that Stanky's tactics were "unsportsmanlike" and would not be tolerated. After Seminick collided with Hank Thompson at third base, knocking him unconscious and loosening several teeth, Durocher allowed Stanky to employ his offbeat strategy yet again. According to one source, he added jumping jacks this time. Lon Warneke thumbed him out of the game, which was marred by a brawl and won by Philadelphia in extra innings. Changes to the rulebook later prohibited deliberate distractions made by members of the defensive team.

June 16, 1951

An Evangeline League game in Alexandria, Louisiana, was disrupted by a horrifying scene. In the sixth inning of the Class-C contest, Crowley Millers outfielder Andy Strong was hit by a bolt of lightning. Witnesses said that the clouds over the park did not appear threatening at the time. The twenty-four-year-old prospect was killed instantly. Strong, who had served in the US Naval Reserve during World War II, was hitting .339 in sixteen games at the time. He was married with one child—a son who later attended Centenary College in Louisiana on a baseball scholarship.

Strong is not the only player to have been killed by lightning. In their 2009 work, *Death at the Ballpark*, authors Robert Gorman and David Weeks assert that thirty individuals at various levels of play have been killed by lightning strikes—including three in one game. That game took place at Baker, Florida, in 1949. The lightning struck a chicken-wire backstop and traveled around the infield, instantly killing Allen Joyner at third and Harry Moore at short. Second baseman Joe Taylor died the next day.

August 19, 1951

Bill Veeck was among the zaniest promoters in baseball history. He believed that any team that relied solely on diehard fans to survive would soon be out of business. Resentful of the establishment in general, he spent his entire career trying to give folks something more. While working for the Cubs, he planted ivy on the outfield wall. On the south side of Chicago, he put showers in the bleachers and introduced an exploding scoreboard. In Cleveland, he broke the American League color barrier with the signing of Larry Doby and Satchel Paige. He also constructed a daycare center at the ballpark. Two of his wildest promotions occurred during the 1951 slate, when he was owner of the St. Louis Browns.

The South End Grounds in Boston was the site of a devastating fire in 1894. The blaze spread to the adjacent neighborhood, damaging or destroying more than two hundred buildings. Library of Congress, LC-DIG-ppmsca-18836.

In 1908, an infamous baserunning error by Giants first baseman Fred Merkle led to a one-game playoff for the NL pennant. A standing-room-only crowd at the Polo Grounds saw the Cubs prevail, 4–2. The precipitating play would forever be labeled "Merkle's Boner." Library of Congress, LC-DIG-ggbain-02280.

Among the most entertaining characters of the deadball era, infielder Germany Schaefer became famous for calling his own shot and "stealing" first base. Library of Congress, LC-DIG-ggbain-13278.

Don't let the smile in this photo fool you. Ty Cobb was one of the nastiest players ever to step onto a diamond. He once climbed into the stands and beat up a disabled man who was heckling him. Library of Congress, LC-DIG-ggbain-08008.

Two of the most clever strategists the game has ever seen. The articulate Johnny Evers (left) had a knack for influencing the calls of umpires. Manager George Stallings (right) once set up a spy operation at Hilltop Park in New York and ended up getting caught stealing signs from opponents. Library of Congress, LC-DIG-ggbain-17512.

Babe Ruth and Ernie Shore (left and second from left) combined for a no-hitter in 1917. Ruth deserved very little credit as he faced just one batter, took a swing at the umpire, and was ejected. Shore came on in relief and retired every batter he faced that day. Library of Congress, LC-DIG-ppmsca-18459.

Cleveland shortstop Ray Chapman was killed after being hit in the head by a Carl Mays pitch in 1920. Mays, who played for the Yankees, would forever be stigmatized as a villain. Library of Congress, LC-DIG-ggbain-27249.

Sam Rice's circus catch in the 1925 World Series remained shrouded in controversy throughout his lifetime. He drafted a letter revealing the truth about the incident and told Hall of Fame officials not to open it until after his death. Rice's message from the grave was: "At no time did I lose possession of the ball." Library of Congress, LC-DIG-ggbain-38192.

Closed in 1938, the Baker Bowl was one of the ugliest ballparks in the majors. The owners failed to properly maintain it, and sections of the bleachers collapsed at two different points in time, killing a dozen people and injuring hundreds. At least players were safe from "B.O.," or so the billboard in the background says. National Baseball Hall of Fame Library, Cooperstown, New York.

The oldest surviving structure in the American League, Fenway Park's unusual facets make it a hitter's paradise. The famous "Green Monster" is situated just 310 feet from home plate and stands thirty-seven feet high. National Baseball Hall of Fame Library, Cooperstown, New York.

Rip Sewell of the Pirates lost part of his toe in a hunting accident and developed a blooper pitch to compensate for it. Nicknamed the "eephus," Sewell's novelty offering brought fans to the ballpark in droves during World War II. National Baseball Hall of Fame Library, Cooperstown, New York.

Among the greatest natural hitters in history, Red Sox outfielder Ted Williams had an ugly temper. In 1956, he was fined for spitting at fans and flipping them the bird. National Baseball Hall of Fame Library, Cooperstown, New York.

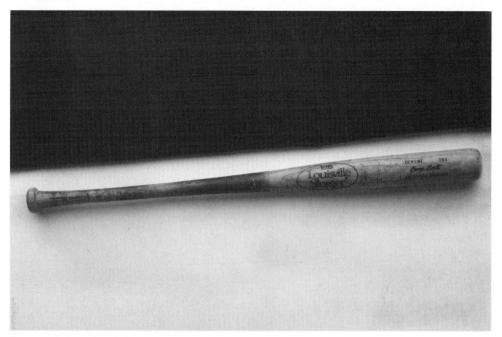

A superficial examination of George Brett's infamous pine-tar bat (which now resides at the Baseball Hall of Fame) reveals that the sticky substance was indeed used excessively. National Baseball Hall of Fame Library, Cooperstown, New York.

Outfielder Jimmy Piersall suffered from bipolar disorder, a serious and persistent mental illness that prompted numerous peculiar episodes on the field. In this photo, he is running the bases backward to celebrate his one hundredth career homer. AP Photo.

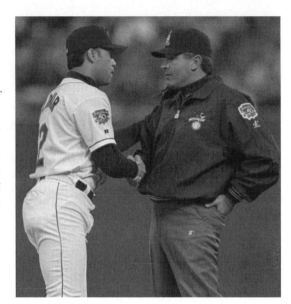

After the infamous spitting incident of 1996, Orioles second baseman Roberto Alomar shook hands with umpire John Hirschbeck and apologized. The memorable moment took place during a game in April of the following year. It was the first time the two had taken the field together since Alomar expectorated on the arbiter. AP Photo/Dave Hammond.

Umpire Charlie Reliford separates Mike Piazza and Roger Clemens during game 2 of the 2000 World Series. Piazza's bat had shattered on contact with a pitch, and Clemens had inexplicably thrown one of the broken pieces at Piazza as he ran toward first. The Mets backstop later referred to Clemens's behavior as "bizarre." AP Photo/Bill Kostroun.

The Browns had a long history of losing. Aside from one World Series appearance in 1944, the club had spent most of its existence in the second division. Desperate to save the ailing franchise, Veeck brought a little burlesque to the ballpark. On August 19, he sent a little person to the plate in a game against the Detroit Tigers. He envisioned the prank as a celebration of the American League's fiftieth anniversary. He also wanted to honor his chief sponsor, the Falstaff Brewing Company. How this morphed into putting a little person on the field has never been adequately explained.

Veeck was inflexible about hiring a "midget" as opposed to a "dwarf" since he wanted someone who appeared athletic. He ended up recruiting a three-foot-seven, sixty-five-pound performer named Eddie Gaedel. Gaedel had worked in circuses, rodeos, and other miscellaneous shows. During World War II, he had served as a riveter, crawling into plane engines where others couldn't fit. For the ballpark gag, Gaedel wore a uniform belonging to the nine-year-old son of club vice president Bill DeWitt. The number was changed from "6" to "1/8" (a joke in reference to Gaedel's diminutive stature). It was listed as "18" on scorecards so as not to arouse pregame suspicion from fans.

Between games of a Sunday doubleheader, Veeck arranged to have a seven-foot cake wheeled out onto the field. Gaedel popped out and received a warm reception from fans. Bob Cain was on the mound for the Tigers, and after he had finished warming up in the bottom of the first, the Browns called for a pinch hitter. As Gaedel strolled to the plate, umpire Ed Hurley reportedly shouted: "What the hell?!" When St. Louis manager Zack Taylor presented the arbiter with a valid contract for Gaedel, Hurley allowed the little man to hit.

The right-handed Gaedel had been instructed to crouch low at the plate, and in a pregame practice session, his strike zone had been determined to be less than two inches. Bob Cain couldn't find it, issuing a four-pitch walk. Gaedel jogged to first and then was immediately replaced with a pinch runner. He got a standing ovation as he exited the field, commenting later: "For a minute, I felt like Babe Ruth."

Gaedel worked with Veeck again on two occasions. In May 1959, he and three other little people landed in a helicopter at Comiskey Park dressed as "Martians." In a bizarre stunt, they "abducted" vertically challenged infielders Nellie Fox and Luis Aparicio, ushering them to home plate for a ceremony. Gaedel worked for Veeck one last time in 1961. Responding to complaints that vendors were blocking the views of fans, Veeck hired Gaedel and several other little people to sell refreshments in the box seats during a game in Chicago.

While Veeck was planning the Gaedel stunt in 1951, "Grandstand Manager's Day" was already in the works. A contest was held by the *St. Louis*

Globe Democrat, allowing fans to pick the starting lineup for an August 24 game against the A's. A limited number of fans who had filled out ballots received tickets in the mail entitling them to sit in a special section behind the Browns dugout. When the contest winners arrived at the ballpark, they were given placards that said "YES" on one side and "NO" on the other. More than a thousand "managers" joined Veeck and special guest Connie Mack in the reserved section. Two fans were assigned as "coaches" on the field.

The game proceeded as follows: Veeck's publicity man, Bob Fischel, stood near the dugout with signs that displayed various managerial strategies (bunt, steal, etc.). Fischel held up the signs, and "managers" voted by holding up their placards. The votes were tabulated and relayed to Browns coach Johnny Berardino by walkie-talkie. Berardino then put the decisions into action.

The A's took a 3–0 lead in the first on a homer by Gus Zernial. Starter Ned Garver then got into further trouble with runners on the corners, setting up the first "managers'" option. Fischel flashed a sign asking whether infielders should position themselves deep for a double play or shallow for a play at the plate. The crowd voted in favor of a double play, and the decision paid off as Pete Suder obliged them with a textbook grounder, ending the frame.

The Browns responded with three runs in the bottom of the first. The "managers" made their first bad call, voting for Hank Arft to attempt a steal of second. Since the A's could see Fischel's sign and the decision of the crowd, Arft was thrown out by a mile. The Browns ended up winning the game, 5–3.

After Zack Taylor returned to his managerial duties, St. Louis dropped five games in a row. The Browns would finish the year at 52–102, and despite Veeck's innovative promotions, attendance continued to sag. The resourceful owner sold his interest in the club after the 1953 slate. Today, the Browns are known as the Baltimore Orioles.

May 21, 1952

After the Dodgers demolished the Reds, the United Press remarked, "It's Ladies' Day in Brooklyn today, but Ebbets Field is no place right now for women or children. The Dodgers are likely to frighten away all but the brave-hearted if they come close to repeating last night's record-breaking 19–1 massacre of Cincinnati."

Coming off six consecutive All-Star selections, right-hander Ewell Blackwell took the mound for the Reds. He was off to a slow start, carrying a 1–5 record into the game. After retiring leadoff man Billy Cox on a grounder to third, he faced five batters and was removed. By then, the Dodgers had already plated three runs. Bud Byerly, Herm Wehmeier, and Frank Smith were all summoned from the bullpen. None of the three was effective, and nineteen straight batters reached base—a new NL record.

During the Dodgers' first run through the batting order, they victimized Blackwell and Byerly for a homer, a double, three singles, and three walks. The second time around, Byerly, Wehmeier, and Smith pooled their efforts in allowing five singles, three free passes, and a hit batsman. Smith finally recorded the third out, getting Duke Snider on a called strike to end the debacle. Pee Wee Reese reached base three times during the frame as the Dodgers jumped out to an insurmountable 15–0 lead.

June 11, 1952

Red Sox center fielder Jimmy Piersall claimed he remembered nothing from the time he reported to training camp in 1952 to the time he was released from a sanitarium in September of that year. During those missing months, he generated a storm of controversy and negative press with his erratic behavior. On May 24, he fought with Yankee bad boy Billy Martin shortly before game time. While changing his bloody shirt in the clubhouse, he got into another scuffle with teammate Mickey McDermott.

On June 11, Piersall resorted to bizarre tactics on the field. Facing Satchel Paige in the ninth inning of a game at Fenway Park, he announced to the legendary St. Louis hurler that he was going to bunt. After doing exactly that and reaching first safely, he began mimicking Paige's motions. Hoot Evers beat out an infield hit, and Piersall continued to taunt Paige from second base, making animal noises. Distracted and aggravated by Piersall's "oink-ing," Paige lost his composure, walking future Hall of Famer George Kell to load the bases. After getting Vern Stephens to pop out, Paige followed with another free pass to Billy Goodman, forcing in a run. A Ted Lepcio single set up a game-winning grand slam by Sox catcher Sammy White. After the game, Browns backstop Clint Courtney said, "I believe that man is plumb crazy. I never saw a man do those things. Anywhere."

Piersall was demoted to the Birmingham Barons of the Southern Association in late June. His antics resulted in numerous ejections, one of them coming after he "shot" umpire Neil Strocchia with a water pistol and then heckled the arbiter from the grandstand roof. Piersall ended up being shipped to Westborough State Hospital in Massachusetts and being diagnosed with "nervous exhaustion." (It was later determined that he was suffering from bipolar disorder.) He missed the remainder of the season.

On returning to action in 1953, he was occasionally taunted by opponents, who warned him that the men in the white coats were coming to get him. He persevered, assembling a seventeen-year career highlighted by two

Gold Glove Awards and two All-Star selections. The book he coauthored with
Al Hirshberg about his rookie experience, *Fear Strikes Out*, was made into a
1957 movie starring Anthony Perkins.

August 25, 1952

Tiger pitcher Virgil Trucks threw two no-hitters in 1952. The first one
came on May 15 against the Senators before a sparse crowd of 2,215 at
Briggs Stadium in Detroit. Trucks, nicknamed "Fire" for his lively fastball,
hit two batters, walked one, and survived three errors by second baseman
Jerry Priddy. Vic Wertz sealed the win with a walk-off homer in the bottom
of the ninth.

Trucks's second no-hitter, on August 25, was open for debate. In the
third inning, Phil Rizzuto led off with a grounder to short. Johnny Pesky
had difficulty getting the ball out of his glove, and Rizzuto was safe at first.
Dan Daniel of the *New York World Telegram* convinced John Drebinger (the
official scorer) to change his initial error ruling to a hit since there was no
obvious misplay on Pesky's part. When Trucks had not surrendered another
safety through six frames, Drebinger called the Tigers dugout from the press
box and asked to speak to Pesky. Questioned about the play in the third inning, Pesky believed he should have been charged with an error. The scoring
was changed yet again as Trucks completed the no-hitter. It was no easy feat
with future Hall of Famers Mickey Mantle, Yogi Berra, and Johnny Mize in
the lineup that day.

Trucks's feat was not unique. Johnny Vander Meer and Allie Reynolds
had both spun a pair of no-hitters in the same season before him. Nolan Ryan
and Roy Halladay would turn the trick years later. But Trucks's statistical
totals during his no-hit season were highly unusual. While all of the other
hurlers posted winning records, Trucks was 5–19 during the 1952 campaign.
In his book, *Throwing Heat: The Life and Times of Virgil "Fire" Trucks*, the
stocky right-hander remembered why: "We were last in runs scored and near
the bottom in fielding, a deadly combination for you if you're a pitcher."

April 17, 1953

The legend of Mickey Mantle was born on this date. Playing in his third
big league season, the twenty-one-year-old center fielder became a mythical figure when he blasted the longest home run in the history of Griffith
Stadium. The clout came off of Senators hurler Chuck Stobbs in the fifth
inning and was witnessed by only 4,206 fans. Mantle launched a belt-high

fastball into center field. It glanced off the Bohemian Beer sign and disappeared out of sight.

Yankee PR man Red Patterson tracked the drive to the backyard of a house on Oakdale Lane, where a ten-year-old boy named Donald Dunaway had allegedly retrieved it. Patterson reportedly offered the boy a dollar and two autographed baseballs for the one hit by Mantle. The savvy executive then returned to the stadium with the ball and a new Mantle myth. His estimate of 565 feet came to be widely accepted as fact. To date, Donald Dunaway has never come forward to challenge the tale, though most experts doubt the validity of Patterson's measurement.

The longest home run in history has been credited to Babe Ruth, who allegedly hit a rocket at Briggs Stadium in Detroit that traveled over six hundred feet. That distance is likely exaggerated, though multiple sources claim that the Babe hit homers of five hundred feet in all eight American League parks during the 1921 slate.

Mantle would launch numerous Herculean blasts during his career. In June 1955, he cleared the roof at Comiskey Park. The clout reportedly landed on Thirty-Fourth Street and broke the windshield of a car. In April 1956, he hit two homers over the thirty-foot center-field wall at Griffith Stadium—the first player to accomplish this twice in one game. In May 1963, he hit the facade of the right-field roof at Yankee Stadium, which was nearly four hundred feet from home plate and roughly 115 feet above the field. Mantle hit the facade more than once but never cleared it. Riddled with injuries throughout his career, he would "settle" for a total of 536 regular season homers. He hit eighteen more in World Series play.

May 24, 1953

Pitcher Russ Meyer developed a well-deserved reputation as a hothead and a poor sport. Nicknamed the "Mad Monk" for his volatile temperament, he didn't take too kindly to being removed from games early—especially if he was losing. On one such occasion, he threw his spikes at the shower ceiling, where they got stuck. Before another premature departure, he bounced a ball so hard off the mound that it rolled all the way to first base.

On the date in question, the tempestuous right-hander was pitching for the Dodgers and facing the Phillies at Connie Mack Stadium. Staked to a 2–1 lead in the bottom of the fourth, he issued two straight walks to load the bases. Incensed by the calls of home-plate umpire Augie Donatelli, Meyer began shouting at the arbiter. He was subsequently ejected but refused to leave, stomping back to the mound and staying put until manager Chuck Dressen came out to get him.

Before making an exit, Meyer picked up the rosin bag and tossed it roughly thirty feet in the air. In a moment of comic relief, it landed on the hurler's head, covering him with powder. Even Meyer chuckled briefly at this turn of events. Not quite finished with his tantrum, he returned to the dugout, where cameras captured him grabbing his crotch and swearing loudly at Donatelli. He missed a wild game as Brooklyn scored twelve runs in the eighth before a single batter was retired. The United Press reported that this was a new record.

Meyer was fined and suspended. Commissioner Ford Frick and NL president Warren Giles were vocal in their opposition to dugout cameras. For several years, dugout shots were expressly forbidden in television broadcasts. This was informally referred to as the "Meyer Rule."

September 6, 1953

It's a rare occasion when a ballplayer benefits from an injury, but that's what happened (more or less) in the aftermath of this game. The Dodgers were facing the rival Giants at the Polo Grounds. In the second inning, New York's Ruben Gomez hit Brooklyn's star outfielder Carl Furillo on the wrist with a pitch. Furillo was restrained from charging the mound and was escorted to first base. While Billy Cox was hitting, Furillo exchanged words with some Giants players and then bolted toward the New York bench. He was greeted on the dugout steps by manager Leo Durocher. The two wrestled each other to the ground, and both men were ejected. In the ensuing donnybrook, Furillo sustained a broken bone in his left hand when it was stepped on by another player.

Furillo later claimed that Durocher had ordered the beaning and vowed to get revenge. "I never landed a punch," he told reporters. "I would have given $1,000 to have hit him with just one good punch." Informed of Furillo's brash statements, Durocher said: "I'll be there."

Kept out of action for the rest of the regular season, Furillo's batting average remained frozen at .344. His inactivity may have helped him as he had enough at bats to qualify for a batting title and eventually won it by two points over Red Schoendienst of the Cardinals. Furillo returned in time for the World Series and hit .333 with a homer and four RBIs against the Yankees, who claimed their fifth consecutive championship—an all-time record.

July 18, 1954

Eddie Stanky was up to his tricks—this time as manager of the Cardinals. After dropping the opening game of a doubleheader to the Phillies at home, the Redbirds fell behind in the fifth inning of the nightcap, 8–1. The first game had been delayed by rain for over an hour, and darkness was fast approaching. Determined to avoid a sweep, Stanky began stalling, encouraging his men to bait their opponents.

It didn't take much to get catcher Sal Yvars going. He had a long-standing vendetta against Philly infielder Earl Torgeson that stemmed from a 1952 incident, when Torgeson was with the Braves and Yvars was with the Giants. Torgeson had hit Yvars's shin guard on a backswing, and Yvars had broken Torgeson's bat in retaliation. The two had been nursing a grudge ever since. After pitcher Cot Deal threw dangerously close to Torgeson, the big first baseman got into a battle of words with Yvars. Words gave way to fists, and when Philly manager Terry Moore rushed to the scene, he was tackled by Stanky. Moore, a former Cardinals star, had been fired as a St. Louis coach by Stanky, and there was bad blood between the two. The benches cleared, and the game, which was not yet official, was delayed for nearly ten minutes.

Stanky resorted to new stalling tactics when play resumed, changing pitchers repeatedly. After "The Brat" had called for Tom Poholsky—the third pitcher of the inning—umpire Babe Pinelli got on the phone and notified the press box that the game was being forfeited to Philly by a score of 9–0. All statistics were erased.

Stanky was hit with a five-day suspension by NL president Warren Giles. Yvars and Torgeson were suspended as well. Moore said that he regretted the fight but defended his team's actions. "We felt their pitcher was throwing at our batter," he told reporters. "You just can't take that. It's only human nature to try to do something about it." The Philly skipper avoided suspension.

September 22, 1954

A game in Milwaukee between the Reds and Braves ended on a very strange note. Trailing 3–1 in the top of the ninth, the Reds had Wally Post on first and Gus Bell on second with one out. Warren Spahn had come on in relief of Ernie Johnson and was dealing to pinch hitter Bob Borkowski. Spahn uncorked a wild pitch, and Borkowski swung at it for strike three. This set the wheels in motion.

Catcher Del Crandall quickly recovered the ball and threw to third to try to get Bell. The relay was late, and Eddie Mathews threw across the diamond in an attempt to nail Borkowski at first. The ball hit Borkowski in the back and bounced into right field. Bell and Post both scored, and the umpires called for time.

After a lengthy conference, plate umpire Hal Dixon called Borkowski out, referring to a rule that prohibits runners from advancing on a dropped third strike if first base is occupied and there are less than two outs. Unhappy with the ruling, Cincinnati manager Birdie Tebbetts protested the 3–1 loss. NL president Warren Giles felt that the umpires had made the right decision, but since the outcome affected the standings of several clubs, he upheld the appeal and ordered the game replayed from the point at which it had been interrupted. The September 24 encore was quite eventful.

Dave Jolly took over for Spahn with two outs and two runners on in the ninth. Reds second baseman Johnny Temple lined a single to center field that was mishandled by Bill Bruton. Both runners scored, tying the game at 3. In the bottom of the frame, Cincinnati's Frank Smith relieved Corky Valentine, who had been spared from a loss. It was Smith who absorbed the defeat when he gave up a game-winning single to Catfish Metkovich. The Braves ended up in third place that year, eight games behind the Giants.

July 17, 1956

In his native Puerto Rico, pitcher Ruben Gomez was known as "El Divino Loco," which translates roughly as "the divine madman." There were times when he looked more unbalanced than godlike, particularly on the date in question, when he was involved in a bizarre incident that would come to define his major league career.

In the second inning of a game against the Braves, he drilled slugger Joe Adcock on the wrist with a pitch. Adcock had been hit nine times previously in his career, and at least one serious injury had resulted. Gomez may or may not have shouted something at the Milwaukee first baseman as he was headed toward the initial sack, but Adcock suddenly changed his course and made a beeline for the mound.

Gomez stood six feet tall and weighed 170 pounds. Adcock was four inches taller and forty pounds heavier. In a cowardly reaction rarely seen in baseball, the panicked hurler turned tail and ran—but not before firing another ball at his pursuer. The point-blank throw hit Adcock in the thigh and served to thoroughly enrage him. Like a scene from a classic *Tom and Jerry* cartoon, Gomez bolted for the safety of the Giants' clubhouse, avoiding a flying tackle executed by third-base coach Johnny Riddle and leaving the slow-footed Adcock in the dust. According to multiple unconfirmed reports, Gomez grabbed an ice pick from the clubhouse and headed back toward the field before being intercepted by teammates. Someone in the press box provided a moment of levity when it was announced over the PA system: "Gomez now running for Gomez."

Besieged by reporters after the game, Gomez said he wasn't trying to hit Adcock and complained that the slugger had been crowding the plate. Questioned about running away, he said: "Why should I be brave and get killed? I'd rather be safe than sorry." Adcock harbored no ill will, commenting, "Maybe I should apologize to him. I'd rather just forget the whole thing."

Gomez had a perfect opportunity to lay the affair to rest a week later when the two teams met again. Photographers sent representatives to both dugouts requesting a picture of the two together. Adcock agreed to do it, but Gomez barked tersely, "No pictures, absolutely no pictures." He would never successfully disassociate himself from the incident.

August 7, 1956

Despite his many positive attributes, Ted Williams maintained a prickly relationship with Boston fans. In front of a record crowd at Fenway Park, "Teddy Ballgame" dropped a windblown fly hit by Mickey Mantle in the eleventh inning of a scoreless tie. As Mantle chugged into second base, a scattering of fans began to boo Williams. Minutes later, a majority of the crowd was on its feet cheering a spectacular catch he made on a Yogi Berra liner against the left-field wall to end the inning. But Williams chose to focus on the negative. On his way to the dugout, the ornery left fielder turned and spat directly into the standing-room-only crowd. Making sure his feelings were clear, he spat at fans a second time and reportedly gave them the finger from the Red Sox dugout.

Don Larsen had pitched brilliantly for the Yankees, but his defense deserted him in the bottom of the eleventh. Pitcher Willard Nixon reached on an error by third baseman Andy Carey. Billy Goodman was safe on a Moose Skowron bungle. Billy Klaus drew a walk with no outs, and Yankee manager Casey Stengel summoned Tommy Byrne from the bullpen. Williams was still irritable when he came to the plate. After drawing a walk that forced in the tying run, he flipped his bat high in the air and had to be instructed by first-base coach Del Baker to touch the bag.

Though Williams was apologetic when he initially spoke to manager Joe Cronin, he was whistling a different tune after the cab ride back to his hotel. "I'm not a damn bit sorry for what I did," he told press members. "I'd spit again on the same people who booed me."

It was not the first spitting incident of the season. Williams had spat at the press corps and fans during a July 20 game at Fenway. Feeling that decisive action needed to be taken, Cronin handed the slugger a $5,000 fine—the largest ever imposed on a player for misconduct. Babe Ruth had been fined the same amount by Yankee manager Miller Huggins in 1925. Grousing to reporters, Williams estimated his actions would cost him one-eighth of his salary and snipped sarcastically, "I wouldn't be at the ballpark tomorrow if I could afford $5,000 fines."

April 21, 1957

More than twenty thousand fans at County Stadium in Milwaukee witnessed one of the most infamous cases of rule fracturing in history. The Reds had runners at first and second with one out against Warren Spahn of the Braves when Wally Post rapped a grounder to short. Don Hoak, the lead runner, improvised a creative strategy to break up the double play. On his way to third, Hoak fielded the ball with his bare hands and flipped it to flabbergasted shortstop Johnny Logan. He was called out for interference, while Post was credited with a single.

This touched off a wave of controversy in the press box, where several reporters argued that Post should not have been given a hit due to Hoak's intervention. Second-base umpire Frank Secory was acting on rule 7.08(f), which states that a runner is out when "he is touched by a fair ball in fair territory before the ball has touched or passed an infielder. The ball is dead and no runner may score, nor runners advance." The official scorer was acting on rule 10.05(e), which at that time stated that a base hit shall be scored "when a fair ball that has not been touched by a fielder touches a runner or umpire."

The ruling had little impact on the game's outcome as the Reds failed to score in the inning and lost anyway, 3–1. But the league decided to act in order to prevent repeat offenses. A rule was established declaring both the batter and the runner out in such cases. Hoak later claimed that he had thrown up his hands instinctively believing that the ball would hit him, but no one was buying his story.

July 9, 1957

The All-Star Game generated excitement and controversy as the American League won for only the second time in eight years. The ninth inning was particularly eventful as the Junior Circuit scored three times off of Dodger closer Clem Labine to take a 6–2 lead. They would barely hold on as the NL came storming back with three tallies of their own in the bottom of the frame. The tying run was in scoring position when Minnie Minoso made a fine running catch on a Gil Hodges liner for the final out of the game.

The events before the annual midsummer showcase were equally intriguing as Cincinnati fans provoked the ire of Commissioner Ford Frick by stuffing the ballot box. When voting was complete, Stan Musial was the only nonmember of the Reds selected as a starter. Around the horn, Cincy was represented by catcher Ed Bailey, second baseman Johnny Temple, shortstop Roy McMillan, and third baseman Don Hoak. The outfield contained a trio of Red Legs: Frank Robinson, Gus Bell, and Wally Post.

After a full investigation, commissioner Ford Frick discovered that the *Cincinnati Enquirer* had tipped the scales in favor of hometown favorites by printing premarked ballots and distributing them in Sunday papers. Rumors even surfaced about various bars in the city withholding alcohol from customers until they voted for Reds players. One woman claimed to have personally mailed in a hundred ballots with plans to send a hundred more.

Frick's reaction was decisive. He stripped fans of the right to vote and inserted Willie Mays and Hank Aaron in place of Bell and Post, who was injured anyway. Bell was not upset about the last-minute change, remarking of Mays, "He's had a better year than me." Reds manager Birdie Tebbetts suggested that the ousted starters be named "honorary members" of the NL squad, but Frick was having none of it. "I strongly object to our league making a burlesque out of the All-Star Game," he told a correspondent from the *Sporting News*. "I never want to see such an exhibition again." From 1958 until 1970, players, managers, and coaches made the annual All-Star selections.

The 1957 affair was not the only controversial one in All-Star history. In 1943, Yankee manager Joe McCarthy had been openly accused of playing favorites when choosing his starting lineup. Silencing critics, he refused to utilize any of the New Yorkers on his bench. Yankee fans in attendance at Shibe Park that day would have been sorely disappointed to see pinstripers Bill Dickey and Joe Gordon (among others) riding the pine for all nine frames. The AL fared just fine without help from the Bronx crew. Red Sox second baseman Bobby Doerr blasted a three-run homer off of Cardinal ace Mort Cooper, and Cleveland's third sacker Ken Keltner doubled and then scored what would prove to be the winning run as the Junior Circuit prevailed, 5–3. Among the Yankee players who sat out that day, Tiny Bonham and Johnny Lindell were cheated the most. Neither had another chance to play in an All-Star Game.

August 17, 1957

What are the odds? In a game between the Phillies and Giants at Connie Mack Stadium, Philly leadoff man Richie Ashburn hit the same fan twice with foul balls. Ashburn was known for his extraordinary bat control and his ability to spoil good pitches by slapping them foul. During a fifteen-year Hall of Fame career spent mostly with the Phillies, he led the NL in walks and on-base percentage four times apiece.

During the game in question, Ashburn hit a foul that broke the nose of Alice Roth, wife of *Philadelphia Bulletin* sports editor Earl Roth. Incredibly, as Mrs. Roth was being removed from the game via a stretcher, Ashburn hit her again, in the leg! Informed of her injury, the congenial center fielder visited her in the hospital the next day and apologized. As the story goes, he didn't even know he had hit her a second time until she told him. Ashburn remained friendly with the Roth family for years as their son served as a Phillies batboy. After his playing days were over, Ashburn moved on to a successful career as a broadcaster.

October 6, 1957

Led by a gaggle of Hall of Famers, the Yankees carried a 2–1 World Series edge over the Braves into game 4 at County Stadium in Milwaukee. The Braves had no shortage of talent on their roster either, sending four Cooperstown greats into action. Milwaukee jumped out to a 4–1 lead in the bottom of the fourth on homers by Hank Aaron and Frank Torre, but the Bombers refused to roll over as Elston Howard tied the game with a three-run clout off of Warren Spahn in the ninth. If not for the astute observational skills of Nippy Jones, the Braves might not have won the game.

Things looked bleak for Milwaukee after Aaron misplayed a ball hit off the left-field wall by Hank Bauer, chasing Tony Kubek across the plate in the tenth. Trailing 5–4, Braves skipper Fred Haney selected Jones to lead off the bottom of the frame in place of Spahn. Left-hander Tommy Byrne hit Jones with a low pitch, but as the seldom-used utility man took off for first, home-plate umpire Augie Donatelli called him back, arguing that the ball had hit the dirt. Jones drew Donatelli's attention to a smudge of shoe polish on the baseball—irrefutable evidence that he had been struck on the foot. Donatelli was swayed by the appeal, awarding Jones first base and setting the stage for a dramatic Milwaukee rally.

The speedy Felix Mantilla was inserted as pinch runner. Red Schoendienst sacrificed him to second, and Johnny Logan followed with a game-tying double. Eddie Mathews was the man of the hour for the Braves, sealing a hard-fought victory with a walk-off homer. The Yankees had no complaints about Donatelli's call reversal. Interviewed after the game, Yogi Berra and Casey Stengel both confirmed the presence of polish on the baseball. The Braves went on to win the Series in seven games.

Mets manager Gil Hodges must have been well versed in Series lore when he orchestrated a similar ruling in the 1969 Fall Classic. With the Orioles leading 3–0 in the sixth inning of game 5, Cleon Jones tried to avoid a pitch in the dirt from left-hander Dave McNally. Umpire Lou Dimuro signaled for a hit by pitch after Hodges advised him to inspect the ball, which was clearly blemished with shoe polish. McNally gave up a two-run homer to the next hitter, Donn Clendenon. The Mets won the game 5–3, claiming the first world title in franchise history.

May 26, 1959

As more than nineteen thousand fans settled into their seats for an evening of baseball at County Stadium in Milwaukee, they had no idea that they would be witnessing a piece of history. Pirates left-hander Harvey Haddix was hardly an intimidating presence on the hill. Listed at 170 pounds, it has been said that he actually weighed closer to 150. He got his nickname "Kitten" from Cardinal teammates, who felt that he looked like a skinnier version of their former staff ace, Harry "The Cat" Brecheen. After winning twenty games in his first full season with St. Louis, Haddix had been hit by a line drive off the bat of Braves slugger Joe Adcock. Left with permanent nerve damage in his knee, Haddix was forced to alter his mechanics. According to Stan Musial, the injury had taken something off of his once-devastating curveball. Traded by the Cardinals after the 1955 slate, he failed to find a home in Philadelphia and Cincinnati. A seven-player swap had landed him in Pittsburgh for the 1959 campaign. Entering the May 26 contest, he carried a 4–2 record with a 2.67 ERA—not bad, but hardly the kind of numbers to instill fear in the hearts of opponents.

The evening was windy and damp. At times, lightning flashed in the distance. Haddix was nursing a nasty cold and had been consuming lozenges all day. Despite the malady, he went through the Milwaukee batting order with remarkable efficiency. Following baseball etiquette, none of his teammates said a word to him about the perfect game he had going into the ninth. After opposing hurler Lew Burdette went down on strikes to end the frame, Haddix's teammates congratulated him on becoming just the seventh pitcher in history to achieve perfection. But Haddix didn't feel like celebrating. There was still a game going on.

Burdette had been fairly masterful himself and had gotten stronger as the game progressed, retiring the Pirates in order during the sixth, seventh, and eighth. He tossed up zeroes through thirteen frames, forcing Haddix to rewrite history. By the end of the twelfth, Haddix had retired every batter he faced—an astounding accomplishment considering what was going on in the Braves bullpen. Using binoculars, Milwaukee relievers were stealing the signs of catcher Smoky Burgess and relaying them to batters using a towel. A towel on the shoulder meant a fastball, and no towel meant a breaking ball. Haddix kept mowing down opponents anyway until the thirteenth, when his luck finally ran out.

Felix Mantilla tapped an easy grounder to Don Hoak at third, but his throw pulled Rocky Nelson off the bag. Eddie Mathews sacrificed Mantilla to second. Hank Aaron was intentionally walked to get to Joe Adcock—the man who had almost ended Haddix's career. Haddix was tired, understandably so, and threw a high slider that Adcock absolutely crushed. Aaron didn't see the ball clear the wall in right center field. After touching second base, he jogged off to the dugout, believing that the game had ended on a ground rule double. Mantilla scored, but Adcock was called out for passing Aaron on the bases. The home run was reduced to a double, and the final score was amended to 1–0.

After the game, Burdette commented sympathetically that Haddix "deserved to win." Joe Adcock echoed the sentiment. Haddix turned down offers to appear on numerous television shows. A year later, he would pitch brilliantly in the World Series against the Yankees, posting a 2–0 record with a 2.45 ERA. Virtually no one remembers that. To most fans of baseball history, he remains "Hard Luck Harvey," the only pitcher to lose a perfect game.

June 30, 1959

Wrigley Field in Chicago has been the site of some perplexing incidents over the years, but in terms of sheer confusion, few plays surpass the one that took place in the fourth inning of this game between the Cubs and Cardinals. St. Louis was leading 2–1 in the top of the fourth. Stan Musial was batting, and Chicago hurler Bob Anderson was behind in the count. During portions of six seasons in the Windy City, Anderson would post a .500 won-loss record just once. He wasn't helping his cause on this particular afternoon as his 3–1 offering went wild, getting a piece of catcher Sammy Taylor and umpire Vic Delmore before bouncing to the screen.

Instead of chasing down the errant pitch, Taylor opted to stand and argue that the ball had nicked Musial's bat. He would ultimately lose the debate. Musial took advantage of the situation, rounding first and heading for second. Perhaps distracted by Taylor's dialogue, Delmore handed the catcher another ball. Taylor then passed it to Anderson. While all this was transpiring, Al Dark rushed to the backstop in pursuit of the original ball. The batboy had gotten his hands on it and flipped it to field announcer Pat Piper. Dark scooped it up as it was rolling along the ground.

When Anderson saw Musial breaking for second, he threw to the bag with the newly acquired baseball. Dark had the same idea, firing to teammate Ernie Banks. The two throws took entirely different courses. Anderson's peg sailed into center field, where it was picked up by Bobby Thomson. Thomson tossed it into the Cubs dugout, hoping to dispose of the evidence. Dark's throw made it to second base in time to catch the sliding Musial. The umpires halted the action at that point to sort out the mess.

After a ten-minute delay, Musial was called out by Delmore despite dissention from Cardinals manager Solly Hemus, who lodged an official protest. Hemus withdrew his objection after St. Louis prevailed, 4–1, their fourth win in a row.

Part 5
THE EXPANSION ERA, 1960-1979

Timeline of Significant Events

1960 Branch Rickey's proposal for a third major league sets the wheels of expansion in motion. The old Senators will move to Minnesota and be replaced by a "new" Washington club. The Los Angeles Angels will boost the number of American League teams to ten.

1961 The regular season is extended to 162 games. Roger Maris breaks Babe Ruth's single-season record for homers with sixty-one. Ty Cobb dies.

1962 The Mets and Colt .45s make their NL debuts. Maury Wills raises the bar for stolen bases in a season with 104. Pittsburgh's Roy Face sets a new save record with twenty-eight. Jackie Robinson is elected to the Hall of Fame.

1963 The Mets lose twenty-two straight road games—a National League record. Warren Spahn notches his 327th career victory, the most by any left-hander.

1964 Shea Stadium opens. Jim Bunning throws a perfect game against the hapless Mets on June 21.

1965 Sandy Koufax establishes a record for strikeouts with 382. Satchel Paige becomes the oldest player to pitch in the majors at the age of fifty-nine. The Houston Astrodome opens.

1966 Frank Robinson of the Orioles captures a Triple Crown. Sandy Koufax wins twenty-seven games and then retires with an arthritic elbow. The first game on artificial turf is played at the Houston Astrodome.

1967 The American League has a Triple Crown winner for the second straight year as Carl Yastrzemski turns the trick.

1968 In what will come to be known as the "Year of the Pitcher," Denny McLain wins thirty-one games, Don Drysdale tosses fifty-eight consecutive scoreless innings, and a total of 339 shutouts are recorded.

1969 Four new teams join the major league ranks—the Padres, Expos, Royals, and Seattle Pilots. To boost offense, the height of the pitcher's mound is reduced along with the size of the strike zone. The League Championship Series is introduced.

1970 Curt Flood files a lawsuit against organized baseball, challenging the reserve contract clause. He loses the case. The Pilots move to Milwaukee, becoming the Brewers.

1971 The American League wins the All-Star Game for the first time since 1962. It won't win again until 1983. Ron Hunt of the Expos sets a painful single-season record by getting beaned fifty times. Later research will place his total at number two of all time behind Hughie Jennings of the Tigers.

1972   The first players' strike results in the cancellation of eighty-six games. As a concession, pension-fund payments are increased. The new Senators move to Texas, changing their name to the Rangers. Pirates great Roberto Clemente is killed in a plane crash on a humanitarian mission to Nicaragua.

1973   Nolan Ryan establishes a new single-season strikeout record with 383. The American League agrees to use designated hitters for a trial period.

1974   George Steinbrenner is suspended after making illegal contributions to the Nixon reelection campaign. Hank Aaron becomes the all-time home run king. A's owner Charles Finley experiments with a "designated runner," hiring world-class sprinter Herb Washington. Washington is released the following year.

1975   Frank Robinson is baseball's first black manager. Rennie Stennet of the Pirates collects seven hits in a nine-inning game.

1977   The Mariners and Blue Jays join the American League. Living up to his own hype, Reggie Jackson hits three consecutive World Series homers. He'll be known as "Mr. October" from that point on.

1978   Pete Rose hits in forty-four straight games, a modern National League record. Yankee hurler Ron Guidry strikes out eighteen batters in a game—the most by any left-hander at the time.

1979   Yankee captain Thurman Munson dies in a plane crash. Major league umpires go on strike for forty-five days, receiving a salary increase.

July 23, 1960

Apparently, Jimmy Piersall wasn't taking his meds at the start of the 1960 slate. During a Memorial Day doubleheader, the erratic outfielder (who was suffering from bipolar disorder) threw an orange at Bill Veeck's exploding scoreboard in Comiskey Park. In another outrageous stunt, he brought a can of insecticide into the outfield and used it to spray bugs while a game was in progress. He earned a slew of ejections before Indians team physician Donald Kelly ordered him to undergo psychiatric treatment on June 26. A week earlier, a *Sports Illustrated* article had described his unpredictable behavior as "sensational, irritating, colorful, heroic and comical."

Piersall was up to the same old tricks when he returned to action a month later. During a July 23 game at Fenway Park, he tried to distract Ted Williams by performing what various sources have referred to as a "war dance," waving his arms and jumping up and down while running around in the outfield. He went through the same routine during multiple at bats by Williams before plate umpire Ed Hurley finally threw him out of the game. Cleveland manager Joe Gordon had threatened Piersall with a $300 fine for his next ejection but ended up getting tossed out himself while arguing that his eccentric center fielder had a right to do what he was doing. A famous photo captured a wild-eyed Piersall being restrained by Indians first baseman Vic Power after his eighth-inning dismissal. Piersall's antics did little to deter Williams, who drew a walk and a homer during the outfielder's performances. The Indians won the game, 4–2.

August 28, 1960

The White Sox had reason to feel cheated on this date. Trailing 3–1 to the Orioles in the eighth inning of a game at Memorial Stadium, pinch hitter Ted Kluszewski drilled a three-run homer into the right-field seats. But home plate umpire Ed Hurley had declared "no pitch" before Milt Pappas's offering when he noticed Floyd Robinson and Earl Torgeson warming up on the right-field sidelines outside the designated area. The White Sox argued for more than ten minutes, and second baseman Nellie Fox got tossed. When "Big Klu" stepped back into the batter's box, he lined out to center field, ending the inning. Chicago manager Al Lopez protested the 3–1 loss, but his complaint was overturned.

Yankees manager Billy Martin stole a win from the Brewers in similar fashion during the 1976 slate. On the second day of the season, Don Money of Milwaukee hit what appeared to be a game-winning grand slam. Having seen his team rally from a 6–0 deficit, Martin was not ready to concede defeat. He charged out of the dugout and confronted umpire Jim McKean, claiming that time had been called for by Yankees first baseman Chris Chambliss prior to pitcher Dave Pagan's windup. McKean admitted that he had approved the time out and, in a rare reverse ruling, discounted the homer. Money flied out to right, and the Yankees ended up winning the game, 9–7. Brewers first-base coach Harvey Keunn disputed the decision. "I did hear Chambliss call for time, but I never heard the umpire call it," he told reporters afterward.

June 29, 1961

In one of the worst cases of overmanaging ever, Gene Mauch of the Phillies engaged in a battle of wits with Alvin Dark of the Giants in the early going of a game at Connie Mack Stadium. With his club mired in last place, Mauch tried to hide the identity of his starting pitcher by penciling four hurlers into the lineup at various defensive stations. His original lineup card had Don Ferrarese batting first and playing center field, Jim Owens hitting third and playing in right, Chris Short catching while hitting out of the seventh slot, and Ken Lehman slated to pitch. Before the Giants came to bat in the first inning, Mauch replaced Ferrarese, Owens, and Short. Lehman faced two batters before giving way to Dallas Green. In the bottom of the first, Dark employed a strategy of his own, pulling southpaw Billy O'Dell after one batter and replacing him with right-hander Sam Jones. Mauch's clever subterfuge failed to work as the Phillies dropped both games of this doubleheader, 8–7 and 4–1.

The Phillies would lose fourteen of fifteen games between June 29 and July 13, but they were just getting warmed up. Beginning on July 29, they would assemble an astounding streak of twenty-three straight defeats. Mauch would remain at the Philly helm for nine seasons, guiding the club to a winning record on six occasions.

July 7, 1961

Wet conditions in Baltimore washed out the second game of a twi-night doubleheader between the Yankees and Orioles at Baltimore. The contest was halted before it was official, nullifying homers hit by Mickey Mantle and Roger Maris. The rainout became historically significant when Maris went on to break Babe Ruth's single-season home run record that year with sixty-one.

The homer would have been Maris's thirty-third of the season. Not only would it have padded the all-time mark, it would also have allowed him to tie Ruth's record several days sooner, though not before the 154-game cutoff. Maris's chase for immortality has become a well-weathered tale—how he suffered the ignominy of having an asterisk placed next to his record by Commissioner Ford Frick because it took him 161 games to accomplish what Ruth had attained in a 154-game season. The pressure of being in the spotlight bothered the media-shy Maris, who was interrogated by reporters on a daily basis. He was under intense scrutiny and pressure, his hair actually began to fall out in clumps.

At times, the strain was quite evident. After a September doubleheader during which Maris had failed to go deep, an army of reporters ambushed him at his locker. The slugger pointed to teammate Elston Howard, who had the adjoining locker, and said bitterly: "He hit a homer, not me. Mr. Howard, why don't you tell these gentlemen about it."

"If I had fifty-five homers, I'd be glad to tell the gentlemen," Howard replied pleasantly.

"Fifty-six!" Maris barked at him. "What are you trying to do—shortchange me?"

September 10, 1961

The Jimmy Piersall saga continued during a doubleheader at Yankee Stadium. On September 8, Piersall had attended the funeral of his father, who had died unexpectedly of a heart attack. In the opening game of this twin bill, the grieving Cleveland outfielder became the target of fan abuse when two spectators rushed onto the field and accosted him. He held his own, knocking one of them down with a punch and then throwing a kick at the other. The entire Indians team rushed to his aid. After the game, he issued a warning to fans that he would swing at anyone who came after him. "I've had 117 fights," he joked with reporters, "and this is my first victory." Nearly every major newspaper in the United States printed a wire photo of the incident.

The second game was equally eventful. The Yankees were leading 4–2 in the sixth and had two men on when third baseman Clete Boyer drove a Jim Perry pitch high into the left-field corner. The ball hit the lower deck and bounced back into fair territory. It was initially ruled a home run by plate umpire Joe Linsalata, but second-base ump Charlie Berry indicated that the ball was in play. Jimmy Piersall, who was not in the lineup, came running out of the bullpen to argue the ruling along with Cleveland manager Jimmy Dykes. In the meantime, the ball was relayed to third baseman Mike de la Hoz, who tagged Boyer out in the middle of his home-run trot. The umpires allowed the out to stand.

The crowd of fifty-eight thousand voiced its disapproval, booing for nearly twenty minutes. Some unruly patrons threw garbage onto the field. Berry, the senior official, assumed responsibility for the blown call. "I waved the ball in play but I didn't make a clear signal and [third-base umpire] Umont misinterpreted it." The Yankees swept the doubleheader by scores of 7–6 and 9–3.

June 23, 1963

Jimmy Piersall captured headlines yet again when he collected his hundredth career circuit blast. It wasn't the hit itself that drew the attention of fans and journalists. In fact, the homer—Piersall's first as a member of the New York Mets—barely cleared the 260-foot foul pole in right field at the Polo Grounds. It was the way Piersall ran the bases that became a conversation piece. After the ball landed in the seats, he proceeded to touch the bags in proper order while running backward—a stunt he had promised to deliver long before he reached the career milestone.

Piersall's "bloop" homer came off of Philly hurler Dallas Green and put the Mets ahead, 2–0. Though Piersall received no formal reprimand,

Commissioner Ford Frick was displeased with the center fielder's antics. An inside source commented, "If Piersall ever does it again, he will hear about it. But then he probably won't hit another one hundred, so the subject won't come up." As predicted, Piersall gathered just four more homers before retiring.

April 23, 1964

The 1964 Houston Colt .45s were an offensively challenged club, averaging fewer runs per game than any team in the majors while compiling the lowest cumulative batting average. No one felt the sting of this more than Ken Johnson, who became the first (and to date the only) pitcher in big league history to lose a nine-inning complete game no-hitter. The disparaging defeat occurred on April 23 against the Reds.

Johnson, a thirty-one-year-old right-hander playing in his seventh season, was masterful that day, striking out nine while issuing just two walks. But his team provided little support, scattering five hits off of Cincy's Joe Nuxhall. With one away in the top of the ninth, Johnson threw wildly to first on a bunt by Pete Rose. Rose advanced to second and then moved to third on a hard grounder by Chico Ruiz. Vada Pinson followed with a routine grounder that was booted by Hall of Fame second baseman Nellie Fox. Rose scored the only run of the game on the play.

"I told Nellie it wasn't his fault," Johnson commented after the game. "It was mine. I put the guy on base and have no one to blame but myself." Asked how he felt about the loss, the hurler said it was "a helluva way to get into the record books." He never came terribly close to pitching another no-hitter, though he did turn in a pair of four-hit complete game efforts—one in 1964 and another in 1966.

August 22, 1965

A shocking display of on-field violence occurred during a game between the Giants and Dodgers at Candlestick Park in San Francisco. There was no love lost between the two clubs, which had battled for supremacy of New York for many years before expansion moved them out West. The 1965 pennant race was tight, and the Dodgers were clinging to a slender half-game lead over the Braves entering this contest. The Giants were finishing up a four-game set with their dreaded rivals that had brought them within a game and a half of the division lead.

Both clubs sent their aces to the hill—Sandy Koufax for Los Angeles and Juan Marichal for San Francisco. The tone had been set two days earlier when

Dodger shortstop Maury Wills made contact with the glove of catcher Tom Haller on a backswing. In the next inning, San Francisco's Matty Alou clipped the glove of John Roseboro, leading the veteran backstop to believe that the act was intentional. The vindictive tone carried over into the series finale.

The largest crowd of the season turned out to see the action. Working on three days of rest, Marichal didn't have his best stuff. Maury Wills led off with a bunt single and then advanced to second on a groundout. An RBI double by Ron Fairly put the Dodgers ahead, 1–0.

In the second inning, LA plated another run on a double by Wes Parker and a single by catcher John Roseboro. When Maury Wills made his second plate appearance, Marichal dusted him off with an inside fastball. Ron Fairly was treated to the same in the top of the third. The game soon turned ugly.

Marichal was due to lead off for the Giants in the bottom of the frame, and Roseboro wanted payback. Since Koufax was not in the habit of brushing back hitters, Roseboro took matters into his own hands, grazing Marichal's ear with a carefully placed return throw to the mound. The exasperated hurler clubbed Roseboro over the head with his bat, opening up a cut that would require medical attention. Blood poured down Roseboro's face as both benches emptied.

The game was delayed for roughly fifteen minutes. When play resumed, Koufax surrendered a three-run blast to Willie Mays that would prove to be the game winner. Mays's clutch homer was, of course, overshadowed by accounts of the brawl. Photos of the incident adorned countless newspapers.

The following day, Marichal issued a public apology. He was suspended for eight games and fined $1,750. Roseboro was back in the Dodger lineup within three days. He sued Marichal for $110,000 in damages but settled for much less when the case was finally adjudicated. The two later became friends.

September 8, 1965

Charlie Finley got rich selling insurance. He then became one of the most innovative promoters in baseball history. After trying unsuccessfully to purchase the Tigers and White Sox, he was initially outbid for the Kansas City A's by wealthy entrepreneur Arnold Johnson in 1960. Biding his time, Finley scooped up a majority of the club's stock when Johnson passed away.

The once proud A's had become little more than a farm team for the Yankees over the years. Finley put an end to the frequent roster raids and began to develop young talent. He also attempted to lure fans through the turnstiles by creating a carnival-like atmosphere. Dressing his players in tacky green and yellow uniforms, he placed sheep with dyed wool (tended by a shepherd) in a pasture beyond the right-field fence. He carried the animal motif to an extreme, setting up a children's zoo in left field and installing a mechanical rabbit named Harvey behind home plate. With a push of a button, "Harvey" popped up and handed baseballs to umpires. Finley later appointed a mule named Charley O as team mascot, allowing the creature to travel with the club and stay in the team's hotel.

There was virtually no limit to how far Finley would go. He even released an armada of helium balloons containing A's tickets into the countryside one day. Not all of Finley's employees were appreciative of his screwball ideas. Coach Whitey Herzog once commented: "This is nothing more than a damned sideshow. Winning over here is a joke."

One of Finley's most curious stunts took place on September 8, 1965, when he announced "Campy Campaneris Night," a promotion designed to showcase the talents of the Athletics' fastest-rising star. Joining the club in 1964, Bert Campaneris would steal at least fifty bases in five consecutive seasons before retiring with a grand total of 649 (among the top twenty marks of all time). On the date in question, the twenty-three-year-old shortstop demonstrated his versatility by changing positions every inning.

In the first, "Campy" enjoyed a quiet inning at his primary defensive station. In the second, he shifted to second base and recorded an assist. In the third frame, he had an uneventful stint at the hot corner. In the fourth, he moved to left field and registered a putout on a fly ball. He duplicated the feat in center field during the following frame, but things turned sour in the sixth, when he muffed a pop fly by Jim Fregosi while stationed in right. Albie Pearson scored on the play, putting the Angels ahead, 2–1.

The most challenging duties were yet to come for Campaneris. In the eighth, he completed his first and only career pitching assignment. He faced five batters in all, yielding a run on a hit and two walks. A ninth-inning catching stint was equally hectic as the Angels tried to take advantage of him with a double steal. "Campy" threw to Dick Green at second as outfielder Ed Kirkpatrick came barreling home. Green's return throw was in plenty of time, and after a hard collision at the plate, Campaneris held onto the ball. The star of Finley's wild promotion celebrated his remarkable single-game accomplishment with a set of X-rays at a nearby hospital. They turned up negative. The Angels eventually won the game in thirteen innings, 5–3.

Finley's elaborate schemes failed to boost attendance in Kansas City, but his luck changed after the team moved to Oakland. With the addition of stars such as Reggie Jackson, Catfish Hunter, and Rollie Fingers, the A's would become the only team aside from the New York Yankees to win three consecutive World Series, from 1972 through 1974.

October 6, 1966

Senators shortstop Roger Peckinpaugh set the all-time record for defensive futility in a World Series when he committed eight errors in the 1925 Fall Classic. Dodgers outfielder Willie Davis was on pace to shatter that record when he made three blunders in a single inning during the 1966 October showcase.

Davis was a competent offensive presence in the Los Angeles lineup. He didn't always hit for a high average, but he had good speed on the bases, swiping at least twenty bags in eleven straight seasons. He was nicknamed "3-Dog" for his ability to leg out triples. He demonstrated excellent range in the outfield but was known to get clumsy from time to time, leading NL center fielders in errors on five occasions. In game 2 of the 1966 Fall Classic, he had an epic defensive meltdown the likes of which had never been seen.

The Orioles held a one-game edge in the Series, having beaten Don Drysdale 5–2 in the opener at Dodger Stadium. The matchup for game 2 pitted Sandy Koufax against Jim Palmer. The two Hall of Famers were at opposite ends of their careers. Koufax was playing in his last season while the twenty-year-old Palmer had enjoyed a breakthrough year, posting fifteen wins. The game remained scoreless until the top of the fifth, when Davis tried to unseat Peckinpaugh as the king of October muffs.

Boog Powell opened with the Orioles' second hit of the game—a single to left. After Lou Johnson popped out on a poorly executed sacrifice bunt, Paul Blair lifted a routine fly to center field. Davis lost it in the sun and Blair ended up on second. Andy Etchebarren followed with another lazy fly to Davis, who again failed to make the play. Powell scored easily, and in his haste to cut down Blair at third, Davis threw the ball away. Blair plated the second unearned run of the frame. Luis Aparicio later doubled Etchebarren home before Koufax retired the side.

Davis was treated to a chorus of boos. Between innings, he skulked to the dugout and apologized to Koufax.

"Don't let it get you down," the congenial hurler replied.

"Hell, forget it," fellow Hall of Famer Don Drysdale added, "You've saved plenty of games with great catches."

Perhaps overcompensating for his fifth-inning gaffes, Davis called Ron Fairly off of a fly ball hit by Frank Robinson at the start of the sixth. Fairly could have made the play but allowed himself to be run off by Davis, who failed to snare the ball. Robinson ended up with a triple and later scored on a single by Boog Powell. Davis was not officially credited with an error, but it was a clear lapse of judgment. Baltimore went on to win the game handily, 6–0.

In 1971, Davis joined a Buddhist sect and could be found in the locker room before games chanting with prayer beads. The extent to which this helped his defense is undetermined, but he did win a Gold Glove Award that year. Some teammates openly complained about the chanting, while others were amused by it.

July 15, 1967

Some pitchers are tougher than others. Bobo Newsom of the Senators pitched a complete game shutout on opening day of the 1936 slate after his jaw had been fractured in two places. Curt Schilling hurled six strong innings for the Red Sox in game 2 of the 2004 World Series despite a serious ankle injury that left him with a bloody sock. On July 15, 1967, Bob Gibson faced three batters with a broken leg!

Known for his intimidating scowl and propensity for throwing at hitters, Gibson was one of the fiercest competitors ever to take the hill. Although he pitched in an era of relief specialists, he still finished more than 50 percent of his career starts. On the date in question, he literally pitched until he dropped.

The Cardinals were ahead, 1–0, in the top of the fourth at Busch Stadium when Roberto Clemente of the Pirates hit a hard liner back to the box and fractured Gibson's right fibula. Incredibly, the hard-nosed hurler soldiered on. Willie Stargell drew a walk. Bill Mazeroski flew out to center, and Donn Clendenon worked another free pass. After throwing ball four, Gibson literally collapsed. He was charged with one earned run as Gene Alley lofted a sacrifice fly to center field, scoring Clemente. The Pirates won, 6–4.

Gibson was out until Labor Day and won three of his remaining four decisions. He was lights out in the World Series that year, compiling a 3–0 record with a 1.00 ERA in the Cardinals seven-game triumph over the Boston Red Sox. Fittingly, he was named Series MVP.

May 2, 1968

During the 1968 campaign, major league baseball toughened its stance against spitballs, prohibiting hurlers from wetting their fingers with their mouths within an eighteen-foot circle around the pitcher's mound. Whenever a pitcher was caught doing so, umpires were obligated to rule the subsequent pitch a ball. During a game between the Phillies and Mets at Shea Stadium, umpire Ed Vargo carried this regulation to an extreme.

Trailing the Mets 3–0 in the seventh, Philly manager Gene Mauch replaced starter Woodie Fryman with a pinch hitter. Right-hander John Boozer assumed pitching responsibilities in the bottom of the frame. When Boozer went to his mouth while warming up, Vargo surprised everyone by declaring,

"Ball one!" Mauch came rushing out of the dugout to protest and the arbiter explained that Boozer had violated the new spitball rule. The disgruntled skipper insisted that the statute did not apply to warm-up pitches and inquired hypothetically what would happen if Boozer went to his mouth again. Vargo assured Mauch he would call "ball two."

Pushing the envelope, Mauch encouraged Boozer to do it again. As promised, the arbiter ran the count up to 2–0. When Boozer went to his mouth a third time at Mauch's bidding, Vargo tossed both men out of the game. He then warned reliever Dick Hall not to try anything funny. This brought Mauch out of the dugout again despite his ejection. With an official protest now in place, the light-hitting Bud Harrelson stepped up to the plate with the distinct advantage of a 3–0 count. He failed to make the most of it, grounding back to the box. Hall shut out the New Yorkers the rest of the way in a 3–0 loss.

After the game, Hall joked that just knowing he couldn't wet his fingers had caused his mouth to water. Mauch commented irritably that he had witnessed cases of overmanaging but had never been a victim of overumpiring. The next day, NL president Warren Giles instructed Mauch not to bother drafting a protest letter since the incident in question had no effect on the game's outcome. Giles did caution umpires that pitchers should not be penalized during warm-ups.

June 8, 1968

Dodger hurler Don Drysdale was one of the most intimidating pitchers of the expansion era. Unafraid to move batters off the plate, he led the league in beanings five times during his career. This included a run of four straight seasons from 1958 through 1961. Mickey Mantle once groused that "after he hit you, he'd come around, look at the bruise on your arm and say, 'You want me to sign it?'"

In 1968, Drysdale's period of dominance reached a peak when he broke Walter Johnson's all-time record of 55.2 consecutive scoreless innings. Drysdale had a little assistance along the way. On May 31, the streak stood at forty-four when the Giants loaded the bases against him with no outs in the ninth. San Francisco catcher Dick Dietz ran up a 2-2 count before he was hit on the elbow with a Drysdale slider. The streak should have ended there, but umpire Harry Wendelstedt invoked a rare ruling, declaring "no pitch" on the grounds that Dietz had made no attempt to get out of the way. Ron Hunt, who was watching from the Giants' dugout, commented years later that Dietz "stood there like a post." Forced to hit again, the backstop lifted a fly ball that was too shallow to advance the runners. Drysdale disposed of the next two batters, keeping the streak alive.

After six consecutive shutouts and four scoreless frames against the Phillies on June 8, Drysdale's incredible run finally ended. With two outs in the fifth inning, Philly outfielder Howie Bedell, recently called up from the minors, hit a sacrifice fly, chasing Tony Taylor across the plate. After Taylor scored, Philadelphia skipper Gene Mauch accused the moundsman of doctoring the baseball. Umpire Augie Donatelli inspected Drysdale's left wrist and hair. He warned "Big D" not to touch the back of his head with his right hand or he would be ejected. Drysdale later spoke at length about the "mental strain" the streak had on him. "I could feel myself go blah when the run scored," he said. "I just let down emotionally."

The record stood until 1988, when another Dodger hurler, Orel Hershiser, extended it to fifty-nine scoreless innings. Interestingly, Hershiser received a little help from an umpire just as Drysdale had. During his last start of the regular season on September 28, arbiter Paul Runge made a controversial interference call at second base on a run-scoring double play to keep Hershiser's streak alive. The hurler put up zeroes for ten innings that day to set the all-time mark.

September 19, 1968

Two milestones were reached at Tiger Stadium in Detroit. Denny McLain recorded his thirty-first win of the season, a mark that has not been surpassed by any major league hurler since. McLain was overshadowed by Mickey Mantle, who blasted the 535th home run of his career, breaking a tie with Jimmie Foxx for third place on the all-time list. The homer came gift wrapped from McLain.

The Tigers were leading 6–1 in the eighth when Mantle came to bat for the fourth time. In the 2002 videography *The American Dream Comes to Life*, Mantle recalled that McLain held a conference with his catcher before the at bat (though Mantle's memory was a bit faulty—he said that Bill Freehan was catching when in fact it was Jim Price). When Price returned to the plate, he informed Mantle that McLain would be throwing nothing but fastballs. Mantle was skeptical and took the first pitch—a fastball right down the middle—for a strike. When McLain gave him a funny look as if to say, "What was wrong with that one?" Mantle knew the fix was on. He overswung at the second offering and fouled it back. He launched the next pitch into the upper deck.

Mantle remembered his trip around the bases as follows: "I'm going around first and second and I kind of peek out at [McLain] and he's looking and grinning. . . . When I come around third, he gives me a big wink." According to multiple sources, Mantle tipped his cap at the hurler in gratitude. A famous photo of the incident shows that the stadium was virtually empty. The attendance was reported at 9,063—surprising, considering that the Tigers were in first place and would win the pennant and World Series that year. On an amusing final note, Joe Pepitone stepped into the box after Mantle and indicated to McLain where he would like the ball. McLain promptly dusted him off.

April 25, 1970

A highly unusual play transpired in a game between the Twins and Tigers at Metropolitan Stadium in Minnesota. With his team trailing 2–1 in the top of the seventh, Detroit pitcher Earl Wilson struck out to end the frame. Twins catcher Paul Ratliff trapped the ball in the dirt, and according to the rules, he was obligated to either tag Wilson or throw to first. Instead, he chose to ignore the situation, rolling the ball back to the mound.

Realizing there had been no call from home-plate umpire John Rice, Wilson alertly began circling the bases while members of the Minnesota squad headed for the dugout. Fortunately for the Twins, not everyone on the field had fallen asleep on the play. As Wilson was rounding second, outfielder Brant Alyea heard Tigers third-base coach Grover Resinger shouting at the runner to keep going. Alyea rushed to the mound to pick up the ball as shortstop Leo Cardenas covered the plate. Alyea had trouble getting control of the ball, and Wilson made it partway home before getting trapped in a rundown. He was tagged out, pulling a hamstring on the play. The Tigers rallied to tie the game after Wilson was removed, but the Twins held on for a 4–3 win.

May 16, 1970

A foul ball hit into the stands normally ends up as a souvenir for a happy fan. On this day, a liner off the bat of Manny Mota became a deadly projectile. The tragedy took place during the bottom of the third inning at Dodger Stadium. Maury Wills opened the frame with a double off of Giants ace Gaylord Perry. Mota came to the plate next and ripped a foul ball along the first baseline near the visiting team dugout. The ball struck a fourteen-year-old fan named Alan Fish.

Fish was sitting in the second row with several other boys from his neighborhood near Santa Monica. The boys were being supervised by David Schur, assistant director of the Poinsettia Park Rec Center. Fish didn't even see the ball coming as it struck him squarely in the left temple. He was unconscious for roughly one minute, and on waking, he exhibited labored speech. An icepack was provided by someone in the visiting team dugout, and the boy quickly regained his faculties. He claimed to be okay, but as a precautionary measure, he was taken to a first-aid station and given two aspirin. He stayed to watch the rest of the game.

On arriving home, Fish became extremely disoriented and began exhibiting odd behavior. His parents rushed him to the hospital, believing he had a concussion. What he had was much worse—an inoperable head injury that cost him his life four days later. Manny Mota tried to visit the boy in the hospital but was thwarted in his attempt. The Dodgers offered prayers and words of consolation. Fish's parents sued the organization anyway.

June 12, 1970

Dock Ellis was an occasionally dominant presence on the mound, winning at least fifteen games three times and making one All-Star appearance during his twelve-year career. During the 1970 campaign, he carved a small niche in baseball history when he tossed a no-hitter against the San Diego Padres. It wasn't pretty as he fell behind hitters all evening, walking eight and hitting one. But the performance became quite remarkable fourteen years later when Ellis admitted to being under the influence of LSD at the time.

A free spirit, Ellis allegedly ingested the drug around noon, believing he was not scheduled to start that day. About an hour later, his girlfriend was perusing a newspaper when she discovered that Ellis was listed as a probable starter for the first game of a twi-night doubleheader against the Padres. She escorted the Pirates hurler, who was now feeling the effects of a powerful hallucinogen known as "Purple Haze," to the airport, where he caught a flight to San Diego.

Ellis remembered very little of the game, which started at 6:05 p.m. He described his mood as euphoric and reported various hallucinations. "The ball was small sometimes, the ball was large sometimes. Sometimes I saw the catcher, sometimes I didn't," he alleged. Years later, he embellished the story even further, claiming that he saw Jimi Hendrix and Richard Nixon at different points in the game. He said that Hendrix was using his famous Stratocaster guitar as a bat and Nixon was the home-plate umpire.

Snopes.com—a website that prides itself on debunking urban myths— posted the story's status as "true," though from a guarded perspective. Ellis's behavior was normal enough not to arouse suspicion from players or umpires. He was lucid during postgame interviews. But what would his motivation be for making such a claim? It only served to tarnish the crowning achievement of his career.

After his playing days were over, Ellis sought help for his substance abuse. He later worked as a counselor to help others combat drug problems. He died in 2008.

July 14, 1970

In 2003, Major League Baseball announced that the All-Star Game victors would receive home-field advantage in the World Series. Before then, there was very little to play for except bragging rights. That's why many fans and participants were somewhat dumbfounded by the play that decided the 1970 Midsummer Classic.

Though baseball had become a kinder, gentler game in many respects by 1970, Pete Rose proved he was old school all the way when he nearly ended the career of Indians catcher Ray Fosse. With the score knotted at 4 in the bottom of the twelfth, Rose lined a two-out single to center field. He moved to second on a Billy Grabarkewitz single. Jim Hickman then dropped another hit in front of center fielder Amos Otis. Rose, who had received the green light from third-base coach Leo Durocher, decided on the way to the plate that he was going in standing up. Fosse came up the line to receive Otis's throw as Rose literally knocked him for a loop, delivering the winning run in an unforgettable 5–4 NL victory.

Whether or not Rose used excessive force has been a source of endless debate since then. According to multiple sources, the impact of the collision separated Fosse's shoulder, but the area was so swollen that initial X-rays failed to reveal the full extent of the damage. Fosse kept playing, aggravating the injury and weakening his swing. After 1970, he never hit more than twelve home runs in a season. His days as a first-string catcher were over by 1974. Years later, Rose remained glib about the incident, joking that if it weren't for him, no one would ever have heard of Ray Fosse.

October 10, 1970

Umpire Ken Burkhart entered the realms of baseball infamy when he made one of the worst calls in World Series history during game 1 of the 1970 October showcase. The score was tied at 3 in the bottom of the sixth at Cincinnati's Riverfront Stadium. Bernie Carbo drew a one-out walk off of future Cooperstown inductee Jim Palmer. Tommy Helms followed with a single that sent Carbo to third, putting Palmer in a serious jam. Reds skipper Sparky Anderson sent Ty Cline to the plate in place of light-hitting shortstop Woody Woodward. Acquired from the Expos in June, Cline's .277 batting average was preferable to the .223 mark put up by the offensively challenged Woodward during the regular season. The play that followed would be re-hashed for years to come.

Cline hit a chopper near home plate. Orioles backstop Ellie Hendricks came out to field the ball as Bernie Carbo came flying home. Burkhart had positioned himself to make a fair or foul ruling on Cline's tapper and was blocking the plate. Carbo attempted a hook slide around the official as Hendricks dove toward the runner with his glove out. Burkhart was in no position to make the call at that point with his back to the play, but he ruled Carbo out. Replays clearly showed that Hendricks tagged Carbo with an empty glove as he held the ball in his right hand. Carbo touched home plate coincidentally when he argued the decision. The game was decided on a Brooks Robinson homer in the seventh as the Orioles won a nail-biter, 4–3. Demoralized, the Reds dropped the Series in five games.

A former major league pitcher, Burkhart served as an umpire in six All-Star Games and three World Series. He was elected to the Knoxville and Tennessee Sports Hall of Fame. Still, the blown call remained a blemish on his record. It was even mentioned in his 2004 obituary.

October 18, 1972

Of all the dirty tricks . . .

A's manager Dick Williams proved he was willing to go to any extreme to win a World Series. Trailing the Reds 1–0 in the eighth inning of game 3 at Oakland Coliseum, he came up with a devious scheme. Joe Morgan was on third and Bobby Tolan was on second with one out. Johnny Bench had worked the count full against Rollie Fingers when Williams called a mound conference. Turning his back on conventional strategy, Williams instructed catcher Gene Tenace to set up for an intentional walk. The move was just a decoy as Fingers was ordered to throw a strike.

The right-handed relief specialist could scarcely believe his ears, commenting incredulously, "Is this Little League or what?" Williams assured him the ruse would work but cautioned Fingers not to throw a fastball, since Bench habitually feasted on them. (His exact words were: "If it's a fastball and somebody figures out what we're doing, Bench can hit the shit out of it.") Following orders, Tenace stood behind the plate, motioning for a free pass. He got into his crouch just in time to catch strike three from Fingers. The hurler later described the pitch as the best slider he had ever thrown.

Despite Williams's underhanded tactic, which he claimed to have borrowed from former Cardinals manager Billy Southworth, the A's lost the game, 1–0. Oakland would go on to win the Series by a 4–3 margin. According to Fingers, Bench continued to bring up the incident for many years, describing it as "the most embarrassing moment" of his life. Bench had nothing to be ashamed of as he won ten Gold Gloves, was named to fourteen All-Star teams, and captured MVP honors twice.

July 15, 1973

Among the most dominant strikeout artists in history, Nolan Ryan set an all-time record with seven career no-hitters. His fastball was once (unofficially) clocked at 102.5 miles per hour. 1973 was a banner year for the right-handed flamethrower as he landed on a very short list of players to record multiple no-no's in a single season. The first gem occurred on May 15 before a scattering of fans at Royals Stadium. The second came on July 15 in front of more than forty thousand witnesses in Detroit.

Ryan mowed down the competition all afternoon, recording seventeen strikeouts—the most ever for a nine-inning no-hitter. But the game is best remembered for a moment of comic relief provided by Tigers first baseman Norm Cash. Dubbed "Stormin' Norman" by broadcaster Ernie Harwell, Cash had captured a batting title in 1961. He never came terribly close to repeating the performance at any other point during his career, but he endeared himself to fans and teammates with his unique sense of humor. He once called for time after getting hung up between first and second base. On another occasion, he was stationed at second before a rain delay. When play resumed, he went to third and told the umpire he had stolen the base during the downpour.

By the time Cash came to the plate with two out in the bottom of the ninth during Ryan's 1973 masterpiece, he had struck out twice. Making a bold and comical statement, he came to the plate with a table leg he had retrieved from the clubhouse. Umpire Ron Luciano noticed the implement almost immediately and, after laughing heartily, ordered Cash to replace it.

"Why? I'm not going to hit him anyway," Cash protested.

Luciano stood his ground.

After returning from the dugout with a regulation bat, Cash promptly popped out to shortstop Rudy Meoli, ending the game. Video footage of the slapstick incident exists.

October 8, 1973

Another unpleasant scene involving Pete Rose occurred during the 1973 National League playoffs. The series was tied at one game apiece, and the Mets had just dealt the Reds a 5–0 loss in the second contest. Before game 3,

New York's weak-hitting shortstop Bud Harrelson joked in self-deprecating fashion that the Reds resembled him at the plate (he finished with a lifetime .236 average). Hall of Famer Joe Morgan took offense to the comment and confronted Harrelson. The two ironed out their differences, but Morgan warned him that Pete Rose was still irritated and would be looking for a way to get at Harrelson on the base paths. After the Mets had jumped out to a comfortable 9–2 lead, Rose followed through, knocking the diminutive infielder flat while breaking up a double play. Rose was solidly built at five foot eleven and two hundred pounds. Harrelson had earned the nicknames "Twiggy" and "Mighty Mouse" for his slight 160-pound frame. When Rose tangled with Harrelson at second base, he came across as a bully.

The benches emptied, and Cincinnati reliever Pedro Borbon sucker punched Mets hurler Buzz Capra. Fans went ballistic—especially in the left-field stands, where someone threw a whiskey bottle that barely missed Rose's head. An announcement over the PA system cautioned fans to stop or risk a forfeit. NL president Chub Feeney, who was sitting near the Mets dugout, asked manager Yogi Berra to talk to the fans. Accompanied by several players, Yogi honored the request. The game eventually resumed, and the Mets won, 9–2. They advanced to the World Series against the A's, losing in seven games.

April 9, 1974

Founded in 1969, the Padres lost no fewer than ninety-five games and finished last in the NL West every year during their first five seasons. Off to a poor start again in 1974, they dropped their first three games by a combined score of 25–2. When they fell behind the Astros, 9–2, in the home opener on April 9, owner Ray Kroc lost his cool.

Kroc got on the PA system and said: "Ladies and gentlemen, I suffer with you." The moment became surreal when a streaker suddenly ran across the diamond. "Get that streaker out of here! Throw him in jail!" the disgruntled owner shouted before continuing his speech. "I have good news and bad news," he told the crowd of thirty-nine thousand. "We have outdrawn the Dodgers. . . . The bad news is I've never seen such stupid ball playing in my life."

The reaction to Kroc's invective was resoundingly negative. Padres slugger Willie McCovey deeply resented the remarks and commented that the words would "ring in players' ears for a long time." Astros player rep Denis Menke said that Kroc had "ruined a big night" in San Diego, while Padres manager Preston Gomez stated bluntly, "Somebody has to talk to that man."

Saving a little face, the Padres rallied for three runs after Kroc had said his piece. They lost anyway, 9–5. The club would not even break the .500 mark until 1978.

April 14, 1974

The Tigers were trailing the Red Sox, 7–5, in the ninth inning at Fenway Park when a bizarre and unfortunate event took place. With two outs and two runners on, Detroit left fielder Willie Horton hit a foul pop that struck a pigeon flying over the stadium. The bird was killed instantly, and the carcass dropped in front of home plate just inches from catcher Bob Montgomery. "It scared the hell out of me," Montgomery admitted. "I jumped about a foot in the air and Willie jumped even higher."

When play resumed, Horton singled to load the bases. Reliever Diego Segui then struck out Norm Cash, ending the game in favor of Boston. The peculiar scene was not the only curiosity in the majors that day. In San Diego, a swarm of bees congregated around home plate. Umpire Doug Harvey, who had suffered an adverse reaction to a bee sting the previous winter, wasn't taking any chances. An exterminator was summoned to get rid of the pests. The game, which pitted the Padres against the Giants, was interrupted for more than thirty minutes.

June 4, 1974

With attendance sagging dramatically in Cleveland during the 1974 slate, executive vice president Ted Bonda called his board of directors together for a brainstorming session. Someone suggested they follow the example of the Texas Rangers, who had hosted a successful "Ten-Cent Beer Night." The board agreed, and the date for the promotion was set for June 4. It was one of the worst ideas ever hatched.

For starters, the Indians neglected to request the presence of the Cleveland police. There were few, if any, on-duty officers at the stadium to help control the crowd of more than twenty-five thousand. There were also no rules in place to control the purchase of beer. Fans were permitted to buy up to six cups at a time. The park was soon filled with two-fisted drinkers, many of whom got in the habit of buying the allotted six and handing them off to companions while they went back for more.

The choice of opponents was awkward as well. Just days before, a full-scale brawl had erupted between the Indians and Rangers at Arlington Stadium. There were still some hard feelings between the two clubs when Texas arrived on June 4 for a three-game set.

Examples of unruly fan behavior during the game were numerous. In the early going, a woman ran into the Indians' on-deck circle and bared her breasts. In the top of the fourth inning, a naked man slid into second base. In the bottom of the frame, the crowd joined together in a hostile chant when Texas pitcher

Fergie Jenkins was struck in the stomach by a line drive. The stadium shook with a refrain of "Hit him again! Hit him again! Harder! Harder!"

The keg party continued in the fifth, when two more men hopped over the wall and mooned Rangers outfielders. Numerous other fans in various states of undress were dragged off the field by security as the evening wore on, prompting a rain of beer cups, batteries, and golf balls. At one point, fire-crackers were thrown into the Rangers' bullpen.

The game itself was close as the Indians rallied from a 5–1 deficit to tie the score in the bottom of the ninth. They had the winning run on second base when a man jumped out of the stands and attempted to steal the cap off of right fielder Jeff Burroughs's head. In the Texas dugout, manager Billy Martin armed himself with a bat and headed toward the outfield accompanied by several players. The battle was on.

Rangers personnel soon found themselves surrounded by drunken hoodlums, some holding knives, chains, and blunt weapons torn from stadium seats. Realizing the danger the visitors were in, Cleveland manager Ken Aspromonte issued a call to arms. Banding together, the ballplayers escaped to their respective clubhouses.

Fans rioted for nearly a half hour, stealing bases and anything they could get their hands on. Umpire Nestor Chylak was almost hit by a thrown hunting knife. He was bleeding from the back of his head when he declared the game a forfeit and exited the field with the rest of the crew. There were nine arrests.

June 10, 1975

A lesser-known promotional disaster occurred at Shea Stadium during a game between the Yankees and the Angels. The Yanks, who were "borrowing" the stadium while their own was being refurbished, organized a "Salute to the Military Night" featuring a visit from a former Vietnam commander and the ceremonial firing of two 75mm cannons.

Honoring the two hundredth anniversary of the US Army, the Bronx Bombers lived up their name as the first cannon shots blew out multiple sections of the center-field fence and set portions of the bleachers on fire. The field was enveloped in smoke, and the game was delayed for nearly forty-five minutes. But the festivities were just beginning.

After the damage was repaired, fans celebrated in their own fashion with numerous fistfights and the release of a live chicken, which strutted on top of the backstop screen for two full innings. A night of mayhem was capped off with an eighth-inning bomb scare directed at the California Angels dugout. A thorough search by New York City police uncovered nothing contraband, and the Yankees moved on to a 6–4 win.

September 6, 1976

Dodgers catcher Steve Yeager was the victim of a freak accident at San Diego Stadium. Yeager was standing in the on-deck circle waiting for his turn to hit against Padres southpaw Randy Jones when teammate Bill Russell made contact with a high fastball, shattering his bat into several pieces. The shards flew in Yeager's direction, hitting him in the throat and piercing his esophagus. He collapsed onto the field with blood seeping from his neck. "I couldn't move," Yeager told reporters. "I knew it was going to hit me, and I had to let it."

The injured backstop was transported to the hospital, where he underwent a ninety-eight-minute procedure to remove nine pieces of wood from his neck. He told reporters he wasn't really scared until the doctor explained that one of the pieces had narrowly missed a major artery and surgery would be necessary. On returning to action, Yeager helped design and popularize a protective throat flap for catchers. Before the advent of maple bats, incidents of such a nature were rare. "The bats broke," Yeager explained in 2008, "but very seldom did you see one explode or see the barrel of the bat go flying."

Now it happens all the time. Popularized by Barry Bonds during his historic seventy-three-homer campaign, bats made of maple tend to shatter rather than crack, spraying fragments in all directions. There were three major incidents during the 2008 campaign. In April, Pirates hitting coach Don Long received a nasty gash under his eye that required ten stitches to close after being hit by a bat fragment in the dugout. Ten days later, a fan named Susan Rhodes was struck by the barrel of Todd Helton's bat, which fractured her jaw in two places. In June, umpire Brian O'Nora was forced out of a game after being hit in the face with wooden shards. He sustained a mild concussion.

By mid-2008, Commissioner Bud Selig could ignore the problem no longer. A special advisory committee was assembled to investigate the phenomenon. After examining thousands of broken bats and hundreds of isolated incidents, members arrived at the following conclusion: the straighter the grain, the less likely the bat is to break into multiple pieces. Beginning in 2009, all maple and birch bats were inspected by manufacturers and then labeled with a black dot. Additionally, the logo was rotated ninety degrees, and players were advised to hit with the emblem facing them.

In 2010, MLB reported that broken-bat incidents had declined by 45 percent. That didn't stop Cubs outfielder Tyler Colvin from being impaled in the chest as he was running from third to home during a game. According to one source, a special kind of clear tape is available that can be applied to bats to prevent them from shattering at a cost of less than five dollars per application. The tape proved 100 percent effective during multiple rounds of tests at the University of Massachusetts, Lowell, but MLB chose not to use it.

October 3, 1976

In 1976, the Royals captured their first division title. They owed much of their success to George Brett and Hal McRae, who battled each other for the batting crown during the second half. The race went down to the wire, and the winner was determined amid a storm of controversy. To this day, there are still lingering doubts as to whether or not there was foul play.

A three-game series in Kansas City between the Royals and the Twins put the American League's top four hitters on the field together. Minnesota's Lyman Bostock injured his hand in the opener on October 1 and dropped out of the running. He finished at .323. Entering the last game of the season, Rod Carew still had an excellent chance of surpassing his Kansas City rivals. His average stood at .329. Meanwhile, McRae led Brett by less than a percentage point.

Despite a 2-for-4 performance, Carew fell just short as McRae and Brett held their ground until their final at bats of the season. Facing right-hander Jim Hughes, Brett lofted a catchable flyball to left field. Steve Brye was playing unusually deep and appeared to lay up as the ball dropped ten feet in front of him and then bounced over his head for an inside-the-park homer. No one was happier than McRae, who greeted his teammate at the plate with a big smile and a high five. McRae now needed just one hit to claim the batting crown. He grounded out to short instead, conceding the honor to Brett.

As he walked back to the dugout, McRae accepted a standing ovation from the Kansas City crowd. He then gestured with his middle finger toward the Twins dugout. After the game, he insinuated that Minnesota manager Gene Mauch was a racist who had ordered Brye to allow Brett's homer to drop in. "This is America and not much has changed," McRae griped. "Too bad in 1976 things are like that." Brett may have inadvertently fueled the fire when he made the following postgame comment: "I think maybe the Twins made me a present of the batting championship, and if they did, I feel just as bad about it as Hal does." Mauch vehemently denied McRae's charge, stating that he would "never do anything to harm the integrity of baseball."

But there are still lingering doubts. Former Royals PR director Dean Vogelaar said in 2012: "To this day, I don't think anybody knows the truth."

June 6, 1977

Broadcaster Howard Cosell was a controversial figure with a robust vocabulary and a knack for being confrontational. Some of his incendiary comments landed him in hot water with producers over the course of his career. During a game at Arlington Stadium in Texas, ball boy Rich Thompson inadvertently shared his feelings about Cosell with a national audience.

Thompson was clowning around with a microphone near the Rangers dugout during an ABC *Monday Night Baseball* broadcast. Assuming the mic had been switched off, Thompson directed a stream of derogatory remarks at Cosell, including the abusive sentiment: "Bite me, Howard. The entire state of Texas hates your guts." Thompson was surprised and embarrassed to discover that his comments were being televised.

Cosell was uncharacteristically tongue-tied, refusing immediate comment, while cohost Keith Jackson referred to the interlude as a "stupid incident." Thompson was called on the carpet by his bosses. He told them he had no idea the microphone was live and that his first indication was when he spoke Keith Jackson's name only to have the broadcaster turn and look at him.

Majority owner Brad Corbett issued an apology to Cosell and suspended the sixteen-year old mischief-maker. Despite the regrettable faux pas, Rangers manager Frank Lucchesi discouraged Corbett from firing the boy. The next time the Rangers were on television, Thompson (who got paid eight dollars per game to keep umpires stocked with balls) was reportedly made to wear a piece of tape over his mouth.

June 18, 1977

When Reggie Jackson arrived in the Bronx for the 1977 season, he immersed himself in his own hype. "I didn't come to New York to be a star," he told reporters, "I brought my star with me." He drove a wedge between himself and team captain Thurman Munson with another arrogant comment made to a correspondent from *Sport* magazine: "I'm the straw that stirs the drink. Maybe I should say me and Munson. But he can only stir it bad."

Reggie had a lot of pop in his bat but displayed an alarming lack of hustle at times. Coupled with his self-serving attitude, this landed him in Billy Martin's doghouse. Martin had made no bones about the fact that he never wanted Reggie on the team in the first place. He had advocated for the acquisition of Joe Rudi, a former teammate of Reggie's who could hit and field equally well (though he didn't have Jackson's power).

On June 18, 1977, the two men nearly came to blows in the Yankee dugout during a nationally televised game at Fenway Park. Martin had asked Jackson to shag some flies before the game, and Jackson had refused. With the Yanks trailing 7–4 in the sixth inning, Reggie loafed after a shallow fly hit by Jim Rice. By the time he relayed the ball back to the infield, Rice had pulled up at second base. Billy was fuming. He came out to the mound to replace pitcher Mike Torrez. He then sent Paul Blair in as a substitute for Reggie. This was obviously an attempt to embarrass the egotistical outfielder, whom Billy more or less despised.

Sensitive about his public image, Jackson stormed into the dugout and demanded to know what he had done wrong. Martin snarled at him: "You know what you did!" Reggie then made the mistake of calling Martin an old man. Billy had never backed down from a fight during his career, and he wasn't about to start. It took three coaches to separate the two

George Steinbrenner, who had watched the game on TV with millions of others, decided to fire Billy two days later. But when the story was leaked by UPI writer Milt Richman, fans were overwhelmingly opposed to Martin's dismissal. George ultimately changed his mind but would fire and rehire Martin numerous times over the next few campaigns. Reggie would spend a few more tumultuous seasons in the Bronx, averaging twenty-eight homers and ninety-two RBIs per year.

April 12, 1978

It was a tough day for the Rangers as they touched up Detroit pitching phenom Mark Fidrych for a pair of runs in the first but then slowly squandered the lead in a 3–2 loss at Arlington Stadium. The events before the game were highly disturbing as Texas hurler Rogelio ("Roger") Moret ended up in a psychiatric hospital.

Moret had risen from poverty in his hometown of Guayama, Puerto Rico, to stardom with the Red Sox. Signed in 1968, the spindly southpaw had shown promise as a swingman, posting a 13–2 record in 1973 and a 14–3 mark in 1975. Described as a "light, free, flighty guy" by teammate Bob Montgomery, Moret was prone to odd behavior. He once took a car on a test drive and kept it for four days. Police eventually came to Fenway Park looking for it. While playing for the Braves in 1976, he drank a mixture of rum and kerosene to keep bad luck away. Later that year, he ended up hospitalized when he reportedly became "hysterical" in his hotel room. It would not be his last meltdown.

Traded to Texas for the 1977 campaign, he struggled to find the plate at times, posting a mediocre 3.73 ERA. On April 12 of the following year, Moret went to the clubhouse in the middle of batting practice and stripped down to his undershorts. He then stood in front of his locker in a catatonic state, with his left arm extended and his right hand holding a shower thong. Unresponsive to teammates for roughly ninety minutes, he was transported via ambulance to a psychiatric center. He returned for a handful of appearances in May and June but was largely ineffective. He never pitched again in the majors after 1978. It was later discovered that Moret was suffering from a psychotic disorder known as chronic undifferentiated schizophrenia, which is characterized by delusions and bizarre behaviors.

July 12, 1979

Not all of Bill Veeck's wild promotions went off without a hitch. His most disastrous scheme took place before the second game of a doubleheader at Comiskey Park. The ill-fated event was actually the brainchild of his son Mike. Billed as "Disco Demolition Night," the promotion coincided with a campaign led by Chicago deejay Steve Dahl to eradicate disco music from the airwaves. Dahl had lost his job at a local radio station when the musical format was switched to disco. He landed a job at a rock station known as WLUP "The Loop" and created the "Anti-Disco Army," a club that boasted thousands of members at its peak. Mike Veeck happened to be the sports commentator at WLUP and, together, he and Dahl came up with the idea of destroying disco records during a White Sox game. The maverick Chicago owner agreed it was a good idea.

If only he had known . . .

The admission price was set at ninety-eight cents (WLUP's number on the dial) for anyone who brought a vinyl record to be demolished. Close to sixty thousand fans showed up, creating standing-room-only conditions. Thousands more were left outside the park as police blocked exit ramps from the highway to discourage new arrivals.

Before the game even started, security guards had their hands full as fans rushed the turnstiles and began climbing Comiskey's two-story chain-link fence. A bin designated to collect the LPs and 45s filled up quickly, and fans took their records inside, tossing them carelessly onto the field. Tigers players donned batting helmets to protect themselves against projectiles, which included fireworks, hot dogs, and garbage.

After the Tigers had won the first game by a 4–1 margin, Dahl—dressed in a green army helmet—played master of ceremonies for the "demolition." The bin of records was placed in the outfield, where it was annihilated with an explosive charge. The crowd roared its approval as bedlam ensued.

Fans rushed onto the field, tearing up grass, setting fires, and toppling the batting cage. Numerous fights erupted, and when Bill Veeck pleaded with fans to settle down, his requests were ignored. Harry Caray tried calming the masses with a rendition of "Take Me Out to the Ballgame," but it had little effect. Eventually, a horde of police officers clad in riot gear were dispatched, promptly restoring order.

Veeck wanted the second game to commence, but the field was in such a dismal state that umpires were forced to postpone the game. The following day, AL president Lee MacPhail declared the contest a forfeit in favor of the Tigers. Veeck criticized the decision but ultimately accepted responsibility for the unfortunate turn of events. He would later refer to the promotion as a "mistake."

Part 6

DAWN OF THE STEROID ERA, 1980–1999

Timeline of Significant Events

1980   A players' strike is narrowly avoided as owners agree to increase minimum salaries and pension-fund contributions. George Brett maintains a .400 average for most of the season but finishes at .390 following a late slump.

1981   Len Barker of the Indians tosses a perfect game. Steve Carlton becomes the first lefty to record three thousand strikeouts. Players go on strike from June 12 to August 10, causing the cancellation of more than seven hundred games.

1982   Rickey Henderson steals 130 bases—a major league record. The Metrodome opens in Minnesota.

1983   Dan Quisenberry of the Royals boosts the single-season save record to forty-five. Steve Howe of the Dodgers and Willie Aikens of the Royals receive a full-year suspension for drug abuse.

1984   Pete Rose plays in his 3,309th game—the most by any major leaguer. Umpires go on strike, forcing college replacement officials to work the first game of the NL Championship Series.

1985   Pete Rose collects hit number 4,192, breaking the old mark set by Ty Cobb. Players go on strike for two days in August. The League Championship Series is changed to a best-of-seven format.

1986   Don Sutton strikes out one hundred batters for the twenty-first consecutive season. Bert Blyleven of the Twins surrenders fifty homers—a single-season record. Roger Clemens fans twenty Mariners during an April contest, establishing an all-time mark.

1987   Mark McGwire hits forty-nine homers in his rookie campaign—more than any freshman in history. Don Mattingly hits at least one homer in eight consecutive games, tying a major league record. His six grand slams are the most by any player in a single season.

1988   Orel Hershiser of the Dodgers hurls fifty-nine consecutive scoreless innings, breaking the old mark set by Don Drysdale. Jose Canseco is the first major leaguer to hit forty homers and steal forty bases in a season. Tom Browning of the Reds pitches a perfect game.

1989   Nolan Ryan registers his five thousandth career strikeout. Pete Rose is banned from baseball for gambling activities. The Sky Dome opens in Toronto. Billy Martin dies in an auto crash.

1990   Carlton Fisk hits his 328th homer as a catcher, a new major league record. Bobby Thigpen raises the bar for saves in a single season with fifty-seven.

1991   Rickey Henderson wins his eleventh stolen-base crown and becomes the majors' all-time leader after swiping his 939th bag.

1992   Ozzie Smith captures his thirteenth straight Gold Glove. Fay Vincent
        resigns, leaving baseball temporarily without a commissioner.

1993   The Colorado Rockies and Florida Marlins join the National League.
        Reds owner Marge Schott is suspended for making racist remarks.

1994   Each league forms three divisions. The wild-card format is added to
        the postseason, which is cancelled due to a players' strike.

1995   Greg Maddux claims his fourth straight Cy Young Award. Cal Rip-
        ken becomes the new "Iron Man," playing in his 2,131st consec-
        utive game. Mickey Mantle dies.

1996   Eddie Murray is the third player in history with five hundred homers
        and three thousand hits.

1997   Interleague play begins. Mike Piazza hits .362—the highest twenti-
        eth-century mark for a catcher. Curt Schilling records 319 strike-
        outs—the most ever by an NL right-hander.

1998   Inaugural seasons for the Diamondbacks and Devil Rays. Mark
        McGwire and Sammy Sosa stage a dramatic home-run race,
        both shattering Roger Maris's single-season record. "Big Mac"
        launches seventy bombs while "Slammin' Sammy" is not far be-
        hind with sixty-six.

1999   Mark McGwire and Sammy Sosa become the first players to record
        consecutive sixty-homer campaigns. Randy Johnson's 364 strike-
        outs are the all-time second-highest number by a lefty.

May 4, 1980

Life is full of choices. During a game between the Dodgers and Phillies at Veterans Stadium, Philly skipper Dallas Green made the wrong one.
Davey Lopes opened the game with a single. Rudy Law reached on an error
by second baseman Luis Aguayo, which sent the speedy Lopes to third. Law
stole second and, after a pop out by Reggie Smith, Steve Garvey drove Lopes
home with an infield single. Dusty Baker then grounded into a 6–4 force, but
there was a slight problem: he batted out of turn.

Baseball rules stipulate that it is the opposing team's responsibility to
point out such a transgression. Dallas Green did so immediately, and Ron
Cey, the proper batter, was ruled out. Baker then returned to the plate and
deposited a Randy Lerch pitch into the seats for a three-run homer. Green
tried to undo the damage by arguing that Baker should not have batted, but
he ended up being ejected by home-plate umpire Paul Pryor. He missed one
heck of a game.

The Dodgers opened up a 9–0 lead, but the Phillies rallied to tie the score in the eighth. Unfortunately, the Philadelphia bullpen blew it as LA plated three more runs in the final frame. The Phillies brought the tying run to the plate in the bottom of the ninth but came up short in a 12–10 loss. They moved on to capture the first world championship in franchise history that year.

September 8, 1981

A Dominican import, outfielder César Cedeño was compared to the likes of Hank Aaron, Willie Mays, and Roberto Clemente in his prime. Though he never attained that level of success, he did earn five Gold Gloves and four All-Star selections while stealing no fewer than fifty bases every year from 1972 through 1977. Off the field, Cedeño had a checkered past.

While wintering in Santo Domingo in 1973, the highly touted outfielder accidentally shot and killed his mistress at a seedy hotel. He panicked and fled the scene before turning himself in to authorities a few hours later. Because he was a famous ballplayer who invoked a sense of national pride, he was given a ridiculously lenient sentence—twenty days in jail and a fine of one hundred pesos. Though the Astros organization tried to keep the sordid affair under wraps, details eventually became public.

For years, Cedeño dealt with sporadic heckling from fans, some of whom called him "killer" and demanded to know who he was going to shoot next. On September 8, 1981, he finally snapped. During a game against the Braves at Atlanta-Fulton County Stadium, he jumped into the stands and assaulted a man who had allegedly been insulting him for two straight evenings. Several teammates restrained him before anyone was injured.

The reckless act couldn't have happened at a worse time. During the strike-shortened 1981 season, pennant contenders were decided by pitting the first-half winners against the second-half victors in a divisional showdown. At the time of Cedeño's tirade, the Astros were vying for the second-half title, which they would ultimately clinch. Following Cedeño's ejection, Houston blew a 2–1 lead in the bottom of the ninth, losing the game, 3–2.

Cedeño later expressed regret that his actions had hurt the club but stated that his conscience was otherwise clear. "I can take most of the abuse," he said. "But when it comes to my family, no. I will not put up with that." His wife had been sitting in proximity to the heckler and had allegedly been driven to the verge of tears by the man's comments. Cedeño appealed an indefinite suspension through the Players Association and ended up with a $5,000 fine. He was allowed to return to action. The Astros dropped the divisional series to the Dodgers that year after winning the first two games.

April 2, 1982

Steve McCatty's career will always be a case of what might have been. In 1980, the hard-throwing right-hander won fourteen games for the Oakland A's, helping them to a surprising second-place finish. His greatest season was shortened by a strike as he led the league in wins and shutouts while finishing second in Cy Young voting during the 1981 slate. After that, he developed arm problems that reduced his effectiveness and ultimately derailed his path to superstardom. At the very least, he left behind one highly amusing anecdote.

According to some sources, McCatty was an incorrigible practical joker who once set manager Billy Martin's shoelaces on fire while he was calling for a suicide squeeze. During a spring training game against the Padres in 1982, he went to bat with a fifteen-inch toy bat in his hands. It wasn't his idea. Martin was upset that designated hitters were being banned in National League parks that spring. In protest, he sent McCatty (who had never logged an official at bat during the regular season) to the plate with the toy in his hands. Umpire Jim Quick put an end to the joke immediately, and McCatty struck out on three pitches. The A's lost the exhibition game, 6–2, dropping their spring training record to 8–13.

July 24, 1983

Prompted by the conniving managerial tactics of Yankee skipper Billy Martin, the "Pine Tar Incident" is among the most infamous disputes in baseball history. During the first half of the 1983 season, Yankee personnel noted that George Brett's bat was slathered with pine tar. Since the rule book states that a bat cannot be covered by a substance more than eighteen inches from tip to handle, Martin filed the information away as potentially useful.

On July 24, Brett drilled a two-run homer off of Goose Gossage in the top of the ninth to put the Royals up, 5–4. After he crossed the plate, Martin asked umpire Tim McClelland to examine Brett's bat. Using home plate (which is seventeen inches across) as a frame of reference, the umpiring crew determined that the bat was in violation of the rules. McClelland pointed directly at Brett and signaled that he was out.

Brett came flying out of the dugout in an almost psychotic rage, having to be restrained by manager Dick Howser and several teammates. During the heated debate, Howser and Brett were both ejected. According to multiple sources, Kansas City hurler Gaylord Perry (playing in his final season) handed the controversial piece of lumber to the Royals' bat boy with instructions to hide it somewhere. The kid was reportedly chased by security personnel to the clubhouse.

A protest was upheld by AL president Lee MacPhail, who ordered the game replayed from the point of the disruption. Fewer than two thousand fans attended the brief finale on August 18. Brett was conspicuously absent. Billy Martin protested by placing pitcher Ron Guidry in center field and first baseman Don Mattingly at second. In a last-ditch effort to change the tide of the game, he instructed Yankee hurler George Frazier to appeal Brett's homer on the grounds that he had missed first base. When Frazier tossed the ball to first, umpire Tim Welke made a "safe" call. A throw to second prompted the same indication from arbiter Dave Phillips.

Not quite finished yet, Martin came out to argue. He was presented with an affidavit signed by members of the original umpiring crew, each of whom testified to the fact that Brett had touched all the bases. With no more tricks up his sleeve, Martin then retreated to the clubhouse to watch TV.

Hal McRae struck out, ending the Royals' half of the ninth. The Yankees were retired in order in the bottom of the frame, making the 5–4 loss official. Brett's infamous bat now resides in the Museum at the National Baseball Hall of Fame. The unusual 1983 game was not without precedent as a similar scenario had played out in a 1975 contest involving the Royals. The bat in question belonged to Kansas City's first baseman, John Mayberry.

August 4, 1983

Dave Winfield went from All-Star to criminal in the blink of an eye. The Yankee outfielder had just finished warming up in the fifth inning of a game against the Blue Jays when his return throw to the ball boy struck and killed a seagull. He had no idea what trouble the unintentional act would bring. The crowd at Exhibition Stadium booed him lustily as a Toronto bat boy covered the stricken bird with a cloth and carried it off the field. The pinioned creature was reportedly put in cold storage by a humane society official. After the Yankees had completed a 3–1 victory, Winfield was arrested and carted to the Ontario Provincial Police's Toronto station, where he was booked on charges of cruelty to animals.

Winfield maintained his innocence but was forced to post a $500 bond for his release. He was held until after midnight, and the Yankees' chartered flight out of the city was delayed. Yankee skipper Billy Martin came to Winfield's aid (sort of), commenting, "They say Winfield hit that bird on purpose. They wouldn't say that if they saw some of the throws he's been making this year." A UPI article led with the following lines: "New York Yankee slugger Dave

Winfield collected three hits. Two of them are on the scoreboard and one is in the morgue." The charges against him were dropped.

It would not be the last regrettable incident involving thrown baseballs and birds. In March 2001, Diamondbacks ace Randy Johnson hit and killed a dove midflight as he was facing Giants outfielder Calvin Murray during a spring training game. "It exploded," said Murray. "There were nothing but feathers laying on home plate." The umpire ruled "no pitch" as members of the Giants found humor in the situation, teasing Johnson. Never known for his sunny disposition, Johnson commented: "I didn't think it was all that funny."

May 4, 1984

Dave Kingman lived up to his nickname "Sky King" when he propelled a ball more than 180 feet above home plate into the roof of the Metrodome in Minnesota. Twins infielders Houston Jimenez and John Castino stood poised to make the catch as the ball passed through an eight-inch drainage hole in the bottom layer of the fabric ceiling and got stuck. Kingman was reportedly the first batter to accomplish the feat.

There were two outs in the fourth when Twins hurler Frank Viola delivered a low fastball to the A's slugger. "He golfed it up like a drive off a tee," Viola said. Jimenez became jittery when the ball didn't come down and instinctively covered his head. Second baseman Tim Teufel commented that Kingman's hit "was like a rocket going off." The slugger was awarded a double by umpire Jim Evans, and when he arrived at second, he exchanged a smile with Viola.

A prolific home run artist who struck out far too much, Kingman at one time had the most homers of any player not in the Hall of Fame. He downplayed the significance of the Metrodome event, commenting that he had been the first to hit the roof of the Astrodome as well. In 1976, he blasted what is believed to be the longest home run in Wrigley Field history. His drive cleared a thirty-foot screen above the wall and crossed Waveland Avenue before bouncing up onto a neighbor's porch. (The tenant was allegedly inside watching the game.)

May 9, 1984

The White Sox and Brewers weren't in a particular hurry to finish their game at Comiskey Park as they set a new major league record for time elapsed. Though the contest fell short of the all-time mark in terms of innings played, the winning run did not cross the plate until 753 pitches had been thrown and eight hours, six minutes had expired.

A modest crowd of 14,754 got its money's worth as the clubs fought to a 3–3 tie through seventeen innings. The game was suspended due to an AL curfew but resumed the following day. Two and a half more hours of play were necessary to determine a winner as Chicago's Harold Baines finally smashed a walk-off homer in the bottom of the twenty-fifth inning.

A total of fourteen pitchers took the mound, none of them lasting more than 7.1 frames. Both teams combined for eleven consecutive scoreless innings. The Brewers broke through in the twenty-first with a three-run homer by Ben Oglivie, but the White Sox answered with three scores of their own on timely singles by Carlton Fisk and Tom Paciorek. Chicago blew a golden opportunity in the twenty-third frame, when Dave Stegman was physically restrained by coach Jim Leyland while rounding third. Stegman was called out for coach's interference. Tom Seaver picked up a cheap win, facing just three batters before getting the decision. According to the Associated Press, the previous record for major league game duration belonged to the Mets and the Giants, who squared off for seven hours and twenty-three minutes on May 31, 1964.

The longest contest in minor league history took place on April 18, 1981, when the Pawtucket Red Sox and Rochester Red Wings battled for thirty-two innings. The game was suspended at 4:07 a.m. with the score knotted at 2 and concluded on June 23—eight hours and twenty-five minutes after the opening pitch. The International League match established a multitude of records and featured appearances by several notable major league candidates, among them Bruce Hurst, Wade Boggs, and Cal Ripken. When play was suspended during the initial session, fewer than two dozen fans remained, and players were so cold that they were burning bats to keep warm. On a humorous side note, Pawtucket pitcher Luis Aponte was reportedly denied access to his apartment by his wife, who refused to believe his story when he got home at five in the morning. He ended up sleeping in the clubhouse.

August 12, 1984

One of the most violent games in modern history took place at Atlanta-Fulton County Stadium in Atlanta between the Braves and Padres. The trouble began in the first inning, when Atlanta's starter Pascual Perez hit Alan Wiggins in the back as he was leading off the game. San Diego skipper Dick Williams ordered retaliation, and Perez reportedly had to dodge pitches in all four of his plate appearances that day.

Ed Whitson and Craig Lefferts were both ejected for throwing at Perez, who later claimed the first inning beanball was an accident. The contest was marred by two nasty brawls—both stemming from brushback pitches. The second fight took place in the ninth inning after Atlanta's Donnie Moore plunked Graig Nettles.

According to the Retrosheet box score, there were seventeen ejections, including both managers. Newspapers reported five fan arrests as spectators became involved in the fighting. By the end of the game, police were stationed on top of both dugouts. A battle of words continued after the game. "With that much action the fight isn't over with," said Braves third baseman Jerry Royster. "We're looking for it." Atlanta's skipper, Joe Torre, called Dick Williams an "idiot" and told reporters to "spell that with a capital *I*." Williams countered by telling Torre he could "stick that finger he is pointing."

April 28, 1985

What is it with Mookie Wilson and elusive grounders? More than a year before the infamous error by Bill Buckner in game 6 of the 1986 World Series, Wilson plated the winning run during a marathon encounter against the Pirates in comparable fashion.

It looked as if the Mets might breeze to victory when Darryl Strawberry hit a grand slam off of Mike Bielecki in the bottom of the first at Shea Stadium. But it was all the scoring the New Yorkers would manage for sixteen more innings. Pittsburgh knotted the score on homers by George Hendrick and Tony Peña as the game eventually meandered into the eighteenth frame.

The Mets ran out of bench players in the twelfth and ended up installing Rusty Staub in right field. The forty-one-year-old slugger was not exactly in prime condition, having added forty pounds to his frame over the years. Due to his limited range, he switched places with Clint Hurdle in left field several times (depending on which side of the plate batters hit from). Staub was stationed in right field in the eighteenth frame when he made a game-saving catch on a ball hit by Rick Rhoden.

In a scene reminiscent of the 1986 Fall Classic, Gary Carter opened the home half of the eighteenth with a walk. Mookie Wilson was inserted as a pinch runner. He moved to third on a single by Strawberry and then scored the winning run when an easy grounder squirted through the legs of first baseman Jason Thompson. More than forty different players were used in this game, which lasted five hours and twenty-one minutes. Bill Madlock of the Pirates commented: "It was a game that nobody seemed to want to win."

October 13, 1985

With few power hitters in their lineup, the 1985 Cardinals relied heavily on speed and defense to capture the NL East title. Playing in his rookie season, Vince Coleman figured heavily into manager Whitey Herzog's game plan (which was nicknamed "Whiteyball"). Coleman paced the circuit with 110 steals during the regular season and was hitting .286 in the NLCS before succumbing to a bizarre injury before the start of game 4 in St. Louis.

Coleman had participated in some pregame drills and was standing on the field, talking with teammate Terry Pendleton. With a light rain falling, the grounds crew decided to activate the automatic tarp machine. Coleman had his back to the device and had no idea it had been switched on until it rolled over his left leg, badly bruising it and chipping a bone in his knee. He was lost for the remainder of the postseason.

The injured speedster remained jovial about the freak accident, joking that the Busch Stadium crew should install bells on the tarp machine to warn people of its approach. Coleman's replacement, Tito Landrum, hit .385 the rest of the way as the Cardinals won the NLCS over the Dodgers and then lost to the Royals in the World Series. Coleman would reach the Fall Classic with St. Louis in 1987. The tarp-machine incident would follow him for the remainder of his career and beyond. "That's what made me famous," he quipped long after his retirement, "the female tarp looking for a good-looking young man."

October 4, 1986

With 311 wins under his belt, Phil Niekro had reason to be jovial. In a game between the Indians and Mariners, the forty-seven-year-old knuckleballer performed a little vaudeville routine on the bases. Cleveland was leading 5–2 in the eighth with Brook Jacoby on first and Jay Bell at bat. Bell stepped out of the box and called for time as Niekro came out of the dugout wearing a red bandanna over his face. He ran to second and dove headfirst into the bag. After receiving a "safe" signal from umpire Vic Voltaggio, the cheeky hurler uprooted the base and headed back to the dugout with it. The crowd of 11,991 loved it, cheering enthusiastically.

Indians second baseman Brook Jacoby explained that Niekro had come up with the idea since his career was coming to a close and he had never stolen a base before. Jacoby joked with reporters, "A seventy-year-old man stealing second—that's something." Niekro had been caught stealing once in his career back in 1976, when he was playing for the Braves. Though he was not officially credited with a theft after the Cleveland Stadium stunt, he at least retained bragging rights.

October 25, 1986

No discussion of the 1986 World Series would be complete without mention of Bill Buckner's infamous game 6 error. But many accounts of that game are missing details of the bizarre incident that took place a couple of hours before.

In the first inning, a thirty-seven-year-old actor named Michael Sergio parachuted into Shea Stadium with a "Let's Go Mets" banner attached to him. He landed on the infield and was promptly carted off by police. Though he received loud applause from the crowd of fifty-five thousand, prosecutors did not find the gag terribly amusing.

In order to pull off the stunt, Sergio's pilot had disrupted air traffic at La Guardia Airport. When Sergio refused to identify his aviator, he was held in contempt of court. FAA lawyers sought the maximum penalty. He was eventually sentenced to six months in a federal jail, maintaining his code of silence throughout.

Had Sergio entered the stadium in conventional fashion on the evening of October 25, he would have witnessed Mookie Wilson's tenth-inning grounder pass through the legs of BoSox first baseman Bill Buckner, allowing the winning run to score with two outs. It was one of the most iconic moments in Series history. The Mets rallied from a 3–0 deficit in game 7 to capture the championship with an 8–5 victory.

August 3, 1987

In a game against the Angels at Anaheim, Twins hurler Joe Niekro got caught doctoring the baseball. Niekro was facing Brian Downing in the fourth inning when umpire Tim Tschida approached the mound and asked the hurler to empty his pockets. Niekro was found to be in possession of an emery board and a piece of sandpaper. The forty-two-year-old moundsman claimed that the implements were for his fingernails, which needed to be properly groomed in order to throw knuckleballs, but the umpiring crew wasn't buying it. According to arbiter Dan Philips, officials had been gathering evidence for several innings. Niekro was ejected and later suspended for ten days.

The incident was neither the first nor the last of its kind during the 1987 slate. On July 5, Astros pitcher Mike Scott had been accused of scuffing baseballs. Right-hander Kevin Gross, who started for Philadelphia that day, claimed to have gotten dramatic movement on his pitches when he inadvertently used one of Scott's doctored balls. On August 10, Gross got into the act himself in a game against the Cubs. Chicago had two runners on with one out in the fifth when umpire Charley Williams responded to a complaint lodged by Cubs skipper Gene Michael that Gross was tampering with balls. Williams and crew chief John Kibler inspected the hurler's glove and found a substance resembling sandpaper glued to the heel. The glove was confiscated and Gross was ejected. Though he maintained his innocence, he received a ten-day suspension. The "Scuffgate" controversy continued as Angels pitcher Don Sutton was accused of defacing balls on multiple occasions during the season.

August 23, 1989

The second-longest shutout in major league history ended in the top of the twenty-second inning when Dodgers catcher Rick Dempsey—who entered the game with a .168 batting average—deposited a 2-1 pitch off of Expos reliever Dennis Martinez into the left-field seats, breaking a scoreless tie. LA hung on for a 1–0 win, but the game is best remembered for a moment of comic relief provided by Montreal's dynamic mascot Youppi!.

Commissioned by Expos vice president Roger Landry and fashioned by a former Jim Henson Muppet designer, the furry orange character became a fixture at Olympic Stadium games in 1979. On the date in question, Youppi! became the first of his kind to be ejected from a major league contest. It happened in the eleventh inning, when Youppi! was dancing on top of the Dodgers dugout. He took a running leap and landed noisily, provoking the wrath of manager Tom Lasorda. Lasorda complained to umpire Bob Davidson, who promptly threw Youppi! out of the game. The banished mascot was allowed to return in the thirteenth inning. Clad in pajamas and carrying a pillow, he "went to sleep" on the roof of the Expos dugout.

The ejection of Youppi! was not the strangest expulsion in baseball history. During a 1985 Florida State League game at Clearwater, Phillies organist Wilbur Snapp was removed from his post following a questionable call at first base. The umpire took exception to Snapp's rendition of "Three Blind Mice" and promptly gave him the boot. Immediately following the ejection, Snapp, a sixty-five-year-old woodworker, was allowed to wander the stands making balloon animals for fans (fittingly, in the shape of mice). He later appeared on the *Today* show, *Good Morning America*, and Paul Harvey's radio program.

October 17, 1989

The 1989 World Series showdown between the Oakland A's and San Francisco Giants was dubbed the "Battle of the Bay." The A's had been propelled to the Series by prolific home-run artists (and clandestine steroid users) Mark McGwire and Jose Canseco—a.k.a. "The Bash Brothers." Inspired by manager Roger Craig's rallying cry of "Humm-Baby," the Giants had won ninety-two regular season games and disposed of the Cubs in the NLCS. The two cities stand just sixteen miles apart, separated by a vast span known locally as the Bay Bridge. By 1989, the Giants had been excluded from World Series play for twenty-seven years. The A's had not won a Fall Classic in well over a decade. What should have been a jubilant time for both municipalities was marred by a natural disaster.

The A's came out swinging in the first two games at Oakland, winning handily by a combined score of 10–1. The Giants were looking to get back on track at Candlestick Park. The pitching matchup for game 3 featured twelve-game winner Don Robinson for the Giants against Bob Welch, a veteran of six postseasons. Neither hurler would take the mound that day.

At 5:04 p.m., while many fans were still settling into their seats, an earthquake rocked the stadium. Light towers swayed and concrete fell from sections of the upper deck, prompting terrified screams from those in proximity. Communications systems were knocked out, and the scoreboard went on the fritz. When the tremors subsided (roughly fifteen seconds later), fans erupted in cheers. Broadcaster Al Michaels commented: "That's the greatest opening in the history of television—bar none." No one realized that the city had just been hit by one of the most powerful earthquakes in modern history.

The game was postponed, and as news of the disaster began trickling in, baseball became monumentally unimportant. The surface-wave magnitude of the quake had registered 7.1 on the Richter scale, bringing down a section of the Bay Bridge and an elevated expanse of Interstate 880. In all, more than sixty people were killed, and thousands were injured.

Game 3 of the Series would not be played until ten days later. The A's romped to a 13–7 win and then completed a sweep on October 28 with a 9–6 victory. Due largely to the earthquake, ABC's coverage of the Series drew a lackluster Nielsen rating of 16.4. It was the first time in the history of prime-time games that the annual showcase had drawn a rating of less than 20.

July 1, 1990

Yankees pitcher Andy Hawkins nearly missed his shot at infamy. On June 5 of the 1990 slate, the right-hander was carrying a 1–4 record with a bloated 8.56 ERA. Given an option to play in the minors or secure his release, the thirty-year-old moundsman chose to call it quits. His bags were literally packed when teammate Mike Witt sustained an elbow injury. Had Witt remained healthy, Hawkins would never have been given the opportunity to be stripped of a no-hitter.

Hawkins accomplished the rare and dubious feat at Comiskey Park on July 1. He had made the most of his second chance with the Yankees to that point, reducing his ungainly ERA by more than two hundred points over a three-week period. He cruised through seven hitless innings against the White Sox before the Yankee defense completely deserted him. With two outs in the eighth, Sammy Sosa reached on an error by third baseman Mike Blowers. A bit rattled, Hawkins issued consecutive walks to load the bases. Robin Ventura then lifted a catchable fly to left field, which was dropped by Jim Leyritz. Three runs scored on the play. Right fielder Jesse Barfield complicated matters even further when he lost Ivan Calderon's pop fly in the sun. It bounced off his mitt for another run-scoring error. Hawkins completed the no-hitter but lost, 4–0. Surrounded by reporters after the game, he quipped that he would "live forever as the answer to a trivia question."

That trivia question morphed into something entirely different during the 1991 slate, when MLB established new rules that erased no-hitters shorter than nine innings. Since the White Sox had never batted in the bottom of the ninth, Hawkins's gem landed on a list of games no longer officially recognized as extraordinary. Hall of Famers Walter Johnson and Rube Waddell were stripped of no-hitters as well.

July 25, 1990

One of the most controversial opening ceremonies in history took place at Jack Murphy Stadium in San Diego. The Padres were in the midst of a disappointing season, mired in fourth place with a 39–54 record. The club had recently been purchased by Tom Werner and his ownership group. Werner was the executive producer of the popular television sitcom *Roseanne*. He invited the show's star, Roseanne Barr, to sing the national anthem in conjunction with a "Working Women's Night" promotion.

The Padres had taken the opening game of a doubleheader from the Reds when Barr strolled to the microphone. She had told a journalist beforehand, "I'm one of the last great singers in the world. You tell me what you think."

Many in attendance did just that.

Roughly five notes into Barr's horrific performance, fans started booing. By the time the actress/comedienne had caterwauled her way through the song, the displeasure of the crowd was palpable. After the final ear-splitting note, Barr mimicked players by grabbing her crotch and spitting on the ground. Few people found this terribly amusing—least of all President George H. W. Bush, who referred to her rendition of the tune as "a disgrace."

Barr later expressed regret to some extent but stated her belief that she was "too hip" for the crowd. "I was trying to be funny," she explained in one of her books. "Sometimes you can't tell if it's funny or not, I guess." In 2011, she sang the national anthem on her reality show, *Roseanne's Nuts*. She did a passable rendition the second time around and referred to her original performance as "a bad mistake."

April 28, 1991

There was no safe haven for players, fans, or coaches during the 1991 campaign as several major leaguers let their tempers get the best of them. Rob Dibble of the Reds began the festivities on April 28 during a relief outing at Riverfront Stadium. Dibble earned his fourth save of the season but pitched somewhat ineffectively, yielding two runs on five hits to the Cubs. After retiring Ryne Sandberg on strikes to end the game, the fiery reliever turned and heaved the ball into the center-field stands, where it struck a twenty-seven-year-old schoolteacher named Meg Porter. She was not seriously injured, but the incident drew the attention of league officials. Dibble was suspended for four games.

It was not Dibble's first angry outburst of the season, nor would it be his last. Earlier in the month, he had deliberately thrown behind the head of Astros utility man Eric Yelding (he served a three-day suspension for that stunt). In July, he would indignantly fire a ball at the legs of a base runner. The runner was Doug Dascenzo of the Cubs. Dascenzo incited Dibble's wrath when he laid down a perfect bunt, allowing teammate Rick Wilkins to score from third. With no play at the plate, Dibble aimed the throw at Dascenzo instead. The irascible right-hander denied he had done it on purpose, commenting, "It's ludicrous to think I'd come off suspension to do something to get suspended again."

Another notorious hothead, Albert Belle, captured headlines in May for his abuse of a spectator. Belle had gotten off to a slow start in the majors, hitting just .225 in his 1989 major league debut. He suffered from alcohol problems and would spend ten weeks in rehab after ripping apart a bathroom during a Triple-A assignment the following year. On completing the program, he ditched his childhood nickname of "Joey" in an effort to get a fresh start. On May 11 of the 1991 slate, Belle was warming up in the outfield when an insensitive fan named Jeff Pillar taunted him from the cheap seats. "Hey, Joey," Pillar shouted. "Keg party at my house after the game, c'mon over!" Not to be trifled with, Belle fired a baseball into the stands, hitting the heckler in the chest. He was suspended for a week, the first of multiple suspensions during a highly successful but tumultuous career.

Padres catcher Benito Santiago was known for having a short fuse. On July 2, 1991, he showed his dark side at Jack Murphy Stadium in a game against the Dodgers. In the sixth inning, Santiago grounded out to first against Ramón Santiago, ending the frame and stranding Tony Gwynn at third. Disgusted with himself, Santiago slammed his helmet on the ground. He didn't know his own strength as he took out two of his bosses in one shot. The helmet bounced into the dugout, hitting pitching coach Mike Roarke in the head before crashing into manager Greg Riddoch and knocking him senseless. Riddoch sustained a concussion during the unfortunate mishap. Santiago was reportedly fined $300 for the tantrum. He would later be linked to claims of steroid use (which would perhaps explain his intermittently explosive behavior).

April 17, 1993

Nine games into the regular season, the Orioles were still working out their spring-training kinks. In the eighth inning of a match against the Angels, three Baltimore players simultaneously vied for possession of third base. After umpires had sorted out the mess, Mike Devereaux joined a relatively small group of major leaguers who have singled into a double play.

Baltimore had the bases loaded with one out against right-hander Joe Grahe when Devereaux lined a ball to center fielder Chad Curtis. Lead runner Jeff Tackett thought a catch had been made when Curtis trapped the ball and retreated to third after advancing roughly halfway to the plate. But when Tackett reached the bag, he found teammate Brady Anderson camped out there. The two were joined shortly afterward by pinch hitter Chito Martinez, who had been running hard all the way from first. Angels catcher John Orton arrived on the scene with the ball and, taking no chances, tagged all three runners. Anderson was deemed the rightful owner of the base as both of his teammates were ruled out, completing an inning-ending double play. The Orioles lost, 7–5, rendering the play especially costly.

Third-base coach Mike Ferraro explained that Tackett couldn't hear him shouting to run home over the crowd noise. *Baltimore Sun* correspondent John Steadman urged manager Johnny Oates to take "a hank of rope and tether the players, holding the line when they are to be restrained and releasing them when it's the appropriate time to run." Oates passed on the advice, guiding the club to a third-place finish anyway.

May 26, 1993

Over the course of his career, Jose Canseco became infamous on a number of levels. Off the field, he was known for his steroid abuse and multiple arrests. On the field, he was renowned for his willingness to assist opponents in hitting homers. He earned that reputation on May 26, 1993, in a game against Cleveland.

Canseco was playing right field for the Rangers at the time. Indians designated hitter Carlos Martinez was leading off the bottom of the fourth against southpaw Kenny Rogers. Martinez lifted a deep fly to right center field. Canseco took off after it and seemed to have a bead on the ball all the way to the warning track. But it bounced off the top of his head and over the wall for a home run. Canseco knew he would not soon live it down, telling reporters after the game, "I'll be on ESPN for a month. I guess I'm just an entertainer."

His clown act continued on May 29, when he persuaded rookie manager Kevin Kennedy to let him pitch the eighth inning of a blowout loss to the Red Sox. The high-priced slugger had been pestering Texas management to give him a shot on the mound all season and had developed a two-pitch repertoire that included a fastball and knuckleball. Canseco threw a total of thirty-three pitches that day, yielding three runs on two hits and three walks. The Rangers' brass found it less than entertaining when he injured his arm during the outing and was lost for the season. "I think if anything is going to happen freakish, it'll happen to me," the slugger commented.

When Canseco returned to action in 1994, he was converted to a full-time designated hitter. The outfield mishap was later voted one of the greatest bloopers in sports history by *This Week in Baseball*. Today, footage of the blunder is still readily accessible on YouTube.

July 14, 1993

Randy Johnson was one of the tallest pitchers in history at six foot ten. Standing on an elevated mound, he was even more imposing. Johnson had a lively fastball, an elusive slider, and an angry demeanor. His questionable control in the early part of his career made him especially menacing to opponents. Before the 1993 slate, Phillies first baseman John Kruk knew Johnson by reputation only. He wasn't relishing the prospect of having to bat against him in the All-Star Game.

As fate would have it, Kruk strolled to the plate against his nemesis with two outs in the third inning and the National League nursing a 2–1 lead. Johnson's first pitch was a ninety-plus miles-per-hour heater that sailed over Kruk's head clear to the backstop. Visibly rattled, Kruk fanned himself off, shook his head, and smiled. He was consoled by AL catcher Ivan Rodriguez before stepping tentatively back into the box. It took just three more pitches to dispose of Kruk. The jittery Philly infielder was standing completely in the bucket when he flailed weakly at the last two offerings. On his way to the dugout, Johnson winked playfully at Kruk. It was his only strikeout in two scoreless innings. The American League breezed to a 9–3 win.

"When I stepped in the box, I said: 'All I wanna do is make contact,'" Kruk told reporters at the game's conclusion. "After the first pitch I said: 'All I wanna do is live' and I lived, so I had a good at bat." Whenever memorable All-Star moments are recounted, the 1993 encounter between Kruk and Johnson invariably comes to the forefront.

July 15, 1994

Washington Post columnist Thomas Boswell once remarked that "cheating is baseball's oldest profession. No other game is so rich in skullduggery, so suited to it or so proud of it." That statement is undeniably correct, especially in regard to bat corking. The practice was declared illegal in 1923 after Babe Ruth and St. Louis Browns outfielder Ken Williams (the founding member of baseball's 30-30 Club) were both caught using bats that did not conform to conventional standards. Williams's bat had a wooden plug in it. Ruth's comprised four separate pieces that had been glued together. Since then, several high-profile players have stepped to the plate with doctored clubs, among them Norm Cash, Graig Nettles, and Sammy Sosa.

Perhaps the most bizarre episode of bat tampering involved universally unpopular slugger Albert Belle. During a tight pennant race between Cleveland and Chicago in 1994, Belle's Indians rolled into Comiskey Park for a four-game series. In the early going of the second contest, White Sox manager Gene Lamont (acting on a tip he had received) asked the umpires to check Belle's bat for anything suspicious. Although a superficial inspection revealed nothing out of the ordinary, the implement was confiscated and locked in the umpires' dressing room.

At some point during the game, one of Belle's teammates crawled above the ceiling and replaced the impounded bat with a "clean" one from the collection of first baseman Paul Sorrento. The half-baked scheme fell apart when umpires discovered broken pieces of ceiling tile on the floor. The original bat was returned, and during a detailed examination, cork was discovered inside the barrel. Belle was suspended for seven games on appeal.

Several years later, pitcher Jason Grimsley admitted to orchestrating the switch. The six-foot-three hurler described his journey through the cramped ceiling space as "hairy." Shortstop Omar Vizquel explained that Sorrento's bat was substituted because Belle's entire cache was corked. On an interesting note, in-depth experiments performed on the television series *Mythbusters* in 2007 strongly suggested that there is no advantage to using a corked bat.

July 30, 1995

1995 was a tough season for player-fan relations. Just two weeks after Bronx hurler Jack McDowell had flipped fans the bird (and been caught on camera doing it) at Yankee Stadium, Angels designated hitter Chili Davis angrily confronted a patron at Milwaukee County Stadium.

The normally mild-mannered Davis was waiting in the on-deck circle during the fourth inning when a twenty-six-year-old spectator named Andy Johannsen began heckling him. Davis snapped at some point and walked to the first-row box seats on the third-base side, poking Johannsen in the face. Booed heartily by fans when he came to the plate, Davis tipped his batting helmet to the crowd. After the game, he was taken into sheriff's custody and charged with disorderly conduct. The citation carried a $287 penalty. Additionally, the AL levied a $5,000 fine.

The incident was unexpected since Davis was such a low-key player and was not in a batting slump at the time. Entering the game, he was hitting .342. Johannsen admitted that he was verbally harassing the slugger but insisted he had said nothing "demeaning or derogatory." Davis was ordered to contribute his fine to the Child Abuse Prevention Fund of Milwaukee. He issued a statement of regret. The incident became the subject of a top-ten list on *The Late Show with David Letterman*.

August 10, 1995

During a "ball day" promotion at Dodger Stadium, fans were given souvenir baseballs as they entered the park. Things turned sour in the ninth inning with the visiting Cardinals leading by a score of 2–1. In the bottom of the frame, Dodger outfielder Raul Mondesi began arguing strikes with plate umpire Jim Quick. He was eventually ejected after he struck out. When Tommy Lasorda came out of the dugout to add his two cents, Quick thumbed him out of the game as well. In particular, Lasorda was miffed about a 3-0 strike call that appeared to be well off the plate. Quick had made a delayed call after Mondesi had started to first base. Lasorda believed that Quick's decision was made solely to assert his authority.

Fans weighed in on the debate by throwing their souvenir balls onto the field. According to multiple reports, as many as two hundred were thrown at once, creating a hazard for St. Louis players. The Cardinals were ordered to their dugout, and after two more volleys, the game was ruled a forfeit. It was the first forfeit in the majors since the disastrous "Disco Demolition Night" in 1979. After the game, Jim Quick pinned the blame on Lasorda, complaining that he had incited fans "by waving his fat little arms."

The Dodger Stadium ball-throwing episode was not the first of its kind. In a 1978 game at Yankee Stadium, hundreds of fans had littered the field with the "Reggie Bars" they had received on entry. In 1993, a "Football Day" promotion went awry at Candlestick Park when fans hurled ornamental baseballs on the field in protest. The 1995 incident prompted the Dodgers to cancel all similar promotions in the future.

September 28, 1995

Baseball has seen hundreds of switch hitters over the years. There have been only a handful of ambidextrous pitchers. Greg Harris of the Expos became the first hurler of the modern era to pitch both right- and left-handed during a major league contest.

Harris had been wanting to get his name in the books for years but had been discouraged by his managers. On September 28, 1995, he got the green light from Expos skipper Felipe Alou. During a 9–7 loss to the Reds, Harris faced four batters—two from his dominant right side and two as a lefty. He accomplished the feat with a specially designed six-fingered glove, which later ended up in the museum at the Baseball Hall of Fame in Cooperstown.

The thirty-nine-year-old reliever entered the game in the ninth. He faced Reggie Sanders right-handed and induced a groundout. After walking Hal Morris as a lefty, he remained a southpaw to retire Eddie Taubensee on a fielder's choice. He then faced Bret Boone right-handed and got him to ground out, ending the frame.

Other players to turn the trick include Tony Mullane in 1882, Elton "Icebox" Chamberlain in 1884 and 1888, and Larry Corcoran in 1889. As of 2012, there was an ambidextrous hurler in the minors, but he had yet to sign with a big league club. A natural right-hander, Pat Venditte learned to pitch with both hands while growing up. Beginning in 2008, he played in the Yankee farm system, notching a 14–12 record with a 2.30 ERA as a closer at various levels. His unusual ability prompted a special set of rules that required him to clearly indicate to umpires which hand he intended to pitch with. Additionally, he was obligated to throw at least one pitch to any given batter before changing hands. Only one switch per at bat was allowed. In 2012, Venditte reportedly suffered a career-threatening injury to his right shoulder.

April 1, 1996

Entering this game between the Expos and the Reds, umpire John McSherry had twenty-five years of experience under his belt. But his belt size had grown considerably since his 1971 debut, raising serious health concerns. By opening day of the 1996 campaign, he was a giant of a man at six foot two and 328 pounds.

McSherry had suffered from weight-related issues in the past. In 1991, he collapsed from dehydration during a game. In 1992, he was forced out of a pivotal NLCS match with dizziness. Three years later, he took a brief leave of absence due to shortness of breath. Just prior to the 1996 season opener, he had been diagnosed with an arrhythmia. He was putting off medical treatment because he didn't want to miss his scheduled game at Riverfront Stadium.

Shortly before the first pitch, the corpulent arbiter was in a jovial mood, joking with Cincinnati catcher Eddie Taubensee that he would allow him to call the first two innings. Just seven pitches into the contest, one of the most horrifying scenes in baseball history unfolded as McSherry backed away from the plate and signalled to other umpires. He took a few steps toward the tunnel leading to the dressing room and then collapsed face-first. A medical crew hustled onto the field in an attempt to revive him, but it was no use. He was pronounced dead of a heart attack at UC Medical Center.

McSherry was esteemed by players and popular with other umpires. Out of respect for him, other members of the crew were willing to continue the game. Players from both squads were far too upset to go on, however, and the match was rescheduled. Reds owner Marge Schott, known for her insensitive comments, darkened the day even further when she complained that the Reds had been "cheated." She later apologized but was snubbed by umpires for some time afterward.

September 27, 1996

At the close of play on September 26, the Baltimore Orioles were in the midst of a tight playoff race, trailing the Yankees by four games in the standings while holding a tenuous lead over Boston, Chicago, and Seattle in the wild-card chase. No one felt the pressure more than Orioles second baseman Roberto Alomar, who irrevocably tarnished his reputation by spitting in the face of umpire John Hirschbeck.

Alomar was arguing a third strike call in the top of the first inning at Toronto's Sky Dome when he lost his composure. Many believed that Hirschbeck had missed the call, but there was no excuse for Alomar's reprehensible act. Making a regrettable situation even worse, Alomar attacked Hirschbeck's character in a postgame interview.

Hirschbeck had suffered a family tragedy in 1993, losing his eight-year-old son, John, to adrenoleukodystrophy. At the time of the spitting incident, Hirschbeck's other son, Michael, was afflicted with the same rare disorder.

Also known as "Addison-Schilder disease" or "ALD" (in its abbreviated form), the illness is an inherited neurological condition that leads to progressive brain damage, paralysis, seizures, and death. When Alomar told reporters that Hirschbeck had become "bitter" due to "a problem with his family," he was universally vilified.

Informed of Alomar's comments, Hirschbeck flew into a rage and was forced to sit out the game he was scheduled to officiate. Taking a lenient approach, American League president Gene Budig issued a five-game suspension to be enacted at the beginning of the 1997 slate. Alomar appealed the ruling and went out and played the same day, clouting a tenth-inning homer that clinched a playoff spot for Baltimore.

In support of Hirschbeck, umpires threatened a postseason strike unless Alomar's suspension was served immediately. By then, the Orioles' star had changed his tune, drafting an apology note to Hirschbeck and offering to donate $50,000 to help find a cure for ALD. The arbiter was somewhat moved by the gesture, giving it his support. A US district court judge ruled that the umpires would be in violation of a collective bargaining agreement if they walked out on the playoffs, and in the end, they decided to go to work.

Making further amends, Alomar withdrew his appeal of the suspension. He was not immediately forgiven by fans, who subjected him to verbal abuse on a regular basis. Some got fairly imaginative, holding up targets and inviting Alomar to spit at them. The heckling continued for several years.

In April 1997, Hirschbeck proved he was a class act when he accepted Alomar's public apology and shook hands with the infielder while standing at home plate before a game at Camden Yards. The two remained friendly from that point on. When Alomar became eligible for Hall of Fame election in 2010, Hirschbeck rallied for the second baseman's enshrinement, stating that he hoped baseball writers were able to look past the incident. Alomar got in on his second try.

October 9, 1996

One of the most infamous cases of spectator interference occurred at Yankee Stadium during game 1 of the ALCS. The Yankees were trailing the Orioles, 4–3, in the bottom of the eighth when Derek Jeter hit a deep fly to right field. Tony Tarasco settled under it and appeared to be poised to make the catch when an eleven-year-old fan named Jeffrey Maier reached over the wall and caught the ball with his own glove.

In cases such as this, the ball is normally ruled dead with a discretionary number of bases or outs awarded by the arbiter. Unfortunately for the Orioles, right-field umpire Rich Garcia blew the call, ruling it a game-tying home run.

Baltimore manager Davey Johnson was ejected following a heated debate, and the Yankees went on to win the game in extra innings.

Garcia reviewed the play after the game and admitted there was inter-ference, though he maintained that the ball was not catchable. AL president Gene Budig rejected an Orioles protest since judgment calls of umpires cannot be officially challenged. The Yanks won the ALCS in five games and the World Series in six. Maier became a celebrity of sorts, appearing on TV talk shows and receiving the ceremonial key to the city from mayor Rudy Giuliani. Following the incident, the Yankees added a railing to the wall in right field, which deterred fans from reaching out for balls in play.

October 7, 1998

Another postseason in New York—another unusual play.

In Game 2 of the 1998 ALCS, the Yankees and Indians were deadlocked at 1 in the twelfth inning. Jim Thome opened the top of the frame with a single off of Jeff Nelson. Employing a small-ball strategy, Cleveland skipper Mike Hargrove installed Enrique Wilson as a pinch runner and gave Travis Fryman instructions to execute a sacrifice (despite his home-run power). Fryman laid down a serviceable bunt that was fielded by first baseman Tino Martinez. Martinez's relay hit Fryman and rolled past Chuck Knoblauch, who was covering the bag. Instead of retrieving the ball, the Yankee infielder stood arguing with officials for an interference call.

In one of the strangest sequences in modern playoff history, Knoblauch continued his debate (with the ball very much alive and resting in the dirt just a few steps away) as Wilson headed home. The obstinate second baseman's eventual throw to the plate was not in time, and New York ended up losing the game, 4–1. One sportswriter referred to him as a "Blauch-Head."

Knoblauch's troubles continued in the field as he inexplicably developed an inability to throw to first base. After the 1998 playoff faux pas, he began double-clutching the ball before throwing. Errors began occurring with alarming frequency. He made twenty-six miscues during the 1999 slate while fielding his position nearly twenty points below the league average. The next year brought more of the same—fifteen muffs in just eighty-two defensive assignments. During a June 2000 contest against the White Sox, he was removed after making three throwing errors in six innings. He contemplated leaving the club but ultimately decided to stay. Before arriving in New York, Knoblauch had won a Gold Glove with the Twins. Many believed his defen-sive woes were brought on by the intense pressure of playing in the Bronx. Manager Joe Torre admitted in his 2009 memoirs that he was surprised to discover how "fragile" Knoblauch was.

September 9, 1999

The seventh inning of a game at Qualcomm Stadium in San Diego was marked by a rare umpiring mistake. After Tony Gwynn of the Padres put his team ahead of the Expos, 8–3, with a two-out RBI single, Reggie Sanders strolled to the plate against rookie hurler Ted Lilly. Sanders struck out to end the frame, but virtually no one noticed. Since no call was made to change sides, the Expos didn't leave the field.

A bit confused, third baseman Phil Nevin stepped in against Lilly, who was unaware that he had already retired three batters. Lilly ran up a 2-1 count on Nevin before someone in the Expos dugout finally shouted to umpire Jerry Layne that the inning should be over. Layne promptly put an end to the at bat, drawing laughter from Nevin. The play, though highly embarrassing to the umpiring crew, had no bearing on the final score (a 10–3 San Diego win).

In addition to Layne, other culpable members of the crew that day were Jeff Kellogg, Paul Schrieber, and Tim Timmons, a minor league ump filling in for one of the regulars on vacation leave. Umpiring gaffes of this nature are few and far between at the major league level.

Part 7
INTO A NEW MILLENNIUM, 2000-2013

Timeline of Significant Events

2000   The Cubs and Mets open the season in the Tokyo Dome—the first regular-season game played in Japan. The United States claims a gold medal in Olympic baseball.

2001   The Seattle Mariners break the mark for most wins in a season by an AL team. Barry Bonds smashes an unimaginable total of seventy-three homers.

2002   The Oakland A's set an AL record with twenty straight wins.

2003   Dodgers relief ace Eric Gagne converts fifty-five consecutive saves—a new record. Roger Clemens becomes the third hurler in history to reach four thousand strikeouts.

2004   Ichiro Suzuki breaks George Sisler's all-time mark for hits in a season with 262. The Red Sox end an eighty-six-year drought with a World Series victory. The Expos leave Montreal.

2005   Jose Canseco's book *Juiced* is released. In it, he admits to steroid use and blows the whistle on many former teammates, among them Mark McGwire, Rafael Palmeiro, Jason Giambi, and Ivan Rodriguez. The Washington Nationals join the National League.

2006   Padres closer Trevor Hoffman becomes the all-time saves leader, passing Lee Smith's career mark of 478.

2007   Barry Bonds breaks Hank Aaron's coveted career home-run record. Former senator George Mitchell releases his infamous report, naming dozens of players under suspicion of using performance-enhancing drugs.

2008   Shea Stadium and Yankee Stadium forever close their doors. Francisco Rodriguez of the Angels breaks Bobby Thigpen's single-season save record with sixty-two. MLB institutes an instant replay system to be used exclusively for home runs.

2009   Joe Mauer of the Twins becomes the first catcher to win three batting titles.

2010   Alex Rodriguez becomes the youngest player to reach six hundred home runs at thirty-five years of age.

2011   Mariano Rivera surpasses Trevor Hoffman's all-time record of 601 saves.

2012   Giants slugger Melky Cabrera qualifies for a batting title but voluntarily withdraws his name after testing positive for steroids. Barry Bonds and Roger Clemens (both suspected steroid users) are denied entry to the Hall of Fame in their first year of eligibility.

2013   Alex Rodriguez launches his twenty-fourth career grand slam, breaking Lou Gehrig's all-time record. Ichiro Suzuki reaches four thousand hits for his career.

April 7, 2000

A dissonant chord was struck during the first week of the 2000 slate when a Florida state jury awarded Andrew Klein more than a million dollars in damages stemming from an incident that took place at Pro Player Stadium during the 1997 campaign. Klein, who was eight years old at the time, was participating in a pregame promotional program known as "Bullpen Buddies." He and roughly one hundred other youngsters had been invited to assemble in the grandstand area before a Marlins game and ask questions of team officials while additionally receiving player autographs. The event could not have been scheduled at a worse time as the visiting Cardinals were in the middle of batting practice. A hot line drive off the bat of Ray Lankford landed in the middle of the group, striking Klein in the left temple. He was left with permanent brain damage.

The Klein family sued the stadium and the franchise. The jury ruled that since Andrew was too young to understand the hazards of standing so close to the field and was technically in custody of the Marlins during the promotion, the team was liable.

May 16, 2000

Members of the Los Angeles Dodgers did nothing to enhance the image of baseball with their unruly behavior on the date in question. In the bottom of the ninth inning of a game at Wrigley Field, the Cubs had crept to within a run of the Dodgers with one out. Possibly intoxicated, a fan hopped the chest-high brick wall separating the stands from the LA bullpen and stole Chad Kreuter's cap. Kreuter, who claimed the fan had slugged him as well, took off in hot pursuit accompanied by various members of the Dodgers relief staff. All hell broke loose after that.

The LA dugout emptied, and more than a dozen players hopped into the stands to tangle with Chicago fans. As the punches started flying, Cubs manager Don Baylor and bench coach Rene Lachemann rushed to the scene, pleading with folks to settle down. The game was delayed for nearly ten minutes as members of the Wrigley security staff struggled to restore order. Three fans were arrested for their participation in the fracas.

After league officials had sorted through various accounts of the melee, sixteen players and three coaches were suspended and fined. The penalties (the most ever imposed on a team for a single brawl) were handed down by Frank Robinson, a Hall of Famer serving as vice president of on-field operations. On April 22, Robinson had suspended sixteen members of the Tigers and White Sox after a nasty brawl between the two clubs. As replays of the Wrigley Field incident saturated television and the Internet, the image of players assaulting those who had paid to see them angered many.

July 8, 2000

An unusual day/night doubleheader was played between the Mets and Yankees in New York. The first game took place at Shea Stadium, and the nightcap was held in the Bronx. The teams had enjoyed a friendly rivalry for years, but on this date, things took an ugly turn.

Through the 1999 campaign, Mets catcher Mike Piazza had accrued an astonishing .583 batting average against Yankee ace Roger Clemens. No one was more aware of this bloated statistic than "The Rocket" himself, who told his personal trainer that he intended to do something about it. Clemens took the mound in the second game and faced Piazza leading off the second inning. Sending a clear message, the aggressive right-hander issued a brushback pitch. It got away from him, however, drilling Piazza squarely in the helmet. The Dodgers backstop sustained a concussion and missed the All-Star Game. When Clemens tried to reach Piazza by phone shortly after the incident, his call was refused.

In the months that followed, numerous media sources blew the confrontation up to mythical proportions, speculating when the two would square off again and what the outcome might be. A grander stage could not have been chosen for the sequel as the crosstown rivals ended up facing each other in game 2 of the 2000 World Series. With a 1-2 count in the first inning, Piazza's bat shattered on contact with a ninety-seven miles per hour laser. The ball eventually rolled foul, but the barrel end of the bat flew toward Clemens, who was so amped up on adrenaline (and quite possibly performance-enhancing drugs) that he threw it belligerently in Piazza's direction. The flabbergasted receiver stopped jogging to first and shouted: "What is your problem?" Umpire Charlie Reliford stepped between the two as both dugouts emptied. When order was restored, Piazza grounded out to end the first inning. Clemens stormed off the field and headed toward the clubhouse, where he reportedly burst into tears. Piazza later referred to the incident as "bizarre" and "idiotic."

June 23, 2001

Manny Ramirez stirred up a great deal of controversy during his career. His nonchalant attitude brought on charges of loafing. His penchant for standing at the plate admiring his home runs invited accusations of hotdogging. But who could blame him? Ramirez hit some of the longest shots in major league history.

On the date in question, Ramirez hit two majestic homers totalling an estimated 964 feet at Boston. Entering the game with an AL best of twenty-one long balls, he lifted a first-inning pitch from Chris Michalak into a billboard above the left center-field screen. The drive was estimated at 463 feet. In the third inning, Ramirez victimized Michalak again, launching a titanic blast that sailed into a row of lights stationed on a tower high above the Green Monster. Naturally, he paused to admire his work before jogging the bases. Club officials surmised the homer to be roughly 501 feet.

The longest homer on record at Fenway was hit by Ted Williams on June 9, 1946—a 502-footer off of Detroit's Fred Hutchinson. The Red Sox commemorated the event by placing a single red bleacher seat in the right-field stands where the ball landed. Red Sox officials may or may not have deliberately underestimated Ramirez's homer to preserve the record for Williams.

Three years later, slugger Adam Dunn of the Reds would upstage Ramirez with one of the longest confirmed dingers in major league history. The ball cleared the center-field wall at Great American Stadium in Cincinnati, bounced onto Mehring Way twenty feet beyond the park, and ended up in the Ohio River. The river itself is technically in the state of Kentucky, possibly making Dunn's homer the first to be hit into a neighboring state. The distance traveled was an impressive 535 feet.

August 7, 2001

The singing of "Take Me Out to the Ballgame" during the seventh-inning stretch is a long-standing tradition at Wrigley Field. The Cubs began using celebrity guests to sing the song after their beloved announcer Harry Caray passed away in 1998. Steve McMichael, a former NFL defensive lineman, became the first guest singer to be tossed out of Wrigley Field. After leading a crowd of 40,266 in a rousing rendition of the classic baseball ditty, McMichael used the PA system as a pulpit to criticize home-plate umpire Angel Hernandez.

In the sixth inning, Chicago's Ron Coomer had tried to score from third when a Denny Neagle pitch got away from Colorado catcher Adam Melhuse.

Melhuse recovered the ball and relayed to Neagle, who was covering the plate. Hernandez called Coomer out despite compelling evidence that the tag was late.

Irritated by the call, McMichael told the crowd he would speak to the umpire after the game. A Pro Bowl selection in 1986 and 1987, McMichael had moved on to a professional wrestling career after leaving the gridiron. Believing his remarks might incite the crowd, Hernandez asked crew chief Randy Marsh to call the press box and have McMichael removed. The crowd stayed calm as the Cubs beat the Rockies, 5–4.

July 9, 2002

The most controversial All-Star Game ever played took place at Miller Park in Milwaukee. It ended as a 7–7 tie when the National League ran out of able bodies on the mound. In an era of pitch counts, both managers were careful not to overwork their moundsmen. Through ten frames, AL skipper Joe Torre and his NL counterpart, Bob Brenly, had conspired to send a total of nineteen pitchers to the hill. On finishing the tenth inning, Phillies right-hander Vicente Padilla told Brenly he couldn't work more than one more inning. Unfortunately, there was no one else to turn to.

Sensing disaster, Brenly and Torre (who was also down to his last hurler) met with officials to devise a solution. It was decided that the game would be called after the eleventh if it remained tied. The National League almost broke through in the bottom of that frame, but catcher Benito Santiago struck out, stranding Mike Lowell at second. Fans littered the field with trash and chanted "Refund! Refund!" Brenly's bench coach, Bob Melvin, commented to members of the press, "Someone should have gone out there and told Freddy [Garcia] to lay one in there for Santiago. . . . We were all praying that he would get a hit."

Commissioner Bud Selig apologized to fans for the "regrettable situation." Determined to prevent future incidents, he expanded the rosters by two players apiece. Adding incentive, he declared that the winning squad would gain home-field advantage in the World Series. The convention has persisted through the 2013 campaign despite opposition from various sources.

September 19, 2002

Two shocking displays of fan violence took place during White Sox games within a year of each other. The first ugly disturbance occurred on September 19, while the Royals were visiting Comiskey Park. The Sox were in the midst of a mediocre season, entering the contest with an even .500 record. They had only a slim chance of capturing a wild-card berth. With one out in the top of the ninth, a drunken spectator named William Ligue Jr. rushed onto the field accompanied by his teenage son. Entering from the first-base side, the two viciously attacked fifty-four-year-old Royals coach Tom Gamboa, leaving him with permanent hearing damage.

Both trespassers were charged with battery. While in police custody, the elder Ligue accused Gamboa of flipping his son the bird. He later admitted to alcohol and drug problems. In a sentence that was perceived as flagrantly lenient to some, both men were placed on probation with no jail time served.

Before the case against Ligue had even been settled, the White Sox were forced to deal with the fallout of another pointless act of fan aggression. In April 2003, a spectator named Eric Dybas stormed the field (again from the first-base side) and grabbed umpire Laz Diaz. This time, it was the arbiter who had the advantage as Diaz used his US Marine Corps training to subdue the inebriated trespasser. Players got in a few shots as well, leaving Dybas scraped and bruised when he was carted out of the stadium by police.

Dybas had reportedly consumed ample amounts of alcohol while attending a Cubs game earlier in the afternoon. His attorney made a plea for leniency, but William Ligue Jr. had set a dangerous precedent several months earlier, and officials wanted to ensure that things were properly handled this time around. Dybas pleaded guilty to aggravated battery and was sentenced to six months in jail along with thirty months of probation.

June 11, 2003

Entering this game against the Astros, the Yankees had not been victims of a no-hitter since September 20, 1958, when Hall of Famer Hoyt Wilhelm accomplished the feat. Their streak of 6,980 games—the longest in major league history—came to an end at Yankee Stadium in front of 29,905 fans. It took six Houston hurlers to get the job done, the most ever for a combined no-hitter.

The Astros were left scrambling for a replacement when Roy Oswalt, one of their top starters, sustained a groin injury in the second inning. Pete Munro, a somewhat unreliable right-hander, was summoned as a hasty replacement. He survived two and two-thirds hitless frames before giving way to Kirk Saarloos. Additionally, the Astros sent Brad Lidge, Octavio Dotel, and Billy Wagner to the hill, completely baffling the New York offense. At one point, eight consecutive Yankees hitters struck out, tying an AL record. The Bombers came close to breaking up the no-no in the fifth inning, when Alfonso Soriano blooped a fly to short left field, but Lance Berkman came racing in to make a tumbling shoestring catch.

Realizing what they were witnessing, Yankee fans stood and applauded as Wagner induced a groundout off the bat of Hideki Matsui to end the game. Joe Torre was frustrated by the loss, which temporarily dropped the Bombers to second place in the AL East. He referred to the game as an "ugly performance" and stated, "We lost our composure."

July 11, 2003

Randall Simon was a hero in his native Curaçao—a small Dutch protectorate in the Caribbean that also produced five-time All-Star Andruw Jones. The easygoing Simon became one of the most vilified players in the majors during the 2003 slate when a prank went awry in a game against the Brewers.

The embarrassing episode happened on the date above during the popular sausage race at Miller Park, a tradition dating back to the 1990s. The race takes place during the sixth inning of every home game as a promotion for a local Wisconsin sausage company. During the event, employees dressed in colorful foam costumes engage in a footrace around the perimeter of the field.

As the costumed characters passed by the Pittsburgh dugout, Simon reached out with his bat and playfully tapped the Italian sausage character. The half-hearted swing was just enough to send nineteen-year-old Mandy Block stumbling into twenty-one-year-old Veronica Piech, who was wearing a hot-dog costume. Both women tumbled to the ground. Though their injuries were very minor, the fallout was immense.

Simon was arrested and booked for misdemeanor battery. He was apologetic when he faced reporters, explaining that he had never intended to hurt anyone. Mandy Block held no grudges, requesting an autographed bat for her troubles. Veronica Piech was not so forgiving. A volleyball player for Harding University in Arkansas, she already had a metal rod in her leg from a previous injury. Perturbed by the fact that her sports career could have been ended, she expressed outrage and "disgust" with Simon.

Video footage of the incident appeared all over television and the Internet for weeks. The affair was mockingly labeled "Sausagegate" as Simon was made to look like a bully. Brewers executive vice president Rick Schlessinger commented that the ill-advised act was among the most "outrageous" things he had ever seen on or off the diamond. Attempting a bit of damage control, the Pirates condemned Simon's actions and issued a formal apology.

In the end, the beleaguered first baseman did his penance, paying a $432 fine for disorderly conduct. He was also penalized $2,000 by league officials and suspended for three games. Traded to the Cubs later in the year, Simon bought Italian sausages for an entire section of fans during a subsequent appearance at Miller Park.

October 14, 2003

Mention the name Steve Bartman to a diehard Cubs fan and you're liable to invoke a barrage of obscenity. Bartman became a scapegoat for the club's failure to reach the World Series when he interfered with a ball during game 6 of the NLCS at Wrigley Field.

The incident occurred in the eighth inning. Chicago was leading the series, three games to two, and stood within five outs of advancing to the Fall Classic for the first time since 1945. Cubs ace Mark Prior was in the midst of a three-hit shutout and had been staked to a 3–0 lead. Juan Pierre of the Marlins was on second base when teammate Luis Castillo lofted a foul pop into the left-field corner. Cubs outfielder Moises Alou tracked it to the first row of seats and appeared ready to make a leaping catch when Bartman, seeking a souvenir, reached out and deflected the ball. Alou slammed his glove on the ground in frustration and shouted up into the stands.

Both Alou and Prior argued in favor of interference, but no call was made since the ball had technically left the field of play. Things fell apart in a hurry for the Cubs as the Marlins rallied for eight runs in the frame and won handily by a score of 8–3. The following night, Florida clinched the NL championship with a 9–6 victory.

Immediately following the foul-ball incident, Bartman's world imploded. TV cameras showed numerous live shots of him, and it didn't take long for his name to appear on MLB's online message boards. He was escorted out of the stadium for his own safety as angry fans peppered him with garbage and verbal abuse. One Chicago newspaper irresponsibly released his address and, though he issued a public apology, he was hounded for weeks. Police were assigned to guard his house, and the governor of Illinois actually suggested he join a witness protection program. Florida governor Jeb Bush offered him asylum. In the end, Bartman dropped off the grid completely. To this day, he has denied all interview requests and his whereabouts are a mystery. His left-field seat remains a popular tourist attraction at Wrigley Field.

September 13, 2004

Relief pitcher Frank Francisco made the wildest toss of his career during a game at the Oakland Coliseum. While Francisco was sitting in the Texas bullpen with teammates, fans in the box seats began making boorish remarks. As Rangers relievers jawed with hostile fans, Francisco grabbed a folding chair belonging to one of the ball boys and hurled it into the stands. His throw bounced off one fan's head before striking a woman named Jennifer Bueno in the face, breaking her nose. The first fan to be hit was Bueno's husband, a season ticket holder and frequent heckler at A's games.

Shortly before the incident, Alfonso Soriano had tied the game for the Rangers with his second home run of the evening. Hank Blalock was at bat with two outs in the ninth when the disturbance took place. Francisco was arrested after the game and charged with aggravated battery. His bail was set at $15,000. Texas manager Buck Showalter felt that the fans involved had "stepped over the line" and complained about similar problems occurring each time the Rangers visited Oakland. The league office was not so supportive, suspending Francisco for the remaining fourteen games of the season. Texas owner Tom Hicks referred to his players' behavior as "unacceptable."

Francisco was later sentenced to thirty days in a Texas jail after pleading no contest to a misdemeanor battery charge. A civil suit against the pitcher was settled in 2007. Bueno had demanded a public apology and an undisclosed sum of money.

August 13, 2006

Royals starter Luke Hudson suffered through one of the most horrific starts in big league history against the Indians. Entering the game, Hudson had a middling 5–3 record with a 4.65 ERA. After just one-third of an inning against the Tribe, the latter statistic would climb nearly two hundred points.

The first ten Cleveland batters who came to the plate in the bottom of the first against Hudson reached base and scored—an astonishing feat that had not been matched in decades. In all, the Indians plated eleven runs in the frame (which lasted for half an hour), matching their highest first-inning total since 1954. They tacked on runs in the fourth and eighth for a 13–0 blowout. According to the Elias Sports Bureau, no pitcher had allowed eleven runs in the first inning of a game since September 21, 1897, when Kid Nichols of the Boston Beaneaters yielded twelve tallies to the Brooklyn Bridegrooms.

"I had one of those days to say the least," Hudson said after the game. "I never expected one this bad." Hudson finished the season with a 5.12 earned run average. After that, he made just one more start in the majors, a disastrous two-inning stint that earned him a demotion to Wichita in the Texas League.

September 18, 2006

In the bottom of the ninth at Dodger Stadium, Los Angeles staged a remarkable rally against the Padres, tying a major league record in the process. Trailing 9–5, four Dodgers batters homered in succession—marking the fourth time in history this had been done. Jeff Kent and J. D. Drew went back to back against right-hander Jon Adkins, who was lifted for bullpen ace Trevor Hoffman. Russ Martin and Marlon Anderson were not fooled by Hoffman's slow offerings, following with a pair of homers to tie the game at 9–9. It was Anderson's second long ball of the game. The Dodgers eventually won in ten innings.

The four homers in a row had not been accomplished since May 2, 1964, when a quartet of Minnesota sluggers (Hall of Famer Harmon Killebrew among them) turned the trick against the A's in extra innings. The 2006 occurrence was inexplicably followed by a rash of others. In 2007, four Red Sox players tagged pitcher Chase Wright of the Yankees for consecutive homers. The following year, the White Sox duplicated the feat against the Royals. In 2010, Adam LaRoche, Miguel Montero, Mark Reynolds, and Stephen Drew of the Diamondbacks went deep off of Brewers hurler Dave Bush. Interestingly, Stephen Drew is the brother of J. D. Drew, the only player to be involved in a four-homer barrage twice in his career (he was among the Red Sox wrecking crew in 2007).

May 30, 2007

An unusual play transpired at the Rogers Center in Toronto. The Yankees were batting in the top of the ninth inning with Hideki Matsui on second, Alex Rodriguez on first, and two outs. Jorge Posada hit a pop-up between third and short. After "A-Rod" had rounded second, he shouted something along the lines of "Hah!" at third baseman Howie Clark and shortstop John McDonald. Clark, who was playing in his first major league game, thought he heard someone yell "I got it!" and backed off from the play. McDonald thought it was Clark's ball as Posada's fly dropped, untouched. Matsui scored to give the Yankees an 8–5 lead.

Blue Jays manager John Gibbons argued for interference, and McDonald became so aggravated during the debate that he had to be physically restrained. No call was made, and Rodriguez could be seen smirking at third base. The Yankees went on to win, 10–5. Gibbons commented that the play was "bush league." Rodriguez defended his actions, pointing out that players yell from opposing dugouts all the time.

July 22, 2007

Mike Coolbaugh got a cup of coffee in the majors with the Brewers and Cardinals in 2001/2002, playing forty-four games as a third baseman, shortstop, and pinch hitter while fashioning a substandard .183 batting average. He refused to let go of the dream, toiling in the minors through the 2006 campaign, after which he was granted free agency by the Kansas City Royals. Finished as a player, he took a job as a coach for the Tulsa Drillers (a Colorado Rockies affiliate) at the request of his two young sons, who loved to see him on the field.

While standing in the coach's box during a Double-A game at Arkansas, the thirty-five-year-old Coolbaugh was struck by a foul liner off the bat of Tino Sanchez. The ball hit Coolbaugh in the head, dropping him to the ground and causing irreparable damage. The game was suspended in the ninth as the fallen coach was rushed to a hospital in North Little Rock. He stopped breathing shortly before arrival. His wife was pregnant at the time, and sadly, Coolbaugh never even learned the sex of his unborn child, which ended up being a girl.

The tragedy brought about new rules for major league coaches, who are now required to wear helmets on the field.

October 5, 2007

It was typical postseason baseball for the Yankees. They had taken a 1–0 lead over the Indians on a clutch homer by Melky Cabrera and were relying on their pitching to carry them the rest of the way. After holding Cleveland scoreless into the seventh, Andy Pettitte left with two runners on and one out. Joe Torre turned the ball over to his latest mound sensation, Joba Chamberlain, who proceeded to blow Franklin Gutierrez away on three pitches and induce a harmless fly off the bat of Casey Blake. Inning over—threat extinguished.

In the bottom of the eighth, a threat of an entirely different variety surfaced as a swarm of insects descended on Jacobs Field. They were referred to as mayflies, midges, gnats, and Canadian soldiers by different sources. *Daily News* reporter Filip Bondy likened them to a "biblical plague" as they swarmed all over Chamberlain "like heat-seeking, Yankee-destroying missiles." The rookie hurler tried to shake them off as coaches sprayed him with repellent, but it was no use. They crawled on his neck and eyelids—at one point he appeared to be spitting them out of his mouth. He lost focus and allowed the tying run without surrendering a hit on a walk and two wild pitches. The game meandered into the eleventh frame, when the Indians scratched out a run to take a two-game advantage in the ALDS.

After the game, Chamberlain bravely shouldered the brunt of the loss, refusing to blame his woes on the insects. "I didn't do my job," he said simply. Three days later, the Bombers were eliminated from the postseason.

It wasn't the first time that flying pests had altered the course of a game. During the nightcap of a doubleheader at Ebbets Field in 1946, Brooklyn pitcher Kirby Higbe was besieged by a swarm of gnats. Higbe threw up his hands and shouted that he was unable to pitch. The field was cleared, and the game was eventually stopped by umpires, who cited that the waving of scorecards by fans to chase off the insects was a distraction to players. The Dodgers won the shortened game, 2–0.

In June 1959, a swarm of gnats gravitated toward Orioles hurler Hoyt Wilhelm at Comiskey Park. Sox trainers tried chasing them off with a towel. When that didn't work, bug spray was used. Finally, smoke bombs were employed. Humans won their battle over nature that day as the invaders left the field.

May 8, 2009

A rare ruling was invoked in a game between the Yankees and Orioles at Baltimore. In the top of the fourth, the Bombers had Nick Swisher on third with one out. Swisher was standing in foul territory, talking with third-base coach Rob Thomson when Baltimore hurler Jeremy Guthrie issued a pickoff throw. Swisher was caught off guard, and Thomson did his part to save the chatty outfielder, literally pushing him back to the bag. The tag was late, but umpire Tim Tschida called Swisher out.

The regulation employed by Tschida was right there in black and white for anyone who cared to look it up: rule 7.09(h) stipulates that a first or third base coach cannot physically assist a runner in leaving or returning to a base. The Yankees had built a 3–0 lead on a homer by Alex Rodriguez, so Thomson's overzealousness didn't hurt the team. C. C. Sabathia pitched a complete game shutout that day (another rarity) as the Yankees prevailed, 4–0.

June 11, 2009

The outcome of yet another game was influenced by uninvited guests. The Royals and Indians were tied 3–3 in the tenth at Progressive Field when KC reliever Kyle Farnsworth coughed up a single to Mark DeRosa and a walk to Victor Martinez. Right fielder Shin-Soo Choo then singled sharply up the middle, straight into a flock of seagulls roosting on the field. Choo's line drive skipped into the grass, bounced off a gull, and caromed to the outfield wall. Center fielder Coco Crisp put his arms up in a gesture of frustration, but he would get no assistance from the umpires.

Baseball rules stipulate that a batted ball that strikes an "unnatural" object over fair territory remains live. This includes birds, other animals, rocks, and dirt clods. Crew chief Mike O'Reilly told reporters after the game: "They're in play—whatever [the ball] does off that bird." Though the Indians scored the winning run on the play, Crisp held no bitterness toward officials. "Crazy things happen in this game," he said. "That's why it's a great game." (Incidentally, the bird was left uninjured on the play.)

June 2, 2010

Almost everyone agreed it was one of the worst calls in major league history—Armando Galarraga of the Detroit Tigers lost his bid for a perfect game when umpire Jim Joyce made a negligible decision on a play at first base. Miguel Cabrera cleanly fielded a grounder off the bat of Indians in-fielder Jason Donald. Cabrera's toss was in plenty of time, but Joyce spoiled Galarraga's shot at immortality when he ruled Donald safe. There were two outs in the top of the ninth at the time.

Detroit manager Jim Leyland hustled out to argue the call, but it was no use. Joyce, a veteran of twenty-two seasons, admitted he blew it after watching a replay. It wasn't even close. Donald was out by a full step. Joyce referred to it as "the biggest call" of his career. It was certainly among the most costly and inaccurate.

Galarraga's gem nearly ended at the beginning of the ninth when Tigers center fielder Austin Jackson was forced to make a circus catch on a fly ball hit by Mark Grudzielanek. Mike Redmond followed with a groundout, bringing Donald to the plate. After the errant call, Galarraga composed himself and went back to work against Trevor Crowe, completing a one-hit shutout. He never confronted Joyce.

The performance was unlikely as Galarraga had suffered through a rough spring, getting demoted to Triple-A Toledo. He didn't make his first start for the Tigers until May 16. Had Joyce made the proper ruling, Galarraga would have recorded the twenty-second perfect game in history. It would have been the third of the season, as Oakland's Dallas Baden had thrown one on May 9 and Philadelphia's Roy Halladay had followed with another three weeks later. To date, there have never been three perfect games in a single major league season.

Galarraga showed remarkable poise and maturity, telling reporters that Joyce was only human and therefore subject to mistakes. The two shared an emotional moment before the next day's game when Galarraga brought out the lineup card. Joyce offered an apology, and the hurler embraced him. "I'm sure the guy feels one hundred times worse than me," Galarraga told reporters.

July 3, 2010

The second inning of a Dodgers and Diamondbacks game at Chase Field in Arizona was one of the sloppiest on record. After James Loney led off with a single, Casey Blake reached on an error by first baseman Rusty Ryal. Home-plate umpire Bruce Dreckman followed with a mistake of his own as he awarded a walk to Xavier Paul on three pitches. (Incredibly, nobody noticed.) Two batters later, the farce continued as Dodger pitcher Clayton Kershaw made it safely to first on an error by shortstop Tony Abreu, scoring Blake and loading the bases.

There were bloopers all around on the next play. Rafael Furcal hit a deep fly to center. Chris Young caught up with it but dropped the ball at the wall. Xavier Paul and Blake Dewitt scored, but Kershaw was oblivious. Believing that Young had made the catch, he reversed direction on his way to third, re-touching second and lumbering back to first. Digging hard, Furcal flew right past Kershaw on the bases. He was called out.

With two outs, Diamondbacks hurler Rodrigo Lopez served up a two-run homer to Sean Kemp. When he finally retired the side, the Dodgers had jumped out to a 6–0 lead. Only two of the nine runs yielded by Lopez that day were earned. The Diamondbacks committed a total of six errors in the humiliating 14–1 loss.

July 7, 2011

Tragedy struck during a game between the Rangers and A's at Arlington. A thirty-nine-year-old firefighter named Shannon Stone was sitting in the left-field seats with his son when a foul hit by Conor Jackson bounced into their vicinity. Stone had purchased a glove for his son before the game, hoping the boy might end up with a souvenir. He shouted at left-fielder Josh Hamilton to toss him the ball, and when Hamilton obliged, Stone slipped through a gap in the left-field railing, plummeting twenty feet below onto concrete. He was conscious as they placed him on a stretcher and was asking for someone to go check on his son. During the ride to a nearby hospital, however, he went into cardiac arrest and died. Rangers president and CEO Nolan Ryan offered sympathy and prayers to Stone's family. Ryan was in attendance when the catastrophe occurred. He was sitting in the front row above the Texas dugout with former US president George W. Bush.

It was the third incident of its kind at Arlington (though neither of the previous two had resulted in fatalities) and the second lethal fall of the season for major league baseball. In May, a man named Robert Seamons was horsing around at Coors Field. Excited to be at a ballgame, he slid down a staircase railing, lost his balance, and fell roughly twenty feet. He suffered massive head trauma and did not survive.

May 5, 2013

A day at the ballpark was filled with horror for a fan named Martin Oleskiewicz as he watched his older sister die from food asphyxiation. Maureen Oleskiewicz, a schoolteacher, was enjoying a hot dog with her brother at Wrigley Field shortly before the first pitch of the Cubs' 7–4 loss to the Reds. Apparently, she did not display the universal signs of choking as Martin didn't know she was in distress until she had fallen to the ground.

EMTs responded quickly, performing CPR while the national anthem was in progress. Oleskiewicz was transported to a nearby hospital, where she was pronounced dead two days later. Her loss was felt deeply at Independence Junior High in Chicago, where she taught language arts to sixth- and seventh-graders. She was kept alive long enough to become an organ donor. Her heart reportedly went to a fourteen-year-old girl in dire need of a transplant. This came as some consolation to grieving family members. The incident was yet another sad chapter in the history of the long-suffering franchise.

April 19, 2013

Jean Segura of the Brewers has a lot to learn about running the bases. In a 2013 game against the Cubs, he demonstrated an alarming unfamiliarity with the rulebook. The twenty-three-year-old Dominican shortstop—playing in his first full major league season—stole second base on a 2-2 pitch to teammate Ryan Braun. Braun drew a walk, and Segura opted to steal third. He should have waited until Chicago pitcher Shawn Camp delivered to the plate. Caught in a rundown between second and third, Segura seemed to lose all sense of where he was in space and time. Braun motored into second. Completely befuddled, Segura joined him. Both players were tagged, and Braun was ruled out. Though the bag legally belonged to Segura, he trotted off toward the dugout believing himself to be retired. When first-base coach Garth Iorg informed Segura he was mistaken, he holed up at first. Then, in an unparalleled display of impulsivity, Segura broke for second again and was thrown out. Commenting on the unusual sequence of events, umpire Tom Hallion said, "Technically, he stole second, stole first, then got thrown out stealing second."

The incident sparked a lively debate, prompting the Major League Baseball operations department to issue a "clarification" memo to umpires. The memo drew the attention of arbiters to rule 7.08(a), which states: "Any runner after reaching first base who leaves the base path heading for his dugout or his position believing that there is no further play may be declared out if the umpire judges the act of the runner to be considered abandoning his efforts to run the bases." Simplifying the language: Segura should not have been allowed to remain at first base!

August 1, 2013

The Houston Astros made a horrific American League debut in 2013. How bad was it?

On April 5, the Astros became the first major league club to record at least thirteen team strikeouts in each of four consecutive games of a season. By April 7, they had raised their cumulative total to seventy-four—the most by any team through six games since the turn of the twentieth century. Their impatience at the plate began to take its toll as they accrued a 10–30 record through May 14, which was officially the worst start in franchise history.

The strikeouts kept coming. On August 1, Brett Wallace got rung up in the fourth inning of a game against the Orioles, raising the club total to one thousand. It took Houston just 107 games to reach that mark, breaking a dubious record set by the Arizona Diamondbacks in 2010. The following players were among the most prolific strikeout artists on the team:

Catcher Jason Castro: One strikeout per every 3.3 at bats
First baseman Brett Wallace: One strikeout per every 2.5 at bats
Center fielder Brandon Barnes: One strikeout per every 3.2 at bats
Designated hitter Chris Carter: One strikeout per every 2.4 at bats

August 18, 2013

Founded by nutritionist Anthony Bosch, Biogenesis of America was a short-lived health clinic located in Coral Gables, Florida. Specializing in weight loss and hormone replacement therapy, it closed in December 2012 after less than a year of operation. In January 2013, the *Miami New Times* obtained evidence linking several major league players who had tested positive for steroids to the clinic. Among those named were Nelson Cruz, Ryan Braun, and Alex Rodriguez.

Major League Baseball launched a full-scale investigation, alleging that the clinic had "actively participated in a scheme" to "solicit or induce major league players to purchase or obtain performance enhancing substances."

"A-Rod" was believed to have engaged in a cover-up, allowing one of his representatives to purchase his medical records and pay a former Biogenesis employee to obtain various other documents.

In July, the plot thickened as major league officials suspended slugger Ryan Braun for the remainder of the 2013 campaign. Twelve other players, including Cruz, were suspended for fifty games apiece. Having admitted to previous steroid use, "A-Rod" received the largest penalty of all—a whopping 211-game suspension that included the entire 2014 season. While all the other players took their lumps, A-Rod opted to appeal the suspension and make his comeback with the Yankees.

Rodriguez had spent most of the season on the disabled list while recuperating from off-season hip surgery. He had already invited an unpleasant outburst from general manager Brian Cashman in late June after he tweeted an update on his recovery to the public. Responding to Rodriguez's claim that a doctor had cleared him to play, Cashman advised "A-Rod" point blank to "shut the f—k up." The troubled slugger eventually returned to the Yankee lineup in August, making claims against the team through his lawyer. Faced with a devastating series of injuries to key players, the Yankees struggled to stay in contention while their clubhouse was enveloped in unwelcome controversy. Cashman commented that Rodriguez had created a "litigious environment" around the Yankees unlike any he had seen in his sixteen years as a general manager. Fans began booing Rodriguez mercilessly during every appearance.

On August 18, Boston pitcher Ryan Dempster resorted to vigilante tactics. In the second inning of a rubber match between the Yankees and Red Sox, Dempster threw behind "A-Rod" on his first offering. His next two deliveries were uncomfortably close, running the count up to 3-0. On the fourth pitch, Dempster sealed the deal by plunking Rodriguez on the elbow.

Home-plate umpire Brian O'Nora issued a warning to both benches but allowed Dempster to remain in the game. In a rare display of unrestrained rage, Yankee skipper Joe Girardi stormed onto the field and confronted O'Nora. He was tossed out of the game when he inadvertently came close to hitting the arbiter while gesticulating wildly. After the Yankees had pulled off a stirring 9–6 victory, Girardi rallied for Dempster's suspension. He got his wish two days later when the hurler was forced to sit out five games and pay a fine. Unlike "A-Rod," he didn't file an appeal.

Afterword

The Colorful Leo Durocher once compared baseball to church, commenting that "many attend, few understand." It's true that baseball is among the most complicated of sports, with a rulebook roughly 125 pages and 50,000 words long. But the rudiments are simple: One pitcher, one batter, three strikes, and three outs.

What could be simpler to comprehend?

The game moves at a leisurely pace and affords spectators the opportunity to debate every pitch. With so many variables in place, virtually anything can happen on the field. Just when you think you've seen it all, you discover you're mistaken as each season brings something new and unique. It's no wonder that baseball has generated more written material than any other sport.

I hope that this book has deepened your appreciation of baseball in some small way. With a lavish history spanning more than 150 years, no American sport is more steeped in tradition. Though the face of the game has changed dramatically over time, one thing has remained constant: there's a story behind every box score. And if you're anything like me, you'll be looking for it.

Play ball!

Bibliography

http://Baseball-almanac.com
http://Baseballlibrary.com
http://Baseball-reference.com
http://Findagrave.com.
http://Hickoksports.com
http://History.com
http://Mlb.com
http://Mlbrulesproject.blogspot.com
http://19cbaseball.com
http://Retrosheet.org
http://Tripleplays.sabr.org
http://Youtube.com

Able, Stephen. "Sam Rice." SABR Baseball Biography Project. Retrieved Dec. 30, 2013. http://sabr.org/bioproj/person/593ed95f.

"American League Notes." *Sporting Life*, Aug. 21, 1909.

"Appleton So Obliging That Superbas Lose." *New York Tribune*, Aug. 7, 1915.

Armour, Mark. "Charlie Finley." SABR Baseball Biography Project. Retrieved Dec. 30, 2013. http://sabr.org/bioproj/person/6ac2ee2f.

"Athletics Take Two." *Washington Herald*, Aug. 4, 1909.

"Athletics Win in Burlesque Game." *New York Tribune*, July 13, 1913.

"Babe Goes into Stand after Insulting Rooter Who Escapes." *New York Tribune*, May 26, 1922.

"The Ball Bouncing off Jose Canseco's Head." *Misc. Baseball* (blog). Retrieved Dec. 30, 2013. http://miscbaseball.wordpress.com/2009/08/14/the-ball-bouncing-off-jose-cansecos-head.

"Baseball: American Association." *Sporting Life*, Sept. 1, 1886.

"Baseball during World War II." Retrieved Dec. 30, 2013. http://www.angelfire.com/ky3/baseballww2.

"Baseball: National League." *Sporting Life*, Aug. 4, 1886.

"Baseball Supply Exhausted, Reds and Red Sox Call Game." Associated Press, Apr. 7, 1939.

"Baseball Today." Amazins.com, Aug. 5, 2007.

"Baseball Yesterday." *New York Tribune*, Aug. 10, 1882.

"Batsmen Tamed by Knockouts." *Mansfield Daily Shield*, July 27, 1907.

"Batting Carnival Gives Washington Easy Victory." *Washington Times*, June 29, 1907.

Berger, Ralph. "Russ Meyer." SABR Baseball Biography Project. Retrieved December 30, 2013. http://sabr.org/bioproj/person/737ae33a.

"Bert Campaneris Plays All Nine Positions in Game (Sept. 8, 1965)." Parallel Narratives. Retrieved Dec. 30, 2013. http://parallelnarratives.com/bert-campaneris -plays-all-nine-positions-in-game-sept-8-1965.

"Bewildering Barters Nothing New for Baseball." *Seattle Post-Intelligencer*, May 24, 2006. Retrieved Dec. 30, 2013. http://www.seattlepi.com/default/article/Bewilder ing-barters-nothing-new-for-baseball-1204464.php.

Biederman, Lester J. "Davis Fumbles into Record." *Pittsburgh Press*, Oct. 7, 1966.

Bingham, Walter. "A Hero of Many Moods." *Sports Illustrated*, June 20, 1960.

Bloom, Barry M. "Safety Tests for Maple Bats Mandated." Mlb.com News, Dec. 9, 2008. Retrieved Dec. 30, 2013. http://mlb.mlb.com/news/article.jsp?ymd=20081209 &content_id=3708319&vkey=news_mlb&fext=.jsp&c_id=mlb.

Blum, Ronald. "Record Six Houston Pitchers No-Hit Yanks." Associated Press, June 12, 2003.

"Bob Shawkey in Fist Fight with Umpire." *New York Tribune*, May 28, 1920.

"Bombs Away! Yanks Christen Nolan, Angels." AP/UPI, June 11, 1975.

Bondy, Filip. "Bugs Irritate Joba Chamberlain, Yankees." *New York Daily News*, Oct. 6, 2007.

"The Boston's Downfall." *New York Times*, Sept. 15, 1872.

"Boston's Narrow Escape." *New York Tribune*, Aug. 27, 1889.

"Boy Injured by Foul Ball Gets $1 Million from Jury." *Los Angeles Times*, Apr. 7, 2000. Retrieved Dec. 30, 2013. http://articles.latimes.com/2000/apr/07/sports/sp-17036.

Boyle, Harvey. "Yanks Win Fourth Game on Error." *Pittsburgh Post-Gazette*, Oct. 6, 1941.

"'Brat' Draws Suspension Pending Hearing Today." Associated Press, July 20, 1954.

"Brawl Breaks Out as Phillies Shade Giants in 11th, 5 to 4." Associated Press, Aug. 12, 1950.

"Brooklyn Beaten Twice." *New York Tribune*, July 5, 1902.

"Brooks Cracking Up? Just Ask the Phillies." United Press, May 25, 1953.

"Brush's Minions in Desperation." *Pittsburgh Press*, Aug. 8, 1906.

"Brush with Death Changes Yeager." Associated Press, May 7, 1977.

"Bugs Gives Game Away." *New York Tribune*, June 18, 1910.

"Bums Smash 5 Records in 19-1 Win." United Press, May 22, 1952.

"Bums Top Cards Under Protest." United Press, July 21, 1947.

"Bums, Yanks Top Loops on Fourth." United Press, July 5, 1949.

"Burke First and Only Woman." United Press International, July 31, 1985.

Calcaterra, Craig. "Hal McRae Thought the 1976 Batting Title Was Stolen from Him in a Racist Plot." *HardballTalk* (blog). Feb. 10, 2010. Retrieved December 30, 2013. http://hardballtalk.nbcsports.com/2010/02/10/hal-mcrae-thought-the-1976 -batting-title-was-stolen-from-him-in-a-racist-plot.

———. "Rollie Fingers, Johnny Bench and the Intentional Walk That Wasn't." *HardballTalk* (blog). Feb. 10, 2011. Retrieved December 30, 2013. http://hardballtalk

.nbcsports.com/2011/02/10/rollie-fingers-johnny-bench-and-the-intentional-walk-that-wasnt.

"Campy Covers Field, Lands in Hospital." United Press International, Sept. 9, 1965.

Caple, Jim. "Dropping the Ka-Boom." *ESPN Page 2* (blog). July 9, 2004. http://sports.espn.go.com/espn/page2/story?page=caple/040709.

Carter, Bob. "Belle Battled Fans, Teammates, Self." ESPN Classic Sportscentury Biography, Sept. 5, 2006. Retrieved Dec. 30, 2013. http://espn.go.com/classic/biography/s/belle_albert.html.

"Catcher Doc Powers Died in Hospital." *Trenton True American*, Apr. 27, 1909.

"Catcher Powers Dead." *New York Times*, Apr. 27, 1909.

"Cedeno Ejected, Chases Heckler." Associated Press, Sept. 10, 1981.

Chapman, Lou. "Better Safe Than Sorry, Says Gomez." *Milwaukee Sentinel*, July 18, 1956.

———. "Hoak Retires Himself: A Hit—Or Not a Hit?" *Milwaukee Sentinel*, Apr. 21, 1957.

"Charlie Sweeney." *Wikipedia*. Last modified Aug. 30, 2013. http://en.wikipedia.org/wiki/Charlie_Sweeney.

Chen, Albert. "The Greatest Game Ever Pitched." *Sports Illustrated*, June 1, 2009. Retrieved Dec. 30, 2013. http://sportsillustrated.cnn.com/vault/article/magazine/MAG1155946.

"Chicago Cubs Fan Chokes to Death on a Hot Dog at Wrigley Field." *New York Daily News*, May 6, 2013.

"Chicago in Uphill Tilt, Beats St. Louis." *Sun* (New York), June 29, 1919.

"Chicago Won Long Battle." *Pittsburgh Press*, Aug. 25, 1905.

"Chili Takes a Poke at Heckler." Associated Press, July 31, 1995.

"Chisox Protest Loss to Orioles." Associated Press, Aug. 29, 1960.

"Clean Sweep for the Cubs." *Sun* (New York), Aug. 31, 1908.

"Close Baseball Races." *Sun* (New York), May 9, 1904.

"Cobb Turns to Boxing." *New York Tribune*, May 16, 1912.

"Cobb Wins for Tigers." *New York Tribune*, May 13, 1911.

Constantelos, Stephen. "George Stovall." SABR Baseball Biography Project. Retrieved Dec. 30, 2013. http://sabr.org/bioproj/person/2eb65ef8.

"Coolbaugh, 35, Dies after Being Struck by Ball." ESPN.com News Services, July 24, 2007. Retrieved Dec. 30, 2013. http://sports.espn.go.com/minorlbb/news/story?id=2945798.

"Cosell-Heckling Ballboy Suspended." United Press International, June 9, 1977.

Costello, Rory. "Shea Stadium (New York)." SABR Baseball Biography Project. Retrieved Dec. 30, 2013. http://sabr.org/bioproj/park/476675.

Cowley, Joe. "Did Babe Ruth Really Call His Shot at Wrigley Field?" *Chicago Sun-Times*, June 16, 2011.

Crasnick, Jerry. "Joba, Yankees Can't Avoid the Plague." ESPN Commentary, Oct. 5, 2007. Retrieved Dec. 30, 2013. http://sports.espn.go.com/mlb/playoffs2007/columns/story?id=3051291.

Cronin, Brian. "Did Sam Rice Reveal a World Series Secret in a Letter Opened after His Death?" *Los Angeles Times*, Sept. 7, 2011.

"Crowd Control: Dodger Players Brawl with Fans in Win over Cubs." *Sports Illustrated*, May 17, 2000. Retrieved Dec. 30, 2013. http://sportsillustrated.cnn.com/baseball/mlb/news/2000/05/16/cubs_dodgers_ap.

"Crush at Baseball Game." *Sun* (New York), Oct. 4, 1903.

"Cubs Lose by Forfeit Route and Pay $1,000." *New York Tribune*, July 19, 1916.

Dashneill, Bennett. "Relive the Majesty and Terror of Ten Cent Beer Night." Deadspin, June 4, 2009. Retrieved Dec. 30, 2013. http://deadspin.com/5278916/relive-the-majesty-and-terror-of-ten+cent-beer-night.

Davis, Aaron, and C. Paul Rogers III. "Stuffy McInnis." SABR Baseball Biography Project. Retrieved Dec. 30, 2013. http://sabr.org/bioproj/person/0bad180f.

Davis, John K. "19th Century Baseball History." *Suite 101* (blog). July 28, 2008. Retrieved Dec. 30, 2013. http://suite101.com/a/19th-century-baseball-history-a62104.

———. "The Youngest Major League Players." *Suite 101* (blog). July 7, 2008. Retrieved Dec. 31, 2013. http://suite101.com/a/the-youngest-major-league-players-a59597.

Davis, Ralph S. "The Cubs Protest Yesterday's Game." *Pittsburgh Press*, Sept. 5, 1908.

———. "Reds Take 10 Inning Contest, Game to Be Protested by Gibson." *Pittsburgh Press,* May 29, 1921.

Day, Frederick J. *Clubhouse Lawyer: Law in the World of Sports*. Lincoln, NE: iUniverse Star, 2002.

Deale, Tim. "Eddie Rommel." SABR Baseball Biography Project. Retrieved Dec. 30, 2013. http://sabr.org/bioproj/person/333594e9.

"Demaree Halts Giants in Their Mad Rush." *New York Tribune*, May 31, 1916.

Dickson, Paul. *The Hidden Language of Baseball*. New York: Walker, 2003.

"Dibble Outburst; Sends Ball into Stands, Hits Fan." *Deseret News*, Apr. 29, 1991.

"DiMaggio Homers as Yanks Beat Sox, 3–2, 6–4." Associated Press, July 5, 1949.

"Dizzy Blanks Tigers, 11–0, in Final Tilt." Associated Press, Oct. 10, 1934.

"Dizzy Gets the Babe in Their First Test of Baseball Rivalry." United Press, May 6, 1935.

"Dock Ellis LSD No-Hitter." Snopes.com. Retrieved Dec. 30, 2013. http://www.snopes.com/sports/baseball/ellis.asp.

"Dodger Fan Hits Umpire as Reds Win." Associated Press, Sept. 17, 1940.

"Dodgers Frustrate Expos in 22." Associated Press, Aug. 24, 1989.

"Doing the Time: Simon Suspended 3 Games for Sausage Incident." *Sports Illustrated*, July 11, 2003. Retrieved Dec. 30, 2013. http://sportsillustrated.cnn.com/baseball/news/2003/07/11/simon_suspension_st.

Donaghy, Jim. "Rule Change Costs Young a No-Hitter." Associated Press, Apr. 13, 1992.

Dow, Bill. "Former Tiger Norm Cash." *Baseball Digest*, Sept. 2001.

———. "When Norm Cash Took a Table Leg to the Plate for the Detroit Tigers." Detroit Athletic Co., Nov. 1, 2011. Retrieved Dec. 30, 2013. http://blog.detroitathletic.com/2011/11/01/when-norm-cash-took-a-table-leg-to-the-plate-for-the-detroit-tigers.

"Doyle's Homer Wins 21-Inning Game for Giants." *New York Tribune*, July 18, 1914.

Dunkley, Charles. "Owen Nearly in Tears in Dodger Dressing Room." Associated Press, Oct. 6, 1941.

Durrett, Richard. "Rangers Fan Dies after 20 Foot Fall." ESPN Dallas, July 8, 2011. Retrieved Dec. 30, 2013. http://sports.espn.go.com/dallas/mlb/news/story?id=6747510.

"Dybas Pleads Guilty, Gets 6 Months." Associated Press, Dec. 4, 2003.

Dykes, Jimmy. *You Can't Steal First Base*. Philadelphia: Lippincott, 1967.

Dzierzak, Lou. "Batter Up: Shattering Sticks Create Peril in MLB Ballparks." *Scientific American*, July 14, 2008.

"Eager to Pass Giants." *Pittsburgh Press*, Aug. 7, 1918.

Eaton, Paul W. "That Forfeited Game." *Sporting Life*, July 29, 1916.

Edgren, Bob. "They Have to Be Good to Take It!" *Lodi News Sentinel*, May 7, 1937.

Elfrink, Tim. "MLB Steroid Scandal: How Porter Fisher Exposed the Coral Gables Clinic." *Miami New Times*, June 18, 2013.

"Elias Says . . ." ESPN, Aug. 14, 2013. Retrieved Jan. 9, 2014. http://sports.espn.go.com/espn/elias?date=20130814.

"Elias Says . . ." ESPN, Apr. 6, 2013. Retrieved Dec. 30, 2013. http://sports.espn.go.com/espn/elias?date=20130406.

Enders, Eric. "George Moriarty." SABR Baseball Biography Project. Retrieved Dec. 30, 2013. http://sabr.org/bioproj/person/44c82f26.

"Episode 83: Baseball Myths." Mythbusters Results. Air date: Aug. 8, 2007. Retrieved Dec. 31, 2013. http://mythbustersresults.com/episode83.

"Ernie Shore's 'Perfect Game' and Ruth's Suspension in 1917." *Misc. Baseball* (blog). Retrieved Dec. 30, 2013. http://miscbaseball.wordpress.com/2011/03/28/ernie-shores-perfect-game-and-babe-ruths-ejection-in-1917.

Eskanazi, Gerald. "Sideline: No Way to No-Hitter; A Late Call on a Bad Hop." *New York Times*, May 13, 1991.

"Fair Triumphs over Fowl." *St. Petersburg Independent*, Apr. 15, 1974.

Fallon, Mike. "Steve Yeager." SABR Baseball Biography Project. Retrieved Dec. 30, 2013. http://sabr.org/bioproj/person/69e2594b.

"Fan Dies after Fall at Coors Field." Associated Press, May 26, 2011.

Feeney, Charley. "Pirates Blow Chances, Fall to Mets in 18, 5–4." *Pittsburgh Post-Gazette*, Apr. 29, 1985.

"Fight Club: Nineteen Dodgers Suspended for Wrigley Brawl." *Sports Illustrated*, May 25, 2000. http://sportsillustrated.cnn.com/baseball/mlb/news/2000/05/24/dodgers_suspensions_ap.

"Fines for Ballplayers." *Sun* (New York), Apr. 27, 1900.

"Fit to Be Tied: All-Star Game Called When Teams Run Out of Pitchers." *Sports Illustrated*, July 9, 2002. Retrieved Dec. 30, 2013. http://sportsillustrated.cnn.com/baseball/2002/allstar/news/2002/07/09/allstar_game_ap.

Fleitz, David. "Cap Anson." SABR Baseball Biography Project. Retrieved Dec. 30, 2013. http://sabr.org/bioproj/person/9b42f875.

Flynn, Karen, and Kevin Flynn. "John Haskell Umpire and Punching Bag." *D.C. Baseball History* (blog). Retrieved Dec. 30, 2013. http://dcbaseballhistory.com/2012/08/john-haskell-umpire-and-punching-bag.

"Four Are Crushed to Death." *Pittsburgh Press*, Aug. 9, 1903.

"Four Pitchers for Giants." *Sun* (New York), Oct. 8, 1911.

"14 Hecklers Banished as Red Sox Win, 9–2." Associated Press, July 20, 1946.

"Fowl Ball: Winfield Arrested after His Pickoff Throw Kills Gull." United Press International, Aug. 5, 1983.

Fralex, Gerry. "Braves, Padres Sign No Treaties." Cox News Service, Aug. 13, 1984.

Francis, Philip C. "The Stories of Jackie and Kitty." *Lakeland Ledger*, Apr. 28, 2002.

"Freak Hit Worries Green." *Evening Post*, Apr. 15, 1912.

Freedman, Lew. "Virgil Trucks Brought the Heat." Call to the Pen, Mar. 27, 2013. Retrieved Dec. 30, 2013. http://calltothepen.com/2013/03/27/virgil-trucks-brought-the-heat.

"Frick Frowns on Piersall's Reverse Run." Associated Press, June 24, 1963.

Frommer, Harvey. "Vandy's Masterpiece: The Double No-Hitter." The Baseball Guru: A World of Baseball. Retrieved Dec. 30, 2013. http://baseballguru.com/hfrommer/analysishfrommer14.html.

Gagnon, Cappy. *Notre Dame Baseball Greats: From Anson to Yaz.* Charleston, SC: Arcadia, 2004.

———. "Red Murray." SABR Baseball Biography Project. Retrieved Dec. 30, 2013. http://sabr.org/bioproj/person/22f8fb88.

"Gamboa Attacker Held on $200,000 Bond." Associated Press, Sept. 21, 2002.

"Gamboa Disappointed." Associated Press, Aug. 6, 2003.

Game recaps. *New York Tribune*, Sept. 5, 1891.

Game recaps. *New York Tribune*, June 30, 1897.

Game recaps. *New York Tribune*, May 4, 1899.

Game recaps. *New York Tribune*, May 6, 1901.

Game recaps. *New York Tribune*, Aug. 22, 1901.

Game recaps. *New York Tribune*, May 22, 1904.

Game recaps. *New York Tribune*, Sept. 4, 1906.

Game recaps. *Pittsburgh Press*, June 19, 1907.

Game recaps. *Pittsburgh Press*, Sept. 2, 1917.

Game recaps. *St. Louis Republic*, Sept. 6, 1901.

Game recaps. *Sun* (New York), July 21, 1894.

Game recaps. *Sun* (New York), July 18, 1896.

Game recaps. *Sun* (New York), June 2, 1897.

Game recaps. *Sun* (New York), June 5, 1897.

Game recaps. *Sun* (New York), June 30, 1897.

Game recaps. *Sun* (New York), Aug. 5, 1897.

Game recaps. *Sun* (New York), Aug. 18, 1900.

Game recaps. *Sun* (New York), June 5, 1901.

Game recaps. *Sun* (New York), July 2, 1901.

Game recaps. *Sun* (New York), Apr. 28, 1902.

Game recaps. *Sun* (New York), July 5, 1902.

Game recaps. *Sun* (New York), May 8, 1904.

Game recaps. *Sun* (New York), June 20, 1905.

Game recaps. *Sun* (New York), Aug. 10, 1905.

Game recaps. *Sun* (New York), June 25, 1906.

"Game Stopped and Players Arrested." *Sun* (New York), May 17, 1897.

"Gehrig Cracks Playing Mark Held by Scott." Associated Press, Aug. 18, 1933.

Ghosh, Palash. "Josh Hamilton Tragedy: Forty Years Ago, Another Fan Died from Foul Ball." *International Business Times*, July 8, 2011. Retrieved Dec. 31, 2013. http://www.ibtimes.com/josh-hamilton-tragedy-forty-years-ago-another-fan-died -foul-ball-296961.

"Giants Downed Again." *New York Tribune*, Aug. 31, 1908.

"Giants Forfeit Game." *New York Tribune*, Apr. 12, 1907.

"Giants Revel in Runs." *New York Tribune*, May 9, 1912.

"Giants Win Double Bill from Cards." *Pittsburgh Press*, July 26, 1935.

"Gomez Passes Up Chance to Mend Tiff with Joe." International News Service, July 25, 1956.

Gorman, Robert M., and David Weeks. *Death at the Ballpark*. Jefferson, NC: McFarland, 2009.

"Grandstand in Flames." *Sun* (New York), Aug. 6, 1894.

Grayson, Harry. "Walker Entertains Fans with Left Field Antics." Newspaper Enterprise Association, Apr. 2, 1941.

"Great Fire in Boston." *Sun* (New York), May 16, 1894.

"Greed Led Canseco to Jeopardize His Career." Associated Press, July 6, 1993.

"Hack Wilson as Pugilist Has Big Day." *Chicago Daily Tribune*, July 5, 1929.

Hand, Jack. "A's on Top, Look Like Serious Pennant Contenders." *Miami News*, May 7, 1948.

"Harris Pitches with Both Hands." *Lakeland Ledger*, Sept. 29, 1995.

Hernon, Jack. "Reflecting on 'The Fight Game.'" *Pittsburgh Post-Gazette*, Aug. 23, 1965.

Hertzel, Bob. "Fenway Park: Where History, Trivia Have Been Made." Scripps Howard News Service, Oct. 21, 1986.

Hill, Thomas. "He's Batty Says Piazza, Charges Clemens Looked 'Unstable.'" *New York Daily News*, Oct. 24, 2000.

"Hillmen Now the Leaders." *Sun* (New York), Sept. 4, 1906.

Hoekstra, Dave. "Steve Bartman Catches More Hell in ESPN Documentary." *Chicago Sun-Times*, Sept. 27, 2011.

Hoffarth, Tom. "40 Years Ago Today: A Death at Dodger Stadium, and Still the Only One of Its Kind at an MLB Game." *Farther off the Wall* (blog). May 16, 2010. Retrieved Dec. 31, 2013. http://www.insidesocal.com/tomhoffarth/2010/05/16/40 -years-ago-to-1.

Holmes, Dan. "Germany Schaefer." SABR Baseball Biography Project. Retrieved Dec. 30, 2013. http://sabr.org/bioproj/person/2594238c.

"Homer Ends 25-Inning Marathon." Associated Press, May 10, 1984.

"Home Run Raises Protest." *New York Tribune*, June 28, 1911.

"Indians Score 11 Runs in First Inning Rout of Royals." Associated Press, Aug. 13, 2006.

"Indians Swamp Yankees, 15–1, Take Lead Again." *Washington Herald*, Aug. 26, 1921.

"Indians Win 8–1, Lead Series, E. Smith's Homer Scores Four." *New York Tribune*, Oct. 11, 1920.

"Indians Win on Rookie's Homer, 4–2." Associated Press, July 24, 1960.

Isaac, A. "Famous Spitting Incidents." Guyism, Nov. 16, 2010. http://guyism.com.

Jackson, Paul. "The Night Beer and Violence Bubbled Over in Cleveland." *ESPN Page 2* (blog). June 4, 2008. Retrieved Dec. 31, 2013. http://espn.go.com/espn/page2/story?page=beernight/080604.

Jaffe, Chris. "10,000 Days since Vince Coleman and the Tarp." *Hardball Times*, Feb. 28, 2013. Retrieved Dec. 31, 2013. http://www.hardballtimes.com/main/blog_article/10000-days-since-vince-coleman-and-the-tarp.

James, Bill. *The New Historical Baseball Abstract*. New York: Free Press, 2001.

Jensen, Don. "Bugs Raymond." SABR Baseball Biography Project. Retrieved Dec. 30, 2013. http://sabr.org/bioproj/person/79835564.

Johnson, James W. "Johnny Vander Meer." SABR Baseball Biography Project. Retrieved Dec. 30, 2013. http://sabr.org/bioproj/person/14ff1abe.

"Jose Canseco Biography." ESPN MLB. Retrieved Dec. 31, 2013. http://espn.go.com/mlb/player/bio/_/id/1626/jose-canseco.

Kaegel, Dick, and Anthony Castrovince. "For the Birds: Gull Struck by Winning Hit." MLB.com News, June 11, 2009. Retrieved Dec. 31, 2013. http://mlb.mlb.com/news/article.jsp?ymd=20090612&content_id=5283376&vkey=news_mlb&c_id=mlb&fext=.jsp.

Kahn, Roger. *Beyond the Boys of Summer*. New York: McGraw-Hill, 2005.

Kaplan, Jim. "Lefty Grove." SABR Baseball Biography Project. Retrieved Dec. 30, 2013. http://sabr.org/bioproj/person/8bc0a9e1.

Kates, Maxwell. "Norm Cash." SABR Baseball Biography Project. Retrieved Dec. 30, 2013. http://sabr.org/bioproj/person/b683238c.

Kay, Joe. "Umpire John McSherry Collapses during Game." Associated Press, April 1, 1996.

Kearney, Seamus. "Roger Moret." SABR Baseball Biography Project. Retrieved Dec. 30, 2013. http://sabr.org/bioproj/person/9e2f0fd4.

Kepner, Tyler. "Whatever Happened to Brett's Pine Tar Bat?" *New York Times*, July 24, 2008.

Kiesewetter, John. "How Dick Williams Fooled Johnny Bench." *TV and Media Blog* (blog). July 8, 2011. Retrieved Dec. 31, 2013. http://cincinnati.com/blogs/tv/2011/07/08/how-dick-williams-fooled-johnny-bench.

Kiesling, Stephen. "Dropping in the Series." *Sports Illustrated*, Oct. 9, 1989.

"Killer Tarp Victim Coleman Hopes to Play." *Chicago Tribune*, Oct. 16, 1985.

"Kingman Fly Never Came Back to Earth." Associated Press, May 6, 1984.

King, Thomas. "Smith May Play at Second Today." *Washington Times*, July 31, 1914.

Kirksey, George. "Brilliant Pitching Wins for Nationals." United Press, July 7, 1938.

———. "Feuding Flatbushers Find Flaming Foes." United Press, July 20, 1940.

———. "Rioting Red Sox Fans Give Yanks Forfeit Win." United Press, Sept. 3, 1939.

———. "'Wait 'til Next Year,' Dodgers Cry as Reds 'Coast In.'" United Press, July 24, 1949.

Kolchak, Carl. "Sam Rice—A Baseball Life Full of Mystery." *Yahoo Voices* (blog). Sept. 26, 2006. Retrieved Dec. 31, 2013. http://voices.yahoo.com/sam-rice-baseball-life-full-mystery-78265.html?cat=14.

Koppett, Leonard, Seth Abraham, Joe Durso, Robert Creamer, John Updike, Shirley Povich, and Joe Reichler. *The All Star Legend*. New York: Major League Baseball Promotion, 1977.

Krabbenhoft, Herm. "Lou Gehrig's RBI Record: 1923–39." *Baseball Research Journal* 41 (Fall 2012). Available at SABR Research. Retrieved Jan. 9, 2014. http://sabr.org/research/lou-gehrig-s-rbi-record-1923-39.

Kroichick, Ron. "Bowled Over/A Collision with Pete Rose in the 1970 All-Star Game Changed Fosse's Career." SFGate, July 10, 1999. Retrieved Dec. 31, 2013. http://www.sfgate.com/sports/article/Bowled-Over-A-collision-with-Pete-Rose-in-the-2919513.php.

Lagerstrom, Hal. "1924 World Series One of the Wildest." *Telegraph Herald*, Oct. 11, 1974.

Lamberty, Bill. "Roy Thomas." SABR Baseball Biography Project. Retrieved Dec. 30, 2013. http://sabr.org/bioproj/person/522fb1e1.

Lang, Jack. "Gene Was Mad Enough to Spit, and Umpire Was in the Wrong." *Sporting News*, May 18, 1968.

LaPointe, Joe. "The Night Disco Went Up in Smoke." *New York Times*, July 4, 2009.

Lardner, Ring W. "Les Giants Sont Massacré Par les Chicago Bas Blanc." *New York Tribune*, October 8, 1917.

"Late Dodger Rally Beats Cardinals." Associated Press, July 21, 1947.

Launius, Roger. "The Great George Brett/Hal McRae Batting Title Race of 1976." *Roger Launius's Blog* (blog). May 21, 2012. Retrieved Dec. 31, 2013. http://launiusr.wordpress.com/2012/05/21/the-great-george-bretthal-mcrae-batting-title-race-of-1976.

Ledger, Kate. "Safety Did Not Come First." *Sports Illustrated*, July 14, 1997. Retrieved Dec. 31, 2013. http://sportsillustrated.cnn.com/vault/article/magazine/MAG1010377/index.htm.

Lee, Henry K. "A's Fan Injured by Flying Chair Settles Lawsuit against Rangers." SFGate, July 2, 2013. Retrieved Dec. 31, 2013. http://www.sfgate.com/sports/article/A-s-fan-injured-by-flying-chair-settles-lawsuit-2624561.php.

Leeke, Jim. "Ernie Shore." SABR Baseball Biography Project. Retrieved Dec. 30, 2013. http://sabr.org/bioproj/person/6073c617.

"Leo Trades Punches with Furillo." Associated Press, Sept. 7, 1953.

Lidz, Franz. "Flashes in the Pan." *Sports Illustrated*, May 4, 1992.

Lindner, Dan. "Kid Gleason." SABR Baseball Biography Project. Retrieved Dec. 30, 2013. http://sabr.org/bioproj/person/632ed912.

"The Longest Game: For Pawtucket, Rochester, It's 32 Innings and Counting." Associated Press, Apr. 20, 1981.

"Longtime Umpire Harry Wendelstedt Dead at 73." Associated Press, Mar. 9, 2012.

Lundquist, Carl. "Red Sox Wreck Records in 29–4 Massacre." United Press, June 9, 1950.

Macgranachan, Brendan. "Tough Week to Be an Ump." Seamheads.com, Sept. 13, 2009. Retrieved Dec. 31, 2013. http://seamheads.com/2009/09/13/tough-week-to-be-an-ump.

Macht, Norman. *Babe Ruth*. New York: Chelsea House, 1991.

"Major League Log." *Pittsburgh Post-Gazette*, Sept. 10, 1999.

"Major League Record Is Broken, Score Is 1–1." *New York Tribune*, May 2, 1920.

"Man Charged for Attacking AL Umpire." Associated Press, Apr. 17, 2003.

Mandich, Steve. "Disco Demolition Night: A Midsummer Nightmare." *Roctober*, no. 37 (Winter 2003).

"Mantle Clouts Longest Homer in History of Griffith Stadium." Associated Press, Apr. 18, 1953.

Mantle, Mickey, and Lewis Early. *The American Dream Comes to Life*, Volume I. Champaign, IL: Sports Publishing, 2002.

Marchand, Andrew. "A-Rod Angers GM Brian Cashman." ESPN New York, June 26, 2013. Retrieved Dec. 31, 2013. http://espn.go.com/new-york/mlb/story/_/id/9422957/brian-cashman-tells-new-york-yankees-alex-rodriguez-shut-up.

Markusen, Bruce. "Cooperstown Confidential: A Tribute to Willie Davis." *Hardball Times*, March 12, 2010.

"Marquard Fired by Brooklyn for Ticket Scalping." *Modesto Evening News*, Oct. 12, 1920.

"Marquard Goes 21 Innings for Pirate Scalp." *Sun* (New York), July 18, 1914.

Martinez, Michael. "2 Days Hawkins Won't Forget." *New York Times*, July 2, 1990.

Marzano, Rudy. *The Last Years of the Brooklyn Dodgers: A History, 1950–1957*. Jefferson, NC: McFarland, 2008.

Masur, Louis P. *Autumn Glory: Baseball's First World Series*. New York: Hill and Wang, 2003.

"Matty's Reds Capture Series from Giants." *New York Tribune*, June 9, 1917.

McCourt, Dan. "August 6th in Yankee History." TakeHimDowntown.com, Aug. 6, 2012. Retrieved Dec 31, 2013. http://takehimdowntown.com/yankee-history/august-6-in-yankee-history.

McGrath, Dan. "A Fan, a Goat and Long Painful Memories." *New York Times*, Oct. 1, 2011.

McKenna, Brian. "Bob Ferguson." SABR Baseball Biography Project. Retrieved Dec. 30, 2013. http://sabr.org/bioproj/person/df8e7d29.

———. *Early Exits: The Premature Endings of Baseball Careers*. Lanham, MD: Scarecrow Press, 2007.

———. "Eddie Gaedel." SABR Baseball Biography Project. Retrieved Dec. 30, 2013. http://sabr.org/bioproj/person/fa5574c8.

———. "Quick Thinking of Stuffy McInnis." *Glimpses into Baseball History* (blog). Aug. 12, 2011. Retrieved Dec. 31, 2013. http://baseballhistoryblog.com/2862/quick-thinking-of-stuffy-mcinnis.

McKenzie, Mike. "Umpires' Ruling Beats the Tar out of Royals." *Kansas City Star*, July 25, 1983.

McKinley, James. "Amateurs Say Easy Throws Can Be the Hardest." *New York Times*, June 17, 2000.

"McMichael Booted from Cubs Game." Associated Press, Aug. 8, 2001.

Merron, Jeff. "Animals Were Harmed in Making This List." *ESPN Page 2* (blog). Retrieved Dec. 31, 2013. http://espn.go.com/page2/s/list/sportanimalcruelty.html.

Merry, Dan. "Lunacy at Shea: Bombs Away for Army, Yankees." *Press Telegram*, June 11, 1975.

Meyer, Paul. "Nothing to Hum About." *Pittsburgh Post-Gazette*, Oct. 17, 1989.

Michael, Matt. "One Hot Day in '85, Ump Gave Organ Player the Heave." *Post-Standard* (Syracuse, NY), Apr. 3, 1990.

"Mick Hits 53rd in Yanks Sweep." Associated Press, Sept. 11, 1961.

Miklich, Eric. "Charles 'Old Hoss' Radbourne." 19th Century Baseball. Retrieved Dec. 31, 2013. http://www.19cbaseball.com/players-charles-radbourn.html.

"MLB Suspends 13, Including A-Rod." ESPN MLB, Aug. 5, 2013. Retrieved Dec. 31, 2013. http://espn.go.com/mlb/story/_/id/9540755/mlb-bans-13-including-alex-rodriguez-new-york-yankees-2014.

Montville, Leigh. *The Big Bam*. New York: Doubleday, 2006.

"More Hard Luck." *Sporting Life*, Apr. 23, 1898.

"More Rowdyism." *New York Tribune*, Aug. 18, 1900.

"Moriarty Breaks Hand as He Kayoes Gaston." Associated Press, May 31, 1932.

Moshier, Jeff. "From Where I Sit: They Will Have a Rugged Time Pardoning the Scorer." *Evening Independent*, July 7, 1959.

Murray, Jim. "Did Babe Herman Triple into a Triple Play?" In *The Complete Armchair Book of Baseball*, edited by John Thorn, 219–21. Edison, NJ: Galahad Books, 1997.

"The National Game." *Pittsburgh Press*, Sept. 5, 1891.

"National League Race Over." *Sun* (New York), Oct. 13, 1911.

"National League Suspends Dibble for 4 Games for Firing Ball into Stands." Associated Press, May 4, 1991.

Neft, David S., and Richard M. Cohen. *The World Series*. New York: St. Martin's, 1990.

Neft, David S., Richard M. Cohen, and Michael L. Neft. *The Sports Encyclopedia: Baseball 2000*. New York: St. Martin's Griffin, 2000.

"New Records Made in Wild Ball Game." *Pittsburgh Press*, Aug. 26, 1922.

"New Yorkers Lose a Close One and Meet with Misfortune." *Sun* (New York), May 13, 1911.

"Niekro Faces Penalty." Associated Press, Aug. 4, 1987.

Nightengale, Bob. "Riddoch Gets Two Headaches." *Los Angeles Times*, July 3, 1991.

"1922 World Series." World History Project. Retrieved Dec. 31, 2013. http://worldhistoryproject.org/1922/10/4/1922-world-series.

"No Balls! So, Game's Off!" United Press, April 7, 1939.

"No Hitter in Defeat Makes Ken Unique." *Miami News*, Apr. 24, 1964.

"No Hitter Loss Is Bittersweet for Hawkins." Associated Press, July 3, 1990.

"No Police, Game Stopped." *Sun* (New York), Apr. 12, 1907.

Ocker, Sheldon. "Pitcher Niekro Steals Second." *Ottawa Citizen*, Oct. 5, 1986.

"Old Man Ruth Whistles Three Homers and a Single off of Pirate Hurlers." United Press, May 26, 1935.

Olney, Buster. "After Three Errors, Knoblauch Walks Out." *New York Times*, June 16, 2000.

———. "Yankee Ends One Corker of a Mystery." *New York Times*, April 11, 1999.

"The Origin of Blue Laws: Understanding Why the Laws Exist." Tree.com/legal.

Overfield, Joe. "George Stallings Used a Midget Long before Bill Veeck." *National Pastime*, no. 10 (1990).

"Owner Goes on PA to Call Padres Stupid." Associated Press, Apr. 10, 1974.

Parker, Blue. *Fouled Away: The Baseball Tragedy of Hack Wilson*. Jefferson, NC: McFarland, 2000.

Passan, Jeff. "Even Santa Believes in Mantle's 565-Foot Blast." Yahoo Sports, Apr. 17, 2008. Retrieved Dec. 31, 2013. http://sports.yahoo.com/news/even-santa-believes -mantles-565-082100864--mlb.html.

Pepe, Phil. *Talkin' Baseball: An Oral History of Baseball in the 1970s*. New York: Ballantine, 1998.

"Perfect Game Pitcher Handles Call with Grace." CNN, June 5, 2010. Retrieved Dec. 31, 2013. http://www.cnn.com/2010/SPORT/06/05/baseball.perfect.game.

Pielli, John. "Dodgers Forfeit Game on Ball Day." *Yardbarker.com* (blog). Aug. 10, 2012. Retrieved Dec. 31, 2013. http://www.yardbarker.com/mlb/articles/dodgers_ forfeit_game_on_ball_day/11422996.

Piersall, Jim, and Al Hirshberger. *Fear Strikes Out*. Lincoln, NE: Bison Books, 1999.

"Piersall Recovery Helps Those with Mental Ills." Associated Press, Apr. 9, 1957.

"Piersall Warns: Stay in Stands." Associated Press, Sept. 11, 1961.

"Pitcher Arrested After Throwing Chair at Fans." *Associated Press*, Sept. 14, 2004.

"Pitcher Is Felled by Lightning Bolt." *Pittsburgh Press*, Aug. 25, 1919.

"Players Fined, Suspended, Moriarty Is Reprimanded." Associated Press, June 1, 1932.

Pollack, Michael. "Disaster in Ruthville." *New York Times*, Apr. 6, 2008.

Potter, Chet. "Boston Fans Howl in Glee at Sewell's Blooper." *Pittsburgh Press*, July 10, 1946.

"Pulls Umpire's Cap Off." *Sun* (New York), May 4, 1913.

"Monster Mash: Ramirez Hits Second Longest Homer in Fenway History." *Sports Illustrated*, June 23, 2001. Retrieved Dec. 31, 2013. http://sportsillustrated.cnn .com/baseball/mlb/news/2001/06/23/ramirez_homers_ap.

"Record Ball Game Is Protested by the Pittsburgh Club." *Pittsburgh Press*, July 18, 1914.

"Record Crowd Sees Cubs and Cards Divide." Associated Press, July 13, 1931.

"Reds Hot Rally in Ninth Beats Cardinals." *New York Tribune*, Apr. 30, 1918.

"Reds Lose Weird Game to Braves, 3–1." Associated Press, Sept. 23, 1954.

"Reds Make Farce out of Finish." *Pittsburgh Press*, Oct. 5, 1902.

"A Remarkable Ball Game." *Sun* (New York), June 19, 1874.

Rice, Grantland. "Crushed and Humiliated Polo Grounders Fleeing toward Coogan's Bluff." *New York Tribune*, October 8, 1917.

———. "Landis Center of Angry and Puzzled Mob." *New York Tribune*, Oct. 6, 1922.

Rice, Thomas. "Harsh Words Used about the Nationals." *Washington Times*, Aug. 29, 1909.

Richter, Francis C. "Black-Letter Day for Philadelphia." *Sporting Life*, Aug. 15, 1903.

"Riot as Giants Win, 10–2, after Phillies, 5–1, Break 17 Straight Game Streak." *Sun* (New York), May 31, 1916.

"Riot When Forfeit Gives Giants Game." *New York Tribune*, Aug. 31, 1913.

Ritter, Lawrence. *The Glory of Their Times: The Story of the Early Days of Baseball Told by the Men Who Played It.* New York: Macmillan, 1966.

"River Invaded Park." *Pittsburgh Press*, July 5, 1902.

"Robins Protest Cross-Diamond Score by Card." *New York Tribune*, June 4, 1918.

Romeo, Joe. "Dock Ellis and the LSD No-Hitter." *Yahoo Voices* (blog). Feb. 9, 2010. http://voices.yahoo.com/dock-ellis-lsd-no-hitter-5410715.html.

Rosciam, Chuck. "The Evolution of Catcher's Equipment." *Baseball Research Journal* 39, no. 1 (Summer 2010). Retrieved Dec. 30, 2013. http://sabr.org/research/evolution-catchers-equipment.

"Roseanne Barr Sang the National Anthem between Padres Games 20 Years Ago Today." *Gaslamp Ball* (blog). July 25, 2010. Retrieved Dec. 31, 2013. http://www.gaslampball.com/2010/7/25/1466280/roseanne-barr-sang-the-national.

"Roseanne Barr Sings National Anthem after 1990 Flop." *Huffington Post* (blog). July 25, 2011. Retrieved Dec. 31, 2013. http://www.huffingtonpost.com/2011/07/25/roseanne-barr-national-anthem-roseannes-nuts-sing-reality-show_n_908417.html.

Rosenberg, Michael. "Twenty Years Ago, an Earthquake Shook a Bay Area World Series." *Sports Illustrated*, Oct. 28, 2009. Retrieved Dec. 31, 2013. http://sportsillustrated.cnn.com/2009/writers/the_bonus/10/27/89.series.

Rosengren, John. "The Iron Horse, Hammerin' Hank and a Chemist's Quest for Accuracy." *Sports Illustrated*, July 11, 2012. Retrieved Dec. 31, 2013. http://sportsillustrated.cnn.com/2012/baseball/mlb/07/03/lou-gehrig-john-rosengren.

Rosynsky, Paul T. "Rangers Player Ducks Trial in Chair-Throwing Case." Inside Bay Area, Jan. 13, 2007. Retrieved Jan. 9, 2014. http://www.insidebayarea.com/oaklandtribune/localnews/ci_5007787.

"Rowdy Fans Cause Dodgers to Forfeit Game." Associated Press, Aug. 11, 1995.

"Rowdyism In Brooklyn." *Sun* (New York), Sept. 20, 1900.

Russo, Frank, and Gene Racz. *Bury My Heart at Cooperstown: Salacious, Sad and Surreal Deaths in the History of Baseball.* Chicago: Triumph Books, 2006.

Sandoval, Jim. "Jake Daubert." SABR Baseball Biography Project. Retrieved Dec. 30, 2013. http://sabr.org/bioproj/person/3fca088a.

Schechter, Gabriel. "Charlie Faust." SABR Baseball Biography Project. Retrieved Dec. 30, 2013. http://sabr.org/bioproj/person/d1ee8535.

Schindler, Kevin. "Fans Lead Veeck's Browns to Victory on Grandstand Manager's Day." *Suite 101* (blog). Sept. 7, 2011. Retrieved Dec. 31, 2013. http://suite101.com/a/fans-lead-veecks-browns-to-victory-on-grandstand-managers-day-a386943.

Schonbrun, Zach. "In Rematch; Memories of a Stolen Moment." *New York Times*, Oct. 6, 2012.

Schott, Arthur O. "A Wild and Wacky Score of a 19th Century Game." SABR New Orleans. Retrieved Dec. 31, 2013. http://www.sabrneworleans.com/publications/arthurschott/NiagaraVsColumbia%2805-2010%29.pdf.

Schwartz, Larry. "Drysdale Sets Consecutive Scoreless Innings Streak." ESPN Classic, Nov. 19, 2003. Retrieved Dec. 31, 2013. http://espn.go.com/classic/s/moment010608drysdale-record.html.

"Score: Braves Get 5, Padres 3, Umps 13, Cops 5." Associated Press, Aug. 13, 1984.

Semchuk, Alex. "Addie Joss." SABR Baseball Biography Project. Retrieved Dec. 30, 2013. http://sabr.org/bioproj/person/5e51b2e7.

"Senators Run Amuck in Detroit Ballpark." *Sun* (New York), July 31, 1914.

"'76 Controversies Begin; Grand Slam Disallowed." Associated Press, April 11, 1976.

Seymour, Harold. *Baseball: The Early Years*. New York: Oxford University Press, 1989.

Shaikin, Bill. "A Bat Accident Waiting to Happen." *Los Angeles Times*, June 1, 2008.

"Sharp Baseball in Brooklyn." *New York Tribune*, July 23, 1884.

Sheinin, Dave. "From Way Out in Right Field." *Washington Post*, June 2, 2006.

"Shut-Out Battle One of Marvels." *Washington Times*, Aug. 5, 1911.

Silverman, Matthew, Michael Gershman, and David Pietrusza, eds. *Baseball: The Biographical Encyclopedia*. Toronto: Sport Classic Books, 2003.

"Simon Says: Infielder Apologizes, Fined for Sausage Race Attack." *Sports Illustrated*, July 10, 2003. Retrieved Dec. 31, 2013. http://sportsillustrated.cnn.com/baseball/news/2003/07/10/sausage_folo_ap.

"A Slight Retrogression." *Sun* (New York), Aug. 14, 1891.

"Smashes Clear Griffith Stadium Center Field Wall." Associated Press, April 18, 1956.

Smith, Brian T. "Astros Pass 1,000 Strikeouts, Continue to Set MLB Records." *Ultimate Astros* (blog). Aug. 2, 2013. Retrieved Dec. 31, 2013. http://blog.chron.com/ultimateastros/2013/08/02/astros-pass-1000-strikeouts-continue-to-set-mlb-records.

———. "With Latest Shortcoming to Tigers, Astros Have Three Times More Losses Than Wins." *Ultimate Astros* (blog). May 14, 2013. Retrieved Dec. 31, 2013. http://blog.chron.com/ultimateastros/2013/05/14/with-latest-defeat-astros-have-three-times-more-losses-than-wins.

Smits, Ted. "Nippy's Natty Shoes Hurt." Associated Press, Oct. 7, 1957.

Snell, Roger. *Root for the Cubs: Charlie Root and the 1929 Chicago Cubs*. Nicholasville, KY: Wind Publications, 2009.

"Sox Pitcher Beaten Up in Battle with Browns." Associated Press, June 21, 1945.

Spatz, Lyle. "Jack Doyle." SABR Baseball Biography Project. Retrieved Dec. 30, 2013. http://sabr.org/bioproj/person/1b894e54.

"Spectacular Catch by Red Murray Robs Pirates of Victory." *Pittsburgh Press*, Aug. 17, 1909.

Spector, Jesse. "Twice as Nice." *New York Daily News*, Aug. 5, 2007.

"Stanky Stalls, Ump Forfeits Second Game to Phils." Associated Press, July 19, 1954.

Stanton, Tom. *Ty and the Babe*. New York: Thomas Dunne, 2007.

Stark, Jayson. "Jean Segura's Baserunning Adventures." *Jayson Stark Blog* (blog). Apr. 20, 2013. Retrieved Dec. 31, 2013. http://espn.go.com/mlb/blog/_/name/stark_jayson/id/9193265/baserunning-adventures-milwaukee-brewers-shortstop-jean-segura.

———. "Jean Segura Should've Been Called Out." *Jayson Stark Blog* (blog). Apr. 25, 2013. Retrieved Dec. 31, 2013. http://espn.go.com/mlb/blog/_/name/stark_jayson/id/9210491/the-final-ruling-jean-segura-baserunning-misadventures.

Steadman, John. "Basepath Stop and Go Signs Are the Answer." *Baltimore Sun*, Apr. 19, 1993.

"Steve McCatty." *1980 Topps Baseball* (blog). Jan. 10, 2010. Retrieved Dec. 31, 2013. http://1980toppsbaseball.blogspot.com/2010/01/231-steve-mccatty.html.

Strecker, Trey. "Fred Merkle." SABR Baseball Biography Project. Retrieved Dec. 30, 2013. http://sabr.org/bioproj/person/372b4391.

"Sunday on the Diamond." *Sun* (New York), June 24, 1895.

Taylor, Charles A. "Harper's Wild Streak Starts Near Riot in Cleveland Park." *New York Tribune*, August 26, 1921.

Taylor, Phil. "Bartman Wasn't Interested in Cashing in on 15 Minutes of Infamy." *Sports Illustrated* (2003). Retrieved Dec. 31, 2013. http://sportsillustrated.cnn.com/2011/writers/painful_moments_in_sports/09/09/Steve.Bartman.Cubs.

"Tenney in Fight with Umpire." *New York Tribune*, Aug. 8, 1906.

"They Kept on Playing and Playing." Associated Press, Apr. 17, 2001.

"This Game Proves Nightmare." *Sun* (New York), July 13, 1913.

"Thousands See the Giants Beaten." *New York Tribune*, Oct. 9, 1908.

"Three Straight for Giants over Cards." *Sun* (New York), May 9, 1912.

"Thunderbolt Puts Caldwell Down, but He Wins Game." *New York Tribune*, Aug. 25, 1919.

"Tigers' Galarraga Robbed by Terrible Call." Associated Press, June 3, 2010.

"Tigers Slug Warhop, Ty Slugs a Spectator." *Sun* (New York), May 16, 1912.

"Tigers Stop Hillmen." *Sun* (New York), Aug. 26, 1909.

"Too Loyal." United Press, Sept. 17, 1940.

Torre, Joe, and Tom Verducci. *The Yankee Years*. New York: Doubleday, 2009.

Tourtellotte, Shane. "The Pine Tar Games." *Hardball Times*, July 28, 2012. Retrieved Dec. 31, 2013. http://www.hardballtimes.com/main/article/the-pine-tar-games.

"Two Balls Used at Once as Cards Win, 4–1." Associated Press, July 1, 1959.

"Two Killed When Fans Stampede in Yankee Stadium." Associated Press, May 20, 1929.

"Two Nines Claim Game." *New York Tribune*, Aug. 8, 1906.

"Umpire and Player Fight at American League Park." *Sun* (New York), July 8, 1903.

"Umpire Burkhart Dies." Associated Press, Dec. 30, 2004.

"Umpire Byron Pulls His Watch and Forfeits Game to Brooklyn." *Washington Herald*, July 19, 1916.

"Umpire Ejects Gross." Associated Press, Aug. 11, 1987.

"Umpire Emslie Slugged." *Sun* (New York), Sept. 8, 1899.

"Umpire's Tragic Death Raises Health Concern." *USA Today*, Apr. 15, 1996.

"Uncorking the Truth." *Baseball Researcher* (blog). Feb. 19, 2011. Retrieved Dec. 31, 2013. http://baseballresearcher.blogspot.com/2011/02/uncorking-truth.html.

Underwood, George. "Reds Register 10 Runs in the Thirteenth." *Sun* (New York), May 15, 1919.

Vecsey, George. "Sports of the Times; Better Late Than Never for Ashburn." *New York Times*, March 8, 1995.

Veeck, Bill, and Ed Linn. *Veeck as in Wreck*. Chicago: University of Chicago Press, 2001.

"Walker, Athletics' First Baseman Hurt as Indians Triumph." *New York Tribune*, Aug. 18, 1921.

"Washingtons Feast on Runs." *Sun* (New York), June 29, 1907.

Weatherby, Charlie. "Mike Grady." SABR Baseball Biography Project. Retrieved Dec. 30, 2013. http://sabr.org/bioproj/person/eabc11fa.

Weber, Bruce. "Virgil Trucks, Who Threw Two No-Hitters in 1952, Dies at 95." *New York Times*, Mar. 26, 2013.

Weeks, Jonathan. *Baseball's Most Notorious Personalities: A Gallery of Rogues.* Lanham, MD: Scarecrow Press, 2013.

———. "Billy vs. Reggie: Remembering the Fenway Flare-up." *Cellar Dwellers* (blog). Mar. 27, 2013. Retrieved Dec. 31, 2013. http://jonathanweeks.blogspot .com/2013/03/billy-vs-reggie-remembering-infamous.html.

Weinbaum, William. "Vander Meer's Unforgettable Feat." ESPN MLB, June 12, 2003. Retrieved Dec. 31, 2013. http://m.espn.go.com/mlb/story?storyId=9387977&wjb=.

"White Shirts of Ball Fans Cause Riot at Philadelphia." *Pittsburgh Press*, Aug. 31, 1913.

Wilbert, Warren N. *Baseball's Iconic 1-0 Games.* Lanham, MD: Scarecrow Press, 2013.

Will, George. *Men at Work.* New York: Macmillan, 1990.

Williams, Joe. "Yankees Too Good." *Pittsburgh Press*, Oct. 9, 1939.

"Williams Threatens to Repeat $5,000 Spitting Incident." United Press, Aug. 8, 1956.

"Wilson Fined $100, Suspended for 3 Days for Kolp Attack." *New York Times*, July 7, 1929.

Wulf, Steve. "The Spit Hits the Fan." *Time*, June 24, 2001.

"Yankees Power Too Much for Feller and the Indians." Associated Press, Aug. 7, 1937.

"Yankees Win, Blue Jays Unhappy with A-Rod's Verbal Antics." Associated Press, May 31, 2007.

Yellon, Al. "MLB Had a Solution to Shattered Bats and Refused to Institute It." SB Nation Chicago, Sept. 20, 2010. Retrieved Dec. 31, 2013. http://chicago.sbnation .com/2010/9/20/1700071/mlb-tyler-colvin-maple-bat-shattered-bat-batglove.

"Yesterday's Great Game." *Sun* (New York), July 25, 1873.

"Young Downs Pirates." *Pittsburgh Press*, Aug. 10, 1905.

Index

About the Author

Jonathan Weeks would have given his right arm to play ball professionally but realized that doing so would have seriously hampered his abilities. *Mudville Madness* is Weeks's third jaunt into the realm of baseball. His previous books, *Cellar Dwellers* and *Baseball's Most Notorious Personalities*, were both published by Scarecrow Press. A lifelong student of the game, he is a member of the Society for American Baseball Research. He has worked in human services for the better part of two decades.